feel like you've been pulled through a knothole.

Emotionally, you're drained. If it isn't the kids fighting, it's the Ex putting you down. If it isn't your parents telling you what you ought to do, it's the babysitter changing schedules and throwing you another curve. You have no place for solitude unless you lock yourself in the bathroom, and even then the children bang on the door.

Socially, you don't even exist. Old friends are too busy; the family can't get over; the wrong people keep calling; and you're not ready to go out and make new friends yet.

Sexually, you're frustrated. You're not close to anyone anymore. You're scared no one will ever want you. You can hardly remember what it is to feel someone's touch.

Spiritually, you're confused. You thought God was in your marriage. You thought you were doing the right thing. You prayed things would straighten out but they only got worse. You were supposed to "live happily ever after," but it didn't work out that way.

A DEEPER QUESTION

You've told me how it's going, but suppose now I ask you a deeper question: *How would you like it to be going?*

Physically, you want peace and well-being that will energize you for the home, office, church, and lots of play with the kids. You never again want to say, "Not now, I'm too tired," and see the hurt and confusion in their eyes.

Emotionally, you'd like to love life and all those around you, including yourself. You want to feel loved and affirmed. You want to be ready to tackle anything and give it your best shot.

Socially, you want to be alive, open, spontaneous and caring. You want to listen to the kids, share with friends, and be supported by all kinds of people.

Sexually, you need to affirm your own sexuality and you want to be affectionate and intimate. You want a profound respect for your own needs, and you want to be able to give yourself fully in a cherished lifetime commitment.

Spiritually, you want to feel forgiven and forgiving. You'd like to know God is in you and you are in Him. You would be truly one!

THE BOTTOM LINE

Taking the question even deeper, let me ask you this: *How would God want things to be going for you?* Does He not want more for you than you could ever want for yourself? Then you can understand why this journey is important to Him. He has placed His Holy Spirit within you to guide you, empower you, and motivate you to see it through. This is a part of why Jesus Christ died for you.

He did not cause your circumstances to bring you to this moment, but He gave Himself to you so that when faced with this moment He could *work all things for good* because He loves you and because you are called according to His purposes. Things do not necessarily always work for good, but whatever you commit to Him He is able to work for good. He is doing the real work, and you are called to allow Him to do it. This what Romans 8:28 really means.

I would never invite you on a journey at this stage in your life if I did not believe in its necessity. Being a single parent does not create this need in you, but, because you are, your need is increased. You carry an extra heavy load.

NOT AN EASY JOURNEY

No journey is easy when you're hurting. No uncertainty seems worth a risk when you're confused. No path seems inviting when the end result cannot be seen. But there is something — *Someone* — to cling to. He promised, "I will be with you always" (Matthew 28:20), and He will lead you to the truth of who you really are — and that will free you to be the parent you want to be. He says to you, "You will know the truth, and the truth will set you free." You will be set free to be, to become, and to work for His own purpose (John 8:32 and Philippians 2:13).

All right, let's take that journey. Let's find the real you — and the parent you can become.

Δ

TAKING ACTION: BACKGROUND INFORMATION

Write out your responses to the following and refer to them after you complete Part I of this book. See how your perceptions have changed by that time.

1. How old were you when you became a single parent?

2. How long have you been a single parent?

3. How many children does this involve?

4. What were their ages when you all became a single-parent family?

5. How did you become a single parent, through divorce, the death of your mate, or never having married?

6. Do the children live with you most of the time or just some of the time? (If some of the time, how often and for how long?)

7. How many miles do your own parents/family live from you?

8. Describe the levels of support and encouragement you receive from the following:

   Family members

   Close friends

   Singles group

   Church family

   Pastor/staff

   Single-parents group

   Other sources

10. List the two or three main problems you encounter as a single parent.

11. List the kinds of help you need most.

12. What has been the hardest task for you as a single parent?

13. What has been your deepest fear?

14. What has been your deepest satisfaction?

15. What has been your greatest surprise?

16. What has been your worst frustration?

17. What are your main concerns for your children at present?

18. What are your main concerns for yourself?

On the following scale, circle the number that indicates where you see yourself at this time in your life.

Pitsville **0 1 2 3 4 5 6 7 8 9 10** A-Okay

2

SELF-DISCOVERY NEEDS

I always appreciate the map at a service station when I need to locate a place I want to go to. The owner knows I will have difficulty reading the tiny print so he attaches a little sign that says, "You are here!"

It isn't always easy to figure out where you are in life either, especially after a trauma has thrown you off course. And there isn't any "You are here!" sign around anywhere. So how do you get to where you want to go when you aren't sure where you are starting from?

For our journey together your eventual destination is the spot where you can begin maturing in Christ, finding personal fulfillment, and becoming all you need to be. But where are you now? Knowing that point is essential in planning your route, but finding it can be a problem. As a result of your early years, a marriage that may or may not have been need-satisfying, and a divorce or the death of your mate, you may have become confused, frustrated and angry, and may even be going around in self-defeating circles. (See Ephesians 4:11-16. Your goal is to "grow up into Christ.")

All this adds up to a need for self-discovery. This need isn't just the result of your divorce or of the death of your mate. It has arisen from an accumulation of a lifetime of experiences, situations and relationships, and has been deepened by your recent traumas. Coming to the Lord brought you new life in Him, but you still have been dealing with the same old you in so many ways. You may not have been taught just what became new. If not, you probably have remained in the same old mindset regarding your self-perceptions.

People come to me in their quest for self-discovery, but almost without exception, at the same time they are asking for help, they resist it. They are convinced that their deep, inner fears are right and that when they do discover themselves they will find a person who is unlovable, not worth knowing, and who *ought* to feel the guilt, fear and anger they have wrestled with most of their lives.

When I first met Cindy, she had been a single parent for almost three years. Although she came to me because of some serious problems in parenting her three boys, ages seven, five and two, it soon became apparent that her deep struggle was with herself, not her parenting. She was unable to cope with her boys' needs because of her own lack of self-awareness and self-acceptance. In essence, she was putting her own *unfinished business into her relationships with her boys,* and that was causing confusion.

WHO YOU ARE

When asked, "Who are you?" some answers I have heard are:

"I'm Susie's mother."

"I'm my parent's child."

"I'm a secretary."

"I'm a person."

"I'm John."

"I'm a widow."

"I'm a divorcée."

What comes to mind for you? How do you see yourself? Take a moment and jot down a few comments you would use to describe yourself to others.

Pause a moment.

Now take a look at what you have jotted down. How you describe yourself betrays your self-perception. What does your description tell you about you? Would it help another person to understand you? Does it express your uniqueness, set you apart from the other five billion people on this planet? Or does it only say what might be said of hundreds and thousands of others?

How you perceive yourself is the basis of how you feel about being you, how you act, how you relate to others, and especially how you parent. Any distortion in your perception will result in a distortion in your levels of living. Where did your self-perception come from and how did it become distorted?

YOUR "INNER CHILD OF THE PAST"

Inside you is the little child you once were, your inner child of the past. (The term, *inner child of the past,* has been popularized by Eric Berne, Thomas Harris, and other transactional analysis writers. It refers to the child egostate.) Paul writes about his in 1 Corinthians 13:11: "When I was a child, my speech, feelings, and thinking were all those of a child." This is the person you were way back when you were two, three, four or five years of age. Although you went on to become an adult, that little child is still there, still a part of you. Right now if you call to mind something from those years, that inner child is activated and his thoughts and feelings become present all over again. For example, if I invite you to go with me and have a hot fudge sundae topped with lots of whipped cream, chopped nuts and a big, red cherry, your inner child remembers a similar treat in the past and your salivary glands go to work anticipating all that yummy goo. (1 Corinthians 13:11 refers to acting as well as thinking and feeling.)

Or, recall the time you realized your marriage was ending. Remember those engulfing fears of copelessness? They reminded you of a childhood experience and how you felt when you were positive your mother had rejected you and your life was about to end. The knowledge of an impending divorce triggered that stored-up memory and at that moment your inner child was back there dealing with mother's rejection all over again. You recall all the pain and anxiety just as when you first experienced it. Whenever you allow that inner child to surface he can take control and you think, feel and act just like you did back then. You want to run and hide from the present reality just as you wanted to at that time.

THE RUB

There is something in that inner child of the past that you need to examine very carefully. This aspect is crucial to your total life's journey—past, present and future:

**Your earliest perceptions of yourself came
through the eyes of this inner child of the past.**

Relating with Dad and Mom, grandparents, brothers and sisters, aunts and uncles, caused this child in you to put together a set of beliefs from the viewpoint of how you thought they saw you. You didn't ask questions like, "Why do you relate with me as you do?" You merely assumed they had a reason, and that reason told you about yourself. Not only did you not raise questions, but also your observations were not reality tested. (*Reality testing* is a thought process by which one checks out an event or experience in terms of reality. Its validity is established after having thought it through and confirming it.) How you thought they saw you may not have been how they saw you at all, but you knew the "truth" — at least your interpretation of the truth.

How could a two-foot-tall three-year-old figure all that out? How could he ask, "Dad, why is it you work all the time and never spend any time with me?" Instead you just concluded, *I guess my dad doesn't want to spend time with me became I'm not worth spending time with.* A child's reasoning is always self-directed. You had such a need to be loved by your dad, how could you blame him and risk losing even more of what you needed most? The only person you could blame safely was you. And how were you, a two-foot kid, to know it was not your fault? Most everything else seemed to be.

STILL WITH YOU

Whatever the little child perceived, he still believes today. I hope you get that point because it is crucial. If that child is allowed to go unchallenged, his views never get updated. Just think that through for a moment. A four-year-old inside you can be telling you how to see yourself. He cannot cope with marriage, a career, a broken relationship, parenting, or any other adult concern. If you allow him to control you, where does that leave you?

Paul goes on to state in 1 Corinthians 13:11 that "now that I am [an adult], I have no more use for childish ways." Parts of those past responses may work all right at the beach or at a birthday party, but not in operating a responsible adult life. You know of "children" in adult bodies, and you know how destructive they can be. You also know, firsthand, when the child of the past in you blew a relationship or destroyed an opportunity. Marriage, parenting and the Christian walk all make demands on the adult in us. (*Adult* refers to the adult egostate that is formed through a thought process, beginning as soon as we are able to reason.) A person with sufficient ego strength can control the inner child of the past.

FLASHBACK

When it became clear your marriage was not going to make it, how easily your inner child was hooked. (*Hooked* means I allowed what happened to engage the child in me so now I am angry, upset, hurt, afraid, or all of the above.) You may have felt like running home so the folks could fix the hurt. You may have felt guilty because you hadn't been easy to live with. You may have covered the guilt with anger and dumped the whole thing on your Ex. Or, you may have dumped the whole thing on yourself, feeling that "it's always me who is to blame. Who could ever love me?" When the child got hooked, the adult in you got squeezed out of the picture.

You need to bring the adult back in. He is your contact with reality, the part of you whom the Holy Spirit can reason with.

HOW YOU SEE YOU

When you see yourself as weak, dependent, not worth loving or knowing, always failing, not able to cope, you can know that the inner child of the past is in control.

If you see yourself as a unique, wonderfully made creation of God, fully and completely restored in Jesus Christ, unconditionally loved by your Heavenly Father, loaded with spiritual gifts, talents and skills, then you are on target. The adult in you is the part of you that can be open to God's truth about who you really are. St. Augustine once wrote, "God loves you as if He didn't have anyone else to love."

You are worth Jesus Christ to Him.

That is what He paid to reconcile you to Himself. There is no other human being on this planet worth more to God than you.

WHY YOU SEE YOURSELF AS YOU DO

You are not who that child says you are. *You are who God says you are.* He says you are only a step below the angels, the object of His unconditional and eternal love. You are the apple of His eye, the object of all His giving. He has graced your life with His own presence. He has chosen to dwell in you. He gives Himself to you. Paul's theology centers in the term, *in Christ.* To God we are in Christ. He sees us no other way.

To see yourself otherwise is to contradict what God says about how He sees you. Just as you projected your own conclusions onto your parents, now you project them onto your Heavenly Father. *(Projection* is a mechanism whereby we attribute thoughts and feelings to others that are our own.) You're trying to tell God how He sees you instead of letting Him speak for Himself. Satan's trick is to keep you from discovering how God really sees you. Satan knows the truth would set you free from the prejudice and delusion of the inner child. As long as the child dominates, the enemy has you in his pocket. You will continue to struggle, and you will miss the entire idea of Isaiah 40:31: "[to] rise on wings like eagles."

WHO YOU ARE REALLY

None of us knows fully who we are. We all struggle with self-prejudice and delusion. We all have inner filtering systems that alter reality until it fits where we want it to. The difference is in the degree each of us perceives reality. Some of us have matured more than others. So, if you are not who you perceive yourself to be, you are not alone. But you do have a lot of work to do in allowing that perception to be changed by His Spirit.

First, you must allow God to speak for Himself and you must seek, with all your heart and mind, to perceive His thoughts about you. I know this is easier said than done because your self-prejudices are so real to you that you believe them to be His thoughts.

Second, you need a circle of trusted friends who are willing to help you discover your true self. Those who truly love you affect you greatly when it comes to self-discovery. They know all there is to know—and still they love you. You need to discover why. Ask them to share this with you.

Third, you need to gain a fuller understanding of why the inner child of the past sees you as he does. Some good reading here could take you a long way in self-awareness and self-understanding.

Fourth, you need to get in touch with your fear of change. As miserable as these inner feelings are, they are familiar and you feel in control of them. If you discovered the truth about you, how might you change? How do you know you will want the changes? If you don't like them, could you ever go back? You have a lot to deal with.

KNOWING YOU ARE ON THE RIGHT TRACK

You tend to allow yourself to be kept in the enemy's prison by telling yourself you might dishonor the Lord by changing. After all, if you were to see yourself as ten feet tall in Him, that might lead to pride and even a spirit of independence from the Lord—and of course that would be wrong.

But wait a minute. How could you be any more independent of Him than you already are? Your view of yourself is totally independent of His truth about you. This concoction of the inner child of the past has been reinforced by subsequent failures, sins and mistakes. So how are you to judge it accurately?

BLOCKS TO SELF-DISCOVERY

You need to recognize at this time that certain things can constitute blocks to your self-discovery. These are not born of the Spirit; rather, they are born of the enemy and of yourself. Paul points out in 2 Timothy 1:7 that God's Spirit "fills us with power, love, and self-control." The fears that block self-discovery are born of your own need. And the enemy seeks to convince you of their validity.

A false sense of humility is perhaps one of the greatest blockers of all. A "humble" response sounds so good and so "Christian," but it can cover a strong feeling of self-righteousness.

Self-denial is another one, at least the way many use it. It appears so spiritual, but when you think it through, it usually is used in such an unbiblical way. Why should it surprise us when the enemy misuses spiritual realities to cripple us? And what about when he uses non-realities in spiritual garb to mislead us? This will be explored more in a later chapter on spiritual needs.

THE BASIS FOR A NEW PERCEPTION OF YOU

Now we come to where you need to deal with your distortions (false beliefs or prejudices). The best way to do this is to bring your perceptions into line with what God has to say. This will update your self-perception and allow a close scrutiny of your feelings. Some people are good at getting new concepts into their head but slow at feeling them, so be prepared—it may take some time.

What becomes real to you is that which translates into feelings, and it won't be real for you until that happens. For example, when you *feel* you are worth loving, you can know your mind has grasped the truth—you *are* worth loving and you really are loved.

When you begin to feel good about being you, you can act on it genuinely, out of your true inner self, much like you see so clearly demonstrated by Jesus. John says, "We saw Him living among us and He was full of grace and truth" (see 1 John 1:1 and John 1:14). The true self is a *manifestation of the true life of Christ.* Finding your true self is part of becoming Christlike. Your true self was born of the Spirit to that journey and cannot be discovered, enhanced, or given away *apart* from that journey (John 1:18). The enemy certainly doesn't want you to know this (Ephesians 4:11-16).

THE NEW PARENT EMERGING

I hope you sense where we are headed: your self-discovery and the fulfilling of your true needs in Part I, and into parenting itself in Part II. Our journey is doubly exciting: We will see the new you, and the beautiful parent your children will be gaining.

Δ

TAKING ACTION: SELF-DISCOVERY NEEDS

1. On a sheet of paper make two columns of numbers, 1 to 25 in each. In the left column, list qualities, characteristics and things you like about yourself. In the right, list what you dislike. After completing your lists, ask yourself:

   (a) Which list was easiest to complete?

   (b) Which list contains the most?

   (c) Are they evenly balanced or was I harder on myself on the right and softer on the left?

   (d) What does this tell me about my perception of myself?

2. On another sheet of paper, plan out a diagram of the family you grew up in. Put yourself in the center with spokes like in a wheel going out to Dad, Mom, brother, sister, etc., until all the significant others have been included. After you have completed your configuration, ask yourself the following questions of each relationship:

   (a) How did _____ see me?

   (b) Why did I feel _____ saw me that way?

   (c) Do I still feel _____ sees me that way?

   (d) If went to _____ and asked, "How do you really see me?" what might that person say?

   (e) Was my earlier perception of how that person saw me correct?

3. Get in touch with ways the inner child of the past may be dominating you. On a sheet of paper respond to this question: In relating with others, what do I fear most, and why? Study your lists before going on to the next chapter, which is on spiritual needs.

3

THE KEY TO YOUR PERSONAL STRUGGLE

When Jesus summed up the Old Testament—and life—in just two commandments (Matthew 22:37-39), He set the stage for your personal fulfillment as well as for your obedience to God's highest ideals. Loving God, others, and self was never presented as an option, because of who God is, what others need, and who you are. It had to be in the form of a command. Nothing less would do.

You know enough about your Heavenly Father to understand that any time He issues a command, there is more in it than a simple, "Because I said so." You may resort to that with your children at times, but God does not. There is a rationale behind every one of His commands that goes much deeper than what may appear on the surface.

You are a spiritual being, fashioned in God's image. The key, then, to understanding your personal struggle is and will always be spiritual, even though the immediate element on which you focus may be physical, intellectual, social, emotional or sexual. Understanding this, you can go directly to the heart of the matter:

Loving is the function of the spiritual being.

To partake of God and the basic essence of His nature, you are commanded to love. To relate adequately with another person—especially your child—love is called for. And to meet your own deepest need, nothing less than love will do. You were made for love.

When you wrap your arms around one of your children expressing your love for him, you acknowledge God's presence in your life, and you symbolically wrap your inner arms around yourself. In that moment you sense a deep, inner peace with Him, with your child, with yourself and with life. Those moments convince you that not only were you made for love, but that it is also the highest experience a person can know. In 1 John 4 we see that God is our source of love, and that John likens loving to knowing God.

A SPIRITUAL BEING

You need to see that you are a spiritual being—clear down to the core of your existence. All other aspects of self relate to that spiritual core and issue from it. Let me illustrate it this way.

You, the spiritual being, possess a physical body, a rational capacity, an emotional capacity, a social capacity and a sexual identity. (See Figure A.) As a spiritual being, your purpose is to mature in love by growing up into Christ (Ephesians 4:11-16). You must interpret your total life in terms of being one with Him, then manifest His love by living that oneness—with others and with your true self. You may have perceived your deepest need as that of being loved. In reality, it is to *be loving*. Your wholeness will manifests itself in your ability to love.

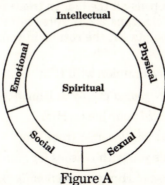

Figure A

John 3:16 tells us that because God loved, He gave. Wholeness always flows outward. God models that for you, as did Jesus and the Spirit. Thus, your deepest need is the ability to flow outward.

All this confirms how you must see yourself. When you see yourself as a spiritual being, suddenly the New Testament makes sense.

THE KEY

The key to who you are is found in your relationship with Jesus Christ: You are in Him and He is in you, and God sees you that way. You are one. You can interpret Galatians 2:20 like this: "And the life I now live in this bodily existence is not really of me, but it is Christ living out in me."

When this truth really dawns on you, your life will be transformed. Not only is Christ living in you, but God is also present in you and you have the Holy Spirit living in you as well. How can there be room for fear or weakness or copelessness? If the triune God is living in you, living a little life does not make sense. Something has to be radically wrong with this *theology*—or with your *experience*. Both cannot exist simultaneously.

PROOF FROM THE WORD

There's a lengthy passage in Colossians 2 and 3 in which Paul addresses self-understanding. He introduces this section by reminding you why he worked so hard on your behalf. It was so you "may be filled with courage and may be drawn together in love, and so have the full wealth of assurance which true understanding brings. In this way [you] will know God's secret, which is Christ Himself. He is the key that opens all the hidden treasures of God's wisdom and knowledge" (Colossians 2:2,3). After setting forth this awareness of Christ, he points out the results in your life by your being in Him:

2:6 - you *live* in union with Him

  :7 - you are *rooted* deeply in Him

     - you *build* your life on Him

     - your *strength* comes from Him

     - He fills you with reasons for *thanksgiving*

  :8 - because of Him you can *remain free* from what once enslaved you

  :9 - the full content of God's nature *resides in Him*

:10 - you have *full life* in union with Him

:11 - He *frees* you from the power of your sinful self

:12 - you have been *baptized* into His death and *raised* with Him to life

     - you have faith in the *active* and *activating power* of God

:13 - you have been brought to *life* in Christ

     - *all your sins are forgiven*

:14 - He did away with all your *past*

:15 - He shares with you His *victory* over all

:19 - you are held *securely* by Christ and in Christ

- you are under His *control*

- you are *growing* in His way

:20 - your real life is in Christ; He *lives* within you

:21-23 - you are called to *full life* in Him

3:1 - you are called to live a life from *above*

:2 - you are called to *think* on these new things

:3 - you are *hidden* with Christ *in* God

:4 - you will one day *share* in His full glory

:9 - you are to put off the *old self*

:10 - you are to put on the *new self;*

:11 - Christ is *in* you

:12 - He *loves* you and has *chosen* you

:13 - you can *love* and *forgive* one another

:14 - you are *bound together* by love

:15 - you can *experience* His *peace*

:16 - you can *live* to His glory and joy

This passage shows you how much you really are a spiritual being. You may be saying, "Okay, so I'm a spiritual being. Now what? What am I supposed to be, know or do?" I'm glad you asked!

YOUR MOST IMPORTANT CONNECTION

Since you are a spiritual being, your most important connection is with the Lord. Your life begins and ends there. It's *"in him we live and move and exist"* (Acts 17:28). Christ and you are partners in your living, your parenting, your relating and your thinking. You are loved, cared for, important, never alone, given resurrection power and led by His Spirit. You have residing in you the very presence, power, person and purpose of God. To define a human apart from his being spiritual is to miss his very essence.

OTHER ELEMENTS

This entire book works on the premise that you are a spiritual being who has physical, intellectual, social, emotional and sexual needs. To divorce any need from your inner spiritual core is to court disaster. The emotional needs relating to your spirituality will be addressed in chapter 4, the social in chapter 7, and the sexual in chapter 8. Chapters 5 and 6 address your need of other people and of the Lord.

THE UNION WITH THE SPIRITUAL

To move beyond each need in these areas is to move into the spiritual, for this is where they all find their full significance. Just as "all roads lead to Rome," so all needs ultimately lead to the spiritual. To understand that whatever need you experience comes from within the spiritual, not from the outside is to be well on the way to understanding how you operate.

TRUSTING GOD

The basis of any significant relationship, human or spiritual, is *trust*. If you are a single parent by virtue of the death of your mate, trust may be flowing easily due to your sense of utter dependence on God. On the other hand, if you believe God took your mate from you, for whatever reason, you may be dealing with a lot of anger, making it very hard for you to trust Him right now.

If you are working through a divorce, you may be at a stage in which you couldn't put one foot in front of another to keep going if it weren't for the assurance of His presence. Your trust level may never have been higher. Or you may be feeling betrayed by your Ex, by others, or even by the Lord Himself. In this case, trust will not come easily nor quickly toward anyone, the Lord included.

Roots of Mistrust

Karen's trust in God began to erode the night she lay in bed, feeling so terribly alone, her face hot with tears, pleading with God to bring her husband back.

"God, I don't have the ability to hold on to him, and if you don't help me, all will be lost. I believed his commitment to me was forever, no matter what, and I need You to hold him to it."

Both had been church leaders and she *knew* it was God's will he come back to her and the children. She bargained with the Lord, telling Him all she'd do for Him once her husband was back and things could go on as before. In spite of her praying and bargaining, her Ex did not return.

When I met her in response to her cry for help and counseling, her trust had been transformed into disillusion, hurt and confusion, and a feeling of having been betrayed. "I prayed God would bring him back to me and the children, but God didn't do it."

At this point, challenging her theology of prayer or her understanding of love wasn't the answer for Karen. She was experiencing a crisis of trust, cut off from the One she needed most. Because it involved a lost love relationship, this would be no small task for her. Trust is a gift we give, and she had chosen to withhold hers for reasons deeper than the trust itself. She also had lost trust in her Ex, in herself, and in the basic assumptions by which she had lived. Our trust levels touch all these relationships. So does our mistrust.

There is no reason for not trusting God except for that which lies within. Trust is a spiritual phenomenon, a spiritual need. There's nothing about God, His Word or any honest experience with Him to merit our mistrust. He is trustworthy.

This is what Jesus meant when He said, "I am the truth": "I am trust-worthy."

The reason you do not trust can be found in your own perceptions of reality. Trust is not earned; it is a gift. Neither God nor your children need to earn your trust. You give them this gift — God, because He is who He is; your children, because they are your children. To withhold the gift is to declare *your lack of being trusting,* and that is a spiritual problem, your spiritual problem. Anyone who sacrifices His Son for your forgiveness has more than demonstrated His trustworthiness. Your children merit your trust because they are living out your expectations of them.

CONNECTEDNESS

Since your deepest inner need is to relate adequately with God, others, and your true self, how you connect is also a spiritual need. (*Connecting* is used in terms of the meaning of John 15:5: "I am the vine, and you are the branches.")

Your inner dialogue connects you with your true self. Spoken dialogue is the way you connect with others. Prayer is the way you connect with God.

Blocks to your connectedness arise from within you. Such negative emotions as bitterness, hostility, misplaced anger, guilt, fear, resentment and jealously cause you to distance yourself, disconnecting from Him, as well as from others and yourself. This ends any sense of belonging, and it destroys fellowship.

Dorothea had been a single parent for seven years when I first met her. Her disconnectedness began as a young teenager when she was repeatedly molested by one of her mother's several husbands. The pain and shame of her experiences left her so devastated she felt no other man would ever want her if he knew. She was fairly sure her mother was aware of what had been going on, but her mother never said anything, nor ever came to her daughter's defense. When Dorothea did marry to escape the home situation, she could never bring herself to any real connectedness with her husband. Their marriage was short-lived, leaving her with a child to raise.

What surprised her most in her counseling, though, was the discovery that she was unable to commit herself to a close relationship with the Lord. She saw her Heavenly Father and His Son as male images, and males always meant pain and suffering for her. Males were not to be trusted. Thus she never felt she belonged. If you can't belong with God, where can you belong at the human level? To paraphrase 1 John 4:20: "How can you connect with one you cannot see if you cannot connect with one you can see?"

HOPE

Christian hope is an assurance based on the faithfulness of God. When the author of Hebrews gave us that Faith Chapter, Hebrews 11, he spoke of the kind of hope faith visualizes: the hope of change, of maturing, of being right with God, of becoming all He wants us to be. It is the parental hope of becoming what our children need. It is the personal hope of growing up into Christ and becoming fully His person. It is the hope of *becoming*.

Hope is a spiritual matter. It is "Christ in you, the hope of glory" (Colossians 1:27, NASB). If you could, apart from hope, become all you desire to be, you'd already be there. You hope because you know how weak and limited you are. To lose hope in a relationship or a marriage is one thing. To lose spiritual hope, which births all other true hopes, is another. Hope means you will never come up empty. Hope means you will allow God to act within all your being. Hope means a partnership with Jesus Christ in the work He has begun in you, a work He has promised to fulfill on His great, coming day.

Immature hope is self-centered, self-limiting and self-destructive. It's what you want, not what He wants for you. It's what you dream, not what He envisions for you, and it's consumed by what you believe you need, not by what your real needs are. Immature hopes tend to be transient, immediate, even self-defeating. True hope, on the other hand, is eternal and always fulfilling. It takes you beyond yourself to all He has for you. The statement Paul made of the future is equally true of the present: "Eye has not seen and ear has not heard . . . all that God has prepared for those who love Him" (1 Corinthians 2:9, NASB). The key to hope isn't in what may result; it's in the one in whom you hope, the one who guarantees the results. (No Christian has ever fully discovered all God has in store for the here-and-now. We tend to be poverty stricken in our imagining of what He has for us now, and even more so regarding the hereafter.)

PURPOSE

Spiritual beings have the highest purpose of all. You are His partner in whatever He is doing. You speak of your children as "my children," yet they are not yours any more than your life is yours. You are His; they are His. He has given you life that you might use it to glorify Him. He has given them to you so that you might be His partner in raising them. Your purpose and their purpose together is in Him, spiritual.

Ephesians 4:11-16 reveals that when you became God's child He shared spiritual gifts with you to carry out His will in your life. This same principle holds true for parenting. When you were granted the privilege of being a parent to others of His children, He offered you the skills and gifts needed to fulfill that task. If you don't understand His purpose, or if you quench the Spirit's working, you are stuck with the natural model of your past to pattern your parenting after. You are on your own, one place you dare not be in the task of parenting.[1]

Proverbs 22:6 (KJV) tells us to "train up a child in the way he [or she] should go." That way is to be *His* way, not yours. It's obvious, looking at the Christian world within our churches, that His way is foreign to many people. They are raising their children in their own way and are giving too little thought to what that way is and what it means for their children. They say, "If it was good enough for me, it is good enough for them." But maybe it *wasn't* good enough for you — it wasn't what you needed — and maybe it is far less than what they need. Part II of this book takes a long, hard look at this.

GUIDANCE

I have crossed the North Atlantic Ocean several times by air and each time it has been overcast so I have yet to see the water below. But no plane ever got lost. Each one had a navigational system that was not dependent on sight but helped the navigator "see" where he was going even when visibility was extremely limited. You also need a navigational system for your personal life, especially for parenting, that allows you to "see" where you are going. That system is divine guidance, which is a spiritual matter, too.

I must confess quite frankly that, if God is guiding all the parents who claim to be under His guidance, I believe God is in big trouble. The fact that He wants to be your guide is indisputable. Look at all the passages of Scripture inviting you to follow. Then think of the contradictory styles represented in books by Christians, all purporting to represent "God's way." Finding a meaningful way through the contemporary clouds of confusion requires divine guidance. The navigational system you grew up under, and tend to duplicate, is inadequate for today's excessive pace. Your children aren't going to retreat to the sixties or seventies, nor are they going to accept any "Because I said so." They need guidance for today's world, and they need it now. Only with the Spirit working through you as their trusted parent can they receive what they truly need.

My mother used to be pretty convincing when she shared her guidance with me, as if she and God were partners in the matter. She spoke with enough authority to convince me that what she said was what God said. Years passed before I discovered she and God were not always on speaking terms, but to this day the little child inside me has a hard time realizing God doesn't speak the way my mother did—He never does. He just loves it into you.

RENEWAL

It has become obvious in our push-and-pull culture, with all its mounting tension and pressure, that our children are being squeezed into their own pressure-cooker existence. A lot of lives lie on trash heaps, and they didn't get there all on their own or by burning out in seeking first His Kingdom. Our parenting failures as a culture are a testimony to our true values. There isn't any parent-child tragedy recorded but what I, as a counselor, have seen it in some family in a local church. Christians are not immune from lousy parenting.

Rapid changes in our culture account for part of this, and because of these constant changes, constant renewal is necessary. You need new information, insights and listening skills. But more important, you need to see that renewal is a spiritual phenomenon, a renewal of the heart, being open to the Spirit's full response. The result, then, can be a renewed spirit, intellect, volition and emotion, and renewed parenting.

Personal maturing and renewal affects the total person, including his parenting. You need spiritual renewal that will allow you to be fresh at each stage of your own development and at each stage of each child's. What worked once at a junior high level for me did not work when my oldest daughter reached junior high. And what worked for her experience still needed up-dating when the youngest got there. To parent both of them on the basis of my experiences would have been to miss meeting their needs. Truth doesn't change; method of application does. Teens need honest answers you may not be prepared to give if you're still stuck back in your own level of experience and understanding.

When they say to you, "But Dad, you don't understand," before you get defensive, back off and take a good look at what you are doing. There may be some truth in their cry.

I used to tell my kids I was in our high school's first driver training class but it had to be cancelled when the mule died.

All children get tired of hearing about "the good old days" as answers to contemporary dilemmas. What they need is someone to listen when they talk about their "present daze."

For example, what one parent needed to *hear* (though it was very painful) was, "Dad, I walk to school alone because I refused to smoke a joint on the way with the other girls that live in our area. They got even by telling me I was too stuck up to associate with them and by telling all the other kids at school I am a lesbian. Do you know how that hurts?"

DIRECTION

Ever since Jesus taught us that the *summum bonum* of life is to "seek first the Kingdom of God," direction has been a prime spiritual concern. Now that you know you can find it, you need to seek it. You can ask directions from the Owner, and then you can follow them to fulfillment (Matthew 6:33).

The average family in our culture is so multi-directioned it appears non-directed. It goes around in circles, yet slowly, inching along, it does move. It really doesn't start from point *A* with any intention of arriving at point *B*. It just sort of arrives somewhere and assumes, "This must be point *B*." Then, in another time, and in another place, it simply announces an arrival at point *C*. It drifts, depending on circumstances. Paul spoke of this in Ephesians 4 when he viewed the little matchbox of life on a wind-tossed sea, being first blown here, then there. It went where circumstances pushed it. Most families are like that. No wonder children feel insecure.

The present generation is called the "me" generation. Why not call it the "lost" generation? Lost in its search for the Kingdom, it is no wonder it feels alone. Darkness is more fearful when all you have is artificial light. Truth always seems strange when you've clung to prejudice and delusion. Without a clear sense of direction any generation can become lost. Remember the reforms instituted by Josiah after the custodian found a lost Bible in a closet of the Temple? (2 Kings 22:3 – 23:27. See also 2 Chronicles 34:3-7,29-33.)

PRAYER

This should be so obvious that only a simple reminder will do; however, there is perhaps no area within the spiritual being that needs more attention. You must begin with the profoundest prayer of all: "Lord, teach me to pray."

Have you ever prayed without an agenda? Most of us pray as if God were a celestial Santa Claus with a bottomless bag of gifts, everything from healing to disciplining. He gets asked to repair cars and marriages, fix plumbing and budgets, find lost kittens and prodigals, heal ingrown toenails and leukemia.

Don't get me wrong—agendas do have a place in praying. You do have real needs to be met; God does invite you to pray with no holds barred; but the main function of prayer often gets overlooked.

For example, you are concerned about the well-being of all your children. Where do you begin to pray in the light of their real needs? Your agenda might touch many of their significant needs but how you pray for them will be determined by how you relate with them. This limits it to your own perception and understanding. When you pray for God to guide them, you are conscious of their need for guidance—the guidance you are (or are not) giving them and that which they may (or may not) be getting elsewhere.

But what if you came to Him, opened yourself up, and prayed this way? "Lord, You know my children better than I do and You care more about them than I ever could. Teach me how to pray for them so that in my praying I can learn how I should live and can be a part of Your divine guidance by interpreting Your will to them."

Now what happens? By setting aside your agenda you now allow the Holy Spirit to give you the Heavenly Father's agenda. There is nothing you need more. Your agenda for your children, as much as you love them, can actually end up being a block instead of a help. Being taught by the Spirit to pray for each of your children, you will know what their real needs are. He will reveal them to you.

This does not mean you cannot or should not pray for what is most obvious to you. It means you need to learn to pray also for what is known to Him and far less obvious to you. At one point you may be praying, "Lord, help my children share my joy in this new relationship in my life," when the Holy Spirit's agenda may be, "Lord, help me hear and share their pain because of this new relationship in my life."

The lost art in prayer is that of listening. Many single parents do a lot of praying. At times it is the only life-line left. But parenting is at its best when you cultivate the art of listening to your true self, to your children's real needs, and most of all to God and His agenda for all of you.

▲

TAKING ACTION:
YOUR SPIRITUAL NEEDS

At this stage in your life's journey, it will be helpful for you to identify the expectations you have. As you respond to each area listed below, you will be making a perception check in terms of what you are looking for, what you consider to be your sources of help and what you may be putting on others. Write out your responses, then study them. What do they tell you about yourself and your deep, inner needs?

1. What do I expect of myself?
2. What do I expect of God?
3. What do I expect of my church?

4. What do I expect of my children?
5. What do I expect of my immediate family?
6. What do I expect of my friends?
7. What do I expect of my Ex?
8. What do I expect of my in-laws?
9. What do I expect of new relationships?
10. What do I expect of dates?
11. What do I expect of marriage?
12. What do I expect of the opposite gender?
13. What do I expect to learn from all this?
14. What do my responses tell me about myself?
15. What spiritual assumptions emerge in my responses? What is it I expect others to do for me?
16. What do I need most for the Lord to do for me?
17. What basic attitude do I have toward life at this point in my journey?

4

YOUR HIDDEN HUNGERS ALONG THE WAY

You have some pretty heavy emotions to deal with, so before diving into this chapter I want you to take a good, deep breath. It may take a little while for your feelings to allow you to surface for another one. May I suggest you pull out the following promise, which God gave to Israel during a troubled time:

Do not cling to the events of the past, or dwell on what happened long ago. Watch for the *new thing* I am going to do. It is happening already—you can see it now! (Isaiah 43:18,19)

Every time negative emotions threaten to hold you under, return to this promise and claim it as your own. The Lord is doing a new thing in your life and, according to Philippians 1:6, He *will* complete it.

THE DEATH OF A MATE

You knew throughout the years of your marriage you had some deep emotional needs. Like many others, though, you buried them under an avalanche of activities: keeping a home, relating to a husband, raising three children who came along within the first ten years, and being busy in the church. You knew that someday you would have to get serious about those inner needs, but at the time things seemed to be in balance. At least you were keeping your head above water for the most part. Then it happened.

The police officer at the door tried his best to soften the blow but there was no way around it. Your mate had been in a terrible accident, and he was pronounced dead at the scene. Your whole world suddenly caved in. You, "Mrs. Dependent," as you perceived yourself, were suddenly faced with widowhood, single parenting and being alone, which meant a zillion problems you never expected to have to face at thirty-two years of age. The emotional needs you had packed away suddenly burst forth and came tumbling down on you with all the force of a house collapsing around your ears.

A DIVORCE

Or . . .

You knew things had not been going well in your marriage the past three years, but his work and your involvement with the family, house, job, church and other activities kept the two of you from talking much about it. During this time your emotional needs had been put on hold as you tried to keep the relationship going. Then it happened.

He wanted out of the marriage, and your world turned upside down. You weren't sure how you would get through it, and the needs you tried to ignore before hadn't gone away. They had been hidden and now what had been a little hill grew to become a mountain. You were in trouble and you knew it. Suddenly you felt something you hadn't experienced since you were a little girl—you were weak, shaken, confused—and *scared*.

EMOTIONAL NEEDS

All of us have emotional needs, and to deny we have them is to court disaster. When you deny an emotion or repress it, you bury it alive. It continues to grow and fester, and it poisons your entire system. (*Repression* occurs when a strong, usually negative, emotion is subconsciously blocked from the conscious mind because the pain is so intense the person cannot accept it. It is still present in the subconscious, though, and very much alive.) What I want you to do right now is assess your needs so some realistic plan of action can be worked out to meet them. Coming through the death of one's spouse or through a divorce takes an emotional toll on everyone involved. Even if you wanted the divorce, sought and pushed for it, you still have an emotional upheaval to deal with.

A TIME FOR REFLECTION

Take a moment and reflect on this question: *What am I feeling right now about the divorce, (or death of my mate), being a single parent or being me?* Get in touch with the feelings that are there. For example, if you have gone through a divorce, you may be feeling scared about where everything will end up, fearful of being a single parent, dependent on others due to a feeling of powerlessness, and angry that it all has come to this. You may feel very unchristian toward your Ex, or like begging for things to be put back together somehow. You have a kaleidoscope of constantly changing feelings, with some that show up more often than others. All these feelings tell you something important about yourself. They reveal your emotional needs. The greater the need, the more complex and intense the feelings. You are struggling for emotional survival.

Here's another question: *What has all this done to me?* The initial shock of sensing your life is about to end is a natural one. But you have gotten through it this far—do you still feel the same way? Or has it lessened? If your emotional needs have not been met in the past, you may still feel life is over for you. Like the prodigal son in the far country, you have been brought to yourself. It *should* put you in touch with what is going on inside you, what your resources are, how well you are able to cope, and how much you can rely on the Lord to see you through. But if the emotional needs are too deep through neglect or a lack of self-awareness, all your needs have been compounded. (See Luke 15:11-32, especially verse 17.)

Another question to consider is: *Where am I now?* You may be stuck in the denial stage even though the death or divorce took place long ago. If you were divorced a year ago and are still wearing your wedding rings, or if your mate died a couple of years ago and you are still saying "we" and "us," you probably are stuck in denial. Your emotional needs have not allowed you to move through this stage toward recovery and adjustment. How does one recover? Each of us takes a private journey into this jungle; however, God's grace is all-sufficient for every need, including this one (2 Corinthians 12:7-10), and if it is allowed to work in us, we can travel *through* the tangles to a meaningful resolution.

WHAT DO OTHERS THINK?

One question we all have asked is: *How do others see me? What do they think of me?* If you are widow or widower, they may have a lot of sympathy, understanding and genuine concern. On the other hand, it may seem like some people you thought you understood have gone crazy. Your very close friend suddenly drops you without any real reason. She just is no longer available. Maybe she is insecure in her own marriage and fears you will steal her husband. If you're divorced, maybe she senses a loyalty to both you and your Ex so is staying away from both, not wanting to take sides.

Other people may move toward you because they want to get out of their own marriages and are envious of your new situation.

In addition, unfortunately, in most every congregation someone will come along and tell you he will do "anything" to help you, but he doesn't mean fix your car, stay with the children, or do the laundry so you can have a Saturday at the park.

You need to realize you cannot control how others see you, or what they think of you, or if they mentally consign all divorced persons to the local leper colony. What matters is how *you* see you — what *you* think of you. If your perception of yourself is within the boundaries of reality and you work at a healthy emotional balance, the Lord will lead you through this with a solid sense of growth and maturing.

If you are too concerned about how others see you, you may isolate yourself from the people who truly care about you. If you need the approval of all those around you, you will be in real trouble because divorce is not easy for everyone to handle. In some circles it is still the "unpardonable sin." In others it is acceptable only if you are the "innocent partner." By giving others the power to tell you whether or not you are worth loving and accepting, you give away something that belongs only to the Lord of your life. Better take it back from them, surrender it to Him and believe what He tells you about you.

HANDLING YOUR ANGER

Now let me ask you: *How do you feel about having to go through all of this?* With the death of a mate your other feelings may be accompanied by anger. You loved him and miss him terribly, but you are also angry.

Normal Anger

You need to know that this anger is natural and normal. You had plans, dreams and needs. With him gone, the plans and dreams are gone too, and the needs are worse than before. More than that, he went before you did. He died on you. That wasn't part of the "unwritten agreement" you had when you married. Now you have to deal with all these enormous emotions, especially the negative, conflicting ones, and he is not there to talk them out with. You *can* love someone and be angry with him at the same time. You know that.

Deal with that anger as a natural feeling—but do deal with it.

Or you have gone through a divorce and are angry. She walked out on you, left you with a pile of bills and two children to care for along with a whole sack of emotions to sort out. What I want to ask you is: What is the real emotion hiding beneath your anger? Is it guilt because you were not a better husband or more attentive to her needs or a better listener? Is it fear that others will see you as a failure, think less of you, question your lovability since she didn't want to stay married to you? Is it hurt because all your dreams have been shattered, your pride stabbed, your ego cut? Maybe it's jealousy over her freedom to walk away from all the responsibility and carve out another life for herself. Or frustration when you think of two children to raise and how you will answer their questions— "Daddy, why did Mommy go away? Did Mommy stop loving you?"

To hide all these things under a blanket of anger is to keep yourself from facing the truth. Maybe you really feel the anger toward yourself, not her. We meet angry people often who never have been able to face the pain inside them, and the anger oozes out of them into every potential relationship. They have never forgiven themselves so they go around continually damning their Ex. They frustrate the grace of God in their lives. Can you be honest enough about your anger to allow the Spirit of Truth to deal with it?

Anger and Sin

Anger is neither right nor wrong. What you *do* with it is right or wrong. Paul states in Ephesians 4:26, "If you become angry, do not let your anger lead you into sin, and do not stay angry all day." Verse 27 goes on to add, "Don't give the devil a chance."

Look for the deeper thing, the emotion that is crippling your recovery. If you get locked into your anger and never get beneath it, you can spend the rest of your life nursing it and sharing it with others.

Your "normal" anger can "lead you into sin" if you continue to vent that anger. You can sin by dumping it all over another person, threatening your relationship. You can sin by swallowing it, making yourself sick. Anger is a signal that something else is wrong. Your emotional system has been thrown out of balance.

Dangerous Anger

I remember well the woman who told me she would not forgive her Ex because to do so would get him off the hook. The doctor called me in to counsel with her because he was losing her and saw no medical reason. She was dying following a surgery that was not that critical. What was killing her, literally and figuratively, was her spirit of revenge and her bitter desire to keep her Ex on the hook. (I'm not sure what that hook is. Maybe it's a cross.)

She needed to realize that her Ex was off building a new life for himself and she was the one on her own hook. She was contaminating her relationships with her children, and she was killing herself. The children continued to relate to their father, but she embittered herself to where she couldn't even stand to be alone with herself. The day she decided to let him off the hook was the day she was free to be healed — physically, emotionally and spiritually, and every other way as well. When the Lord heals, He heals totally!

Fear, anger and guilt can get so mixed up you don't really know which is which. You act angry because you don't want anyone (not even yourself) to know you are afraid. Or, you feel guilty over your lack of meeting another's need so you cover it up with anger. You may be feeling angry toward another person when, if you examined it, you would discover you really are afraid that person will reject you. Yet your anger keeps that person at arm's length. See how confusing it can be? Whenever you experience anger in a relationship, especially a significant one, always ask yourself: *What is beneath it? What am I trying to hide that I would rather not face?*

ANOTHER QUESTION

What will it take to lift you up again? Your are in a pit because of your divorce. What will you have to do to get out of this pit? What will you have to allow the Lord to do in your life? One thing is certain. You can't stay here. You owe the Lord more than this, and you owe your children and family more. You owe yourself more. How can you make the adjustments that will allow Him to change you? Now, at least, your focus is on the sky above rather than on the bottom of the pit, worrying whether it will hold you or allow you to sink deeper.

With that change of focus you notice something you hadn't seen before in your despair. The Lord has carved neat little notches in the side of the pit, going all the way to the top. With your desire and with His strength you're going to start climbing out. This pit is no place for a child of His love to be living in. You're on your way!

I find 2 Timothy 1:7 a real help at this point: "God has not given us the Spirit of fear; but of power, and of love and of a sound mind"(KJV).

Fear here means those inner fears we create to keep us from having to face life or other people. (Normal fear is a reaction from an obvious threat. Pathological fear is a fear of rejection based on self-rejection.) *Power* is strength, the ability to cope. It is the power to live as He has called you to live, to face and overcome the difficulty. *Love* is the ability both to care for others and to allow yourself to be cared for. *Sound mind* means right thinking that leads to proper self-control and self-discipline. Memorize this verse along with its meaning and keep it on hand for quick use.

THIS WAY UP

You have already begun the climb out—you have looked up and you have seen God's blue sky. You feel the warmth of His smile beckoning you to come. The first thing you need to do is what Paul admonishes when you are about to run a race: Jettison the excess baggage (Hebrews 12:1-3). By that I mean, take a good look at your emotional past and get rid of the garbage that is weighing you down.

The climb isn't an easy one and you don't need any hindrances. You need to feel good about being you. Spend time with people who truly love you and allow yourself to feel their love and warmth. The church is to be a mutual affirmation society. If you don't find love and warmth in yours, look for one where you can. Whatever you do, don't let yourself sit in a "judgment corner" while others hack away at you because you've been divorced. Let the Lord deal with them. Find yourself a "love seat" among His true saints and let them love you. You are on your way up, into His joy for you. He's the one inviting you out of the pit, so keep climbing, no matter what.

FACING FACTS

The next step is to come to grips with your stuff in the marriage that didn't work out. This is hard and will take a lot of prayerful insight, but it needs to be done. I know I'm asking you to lance a boil and it hurts like sin, but if you don't, the pus will remain inside and the infection will spread. Claim the Lord's full grace. Take the scalpel of the Spirit and carefully peel back the affected areas. Ask Him to expose the core by pointing out to you where you were wrong, where you failed, where you need to ask forgiveness, where you need to make amends. Don't load your stuff on your Ex and don't allow his or her stuff to get dumped on you. Assess the full relationship and your part in it honestly. No marriage breakup is the fault of just one. It is a shared responsibility.

If you are getting a divorce or have been through it, stand in front of the mirror, look yourself squarely in the eye, and say this to yourself: "I am divorced. This is a fact. My marriage is over. For whatever reasons, it did not work out. I am willing to accept the full blame for my part in its breakup. I have asked for forgiveness and I am learning to forgive myself. I know God has forgiven me. I know He loves me. I am on my journey out of the pit I have been in. I cannot do it alone but He is with me. Together we will make it."

If you lost your husband in death, go back and see what the relationship was like during the years of the marriage and see if there was anything you need to own up to. Your healing will be retarded if you fail to own your part of the relationship. All need to do this, but when a death has terminated the relationship you sometimes end up with a whole lot to face all at once. If your relationship was not doing too well at the time of his death, or if you have had deep struggles throughout the marriage, you may be in real trouble right now. You may have more emotions rattling around in you than you can possibly handle alone. *Get help!*

In both cases, divorce or the death of a mate, how well you relate to your children will be determined by how well you handle your part of the problems in your relationship with your spouse. Your children don't need you putting your stuff on them, either, through discipline or holding back from them because you fear they may discover your inadequacies. It is time to face your hidden hungers, resolve them, and move on up to the next step.

FORGIVENESS AND FORGIVING

One of our deeper struggles centers in the need for both forgiveness and to be forgiving. No element is more intrinsic to our spiritual well-being. You have made as honest an assessment as you could. You have allowed the Holy Spirit to show you your part in all of it. It has not been easy, and the picture that emerged may not be one you want to frame and hang in the living room. You know now, though, that you were a good mate, if less than perfect. You have examined that imperfectness and are ready to deal with it. You can flog yourself with it, wear it around your neck like an albatross, or deny it.

Or you can *deal with it in an effective, productive manner, pos-*

sible only because of the cross of Christ. You can forgive yourself, thus releasing it to Him and allowing Him to nail it to His cross on your behalf. To forgive yourself is to first *own your imperfectness* (it is yours alone)—and to *fully acknowledge your part* in the problems. Then you must *turn it all over* to the one who died for you.

Why keep yourself on the hook when God doesn't keep you there? Why condemn yourself when He does not condemn you? Only forgiveness can free you to live differently. It alone is the key to change. In John 8, Jesus said to the woman, "Go and sin no more," but only after He had forgiven her. You will change after you have accepted His forgiveness and have forgiven yourself (John 8:1-11). You will be freed to become forgiving of all others, no matter what (Matthew 6:12; 18:21-35).

Now you need to forgive your Ex. I want you to let him or her off the hook for whatever was done to you, *no matter what,* even though he may have cheated on you and abused you and the children. Your emotional health is at stake.

Forgiving doesn't mean not fighting for custody if it is needed. It doesn't mean not demanding child support payments on time. It doesn't mean not standing up for your needs. What it does mean is dealing with the past so it can *be* past. It means clearing the relationship of any balance of unmet needs so you can live again. It means giving Jesus any spirit of revenge. It means being free to recover, to grow, to rebuild, and it means having your present unshackled from the spirit of bitterness. Whatever that person owes you, it is nothing compared to what you owed God. And He forgave you *all!*

It may be helpful to write your Ex a letter, sharing your feelings, hurts, disappointments and regrets. You may want to write several and tear them up. But, in time, write one that expresses what is deep inside you. If you can't bring yourself to write anything else, just say, "I forgive you." Let it go. The time has come for healing, and the price of healing is the granting of forgiveness.

I do not say "forgive" as though it were easy or even simple. It may be the hardest step you have to face. Forgiveness is a process much like an oyster goes through when it forms a pearl around an irritant of quartz. Day after day the oyster secretes a milky substance that gradually covers the sharp edges until at last the pain diminishes.

As you go through your process day after day, you will eventually come to where it is easier. The beauty of the final result causes you to forget the pain, and it is a prize which, as God's child, you may one day lay at His feet. In the process of creating that priceless gift for Him, something wonderful also happens to you. It is not by accident that the apostle John pictures the entrance to glory as having gates of pearl.

Forgiveness involves more than forgiving seventy-times-seven sins, or the same person seventy-times-seven times. Every time the offense pops into your consciousness, you need to apply another layer of that milky substance, God's grace. When you relive that experience in your dreams, you need to apply God's grace to it all over again with your first waking moment. You never forget, but you do not have to be forever locked into the icy grip of your memories. Forgiveness frees you from their power. That is the good news of the gospel.

GOD'S PERCEPTION OF YOU

Your major emotional Source is the One who dares to call you His own. It is essential, as noted before, that you understand His perceptions of you. He knows you as you truly are. When you do see His vision of you, *accept it as your own*. Match your feelings to that perception; begin to feel the feelings that grow out of it; then emotionally you will be made whole.

When you finally can believe God's view of you as His child, it also frees you to become what you are designed to be. Through this you learn to love and be loved. There's no better passage for you to examine in regard to this than 1 John 4:7-21. God is love. When you plug into that source, His love flows first to you, then through you to others. Your emotional stability is in direct measure to the ability you have to love and be loved.

Your deep need is to be loving, yet the person with acute, unmet emotional needs is not able to love. Look around in the church where you worship. How many people do you see who are emotionally unable to love or be loved? Most of the people around you are content to stay as they are. What they do is up to them. If you want your emotional needs met, though, you will have to do something more than just sit there and be one of the bunch. You will have to be assertive in seeking sources, helps, information and nourishment that will meet your need in good measure. What you accomplish is up to you and the Spirit's working in your life. There are excellent resources available to you today. Some are listed at the end of this book. Ask your pastor if you can borrow a commentary on 1 John and explore in depth the meaning of 4:7-21. Its truths are profound.

THREE TASKS OF THE SELF

There are three tasks for the self to accomplish as a whole, mature Christian person. The **first,** is to *discover who you are and to know fully whose you are.* Without knowledge of your true self you will be dealing with a "me" you do not understand. If you can't understand you, how can you ever understand another? *(True self,* as used in Scripture and psychology, refers to that person you are in reality, not the one disguised with layers of defenses whom you share with others in safe ways. It is the person God knows.)

The **second** task is to *enhance the self.* You have discovered who you are so you can know yourself; now you need to become, by His grace, the best you that you can become. You have spiritual gifts but you need to enhance them. You have a personality but it needs to be enhanced. You need to grow toward completion as 1 John 4 points out. God gave you life but your enhancement, what you do with it, is your gift to Him in response.

Then comes the **third** and final task, the task that marks true maturity and emotional balance. You are to *give the self away* in love, service, ministry, caring, helping, and whatever He calls you to do. You are learning to spend and be spent for others.

NOT LEVELING OFF

There is no plateau of growth you may achieve that is worth leveling off at. You may be head and shoulders above all those around you, but that plane is easy to reach. Just settle in among a bunch of "spiritual pygmies," and you can look like a giant.

But put the overlay of Christ's full stature against your life. Now who's the "spiritual pygmy"? You are to grow up into Him and this growth is what your children need to see in you. As long as you continue to grow, you will be what they need you to be. Leveling off would rob you, it would rob them, and it certainly would rob Him. So continually re-evaluate your needs, resources and growth to make sure you are moving along well in the emotional and spiritual process of maturing.

REFLECTING ON THE SPIRITUAL

You will not mature emotionally without maturing spiritually, nor will you mature spiritually without maturing emotionally. You cannot separate the two. You will never find a spiritual giant in an immature personality because the emotional limits the spiritual. John says, "Perfect [mature] love drives out all fear" (1 John 4:18). Love has to do with maturity—fear has to do with immaturity. Both are spiritual, but both involve the emotional as well.

As you mature and become stronger in your relationship with the Lord, what happens in your relationship with your children? Do you become more understanding and patient? Is it easier to listen and give of yourself to them? As you move closer to Him, you move closer to them, don't you? At the same time you also feel better about being you—you have moved closer to your true self. You can tell how you are doing emotionally and spiritually by how you relate to Him, to them, and to yourself.

A SUGGESTED PRAYER FOR YOU

"Lord, there are times when the emotional struggle all but overwhelms me. Did it ever seem that way for You? The Word tells me You were tempted in all points such as I am, but at times it is hard to imagine You ever felt like I do. I need to know my feelings are not strange to You and that, even though I may not understand them, You do. Then I can trust You to interpret them to me and to lead me through them to where You want me to be. Help me find answers to my emotional needs. Help me let You be my primary Source. Help me be open to the love of others for me. Help me to be loving. I want so much to be whole. You who are holy and whole—make me whole too. In Jesus' name. Amen."

Δ

TAKING ACTION: EMOTIONAL NEEDS

There are people in your life who help you, or hinder you, in meeting your emotional needs. List those persons in each of the following areas and identify them as helpers or hinderers. Then note what your responses mean in terms of how your emotional needs are or are not being met through these relationships.

1. Emotional security, feeling loved no matter what.
2. A sense of belonging.
3. A sense of freedom to be me.

4. The discipline to set limits on myself.
5. Feeling accepted.
6. Having the approval of significant others.
7. Being affirmed.
8. Being independent at times by depending on myself.
9. Being responsible for myself.
10. Dealing with my fears, keeping them at a minimum.
11. Growing in my ability to love and be loved.
12. Having a true sense of having been forgiven.
13. Having a sense of worthwhileness.
14. Feeling good about being me.

5

WHY GO IT ALONE?

Everyone is on a journey. More accurately, we are on several journeys simultaneously. We have a faith journey, a relational, an intellectual, a physical, a sexual and a social journey. These all combine in what we might call our life's journey. Right now you are assessing where you are on this life's journey which means taking an inventory of each of those mentioned above.

You are also on a parenting journey. You happen to be on a single-parenting one, having come from an earlier dual-parent journey that may or may not have been successful. If you are a typical single parent, you are attempting to go that journey mostly alone. Is this true of you? If so, I want you to answer an important question: *Why go it alone?* At this most critical stage in your life's journey, why attempt to do it alone when help and support are available to lessen the load? Paul taught us to "bear one another's burdens and thus fulfill the law of Christ" (Galatians 6:2), and you need help with yours. Not only that, but you also need all that sharing can bring (Galatians 5:13,14).

WHY YOU ISOLATE YOURSELF

Many single parents, especially near the beginning of their journey, isolate themselves for a number of reasons.

Trauma

If you lost your mate through death, the trauma alone can be isolating. A lot of private grief work must be done and this tends to isolate you. You need to attend to that secluded work so you won't get caught up in a social whirlwind that could distract you from getting through the grief stages, especially denial. A divorce can be just as isolating. The process itself may be messy, never mind the complications of family life, church life, community life, and so on. You probably feel like digging a hole and crawling in. One or two friends may be all you can handle at this time.

Fear

Fear can be a reason for isolating yourself. Having to defend yourself at this point is not enjoyable. The fear of rejection usually accompanies the discomfort of having to explain. You may also fear that previously meaningful relationships will be diminished or terminated because of the attitude of others regarding your divorce.

Guilt

Guilt can be a factor. You wanted the marriage to work, but here you are, re-singled through divorce. Lots of dreams are gone. You aren't exactly feeling your best, and those condescending looks from others hook a very sensitive place inside you. As a Christian you are well aware God has a "best" for your life but right now you feel you have missed it. You don't want to risk people's judgment and your sense of guilt makes it easy to pull back into isolation.

Anger

Anger has its way of isolating you also. You may be angry with a lot of people who failed you (and still may be failing you) as you reached out earlier in your struggle. People can be very disappointing when you truly need them. They can get so wrapped up in themselves they can't see pain in others. Every church has its judgmental persons who have an uncanny skill in saying the wrong thing in the most devastating ways, and they do it with a smile as they promise to "pray" for you.

Though most of us were taught as little children that the eleventh commandment is, "Thou shalt not be angry," we still feel angry, and anger isolates within the Christian community because many see it as inappropriate. (However, God was angry, as was Jesus, at appropriate times. Anger is an emotion generated by a perception of something being wrong. For example, in the face of child abuse and injustice it would be a sin not to be angry.)

Independence

You may feel the need to demonstrate to family, friends, church, community—and your Ex—that you can go it alone. You can be independent. Of course you can, but you don't have to prove it to the point where you isolate yourself and seal your own failure.

You are living in a "macho" age, and that gets interpreted as being independent and going it alone. Most male single parents are locked into this delusion. Well, Dad, can I share an insight with you? You need other people. I need them. We all need them because that is how we are made. That is why God called you to a church body. That's why He created families. That's why He gave you the ability to communicate intelligently. You stand tallest when you stand in relationship with others. The smallest thing you could ever do is try to go it alone when support is available. Your children need the best you have to offer. To be at your best you need to be connected to significant others. True independence means to do what needs to be done for yourself, including the building of a support system to meet your real needs.

YOUR SUPPORT SYSTEM

You have to deal with the temptation to isolate yourself at times just as you have to deal with the temptation not to do it at other times. There is a time to be alone, as we said before, but as a relational being, you also need an adequate support system for your journey.

Now you need to decide to build that support system. You need to bring into your life those persons who can be of effective help to you, in addition to the ones already there.

Some years ago I met two brothers who wanted to make a statement of Christian concern for what is happening in today's world. They felt they could dramatize their message by running from Long Beach, California, to Long Beach, New York. They would run some thirty-two miles each day and complete their journey by the end of the summer in order to be back in college on time.

If they had tried to run it alone, they never would have made it. They needed a support team to carry food, bedding, medical supplies, water, extra shoes and lots of encouragement. They needed an advance team to arrange interviews, others to keep the networks apprised, and a family contact to assure anxious parents all was going well. There were churches to alert along the way so Sundays could be a day of worship and sharing.

Need I say more? Your journey is the most important thing in your life right now and you need a support system if you are going to reach your goal.

Your Unique Journey

You are a single parent, true, but you feel you shouldn't be, and that is your struggle. You feel out of place. Your journey has gone off the map. You feel lost, like Cain, a wanderer. The fact that you feel this way tells you that you have not yet done your homework in dealing with your divorce.

No other person's circumstances are identical to yours. No other single parent is exactly like you with children exactly like yours. No other person's divorce is exactly like yours. Similar, yes, but not the same. The uniqueness you feel inside sets you apart in your own mind. This loneliness is your own creation and you need to discover why you feel you must create it. You are sending yourself on this trip because you do not want to accept the reality of where you are or why you are here.

The events that brought you here undoubtedly were not all of your own making. But here you are. Yet you don't have to stay here. That is what His grace is all about. You are going to trade in your feeling of unique aloneness for a plan that will start you moving.

First, you will assess the kinds of support you need and write them down.

Next, you will assess the kinds of support that are available. You could write those down too.

Finally, you will seek to build the support you need and get growing.

ASSESSING YOUR NEEDS

In writing these out, you will discover a lot of possibilities. You will have to pick and choose what is best for you. No one can build in everything listed and still have time for work, parenting and themselves; however, some of us need more of a network than others. If you make an error in judgment, let it be by adding more than needed rather than less. In time you can adjust as appropriate.

1. You need several *acquaintances,* persons you can touch base with for moral support and encouragement. These will not be heavy-duty friendships involving a lot of time and maintenance; rather, they are fun people you feel a commonness with.

2. A *few close friends* to share more of yourself with. Here you share feelings, get close, laugh, cry and pray together, and you can count on each other day or night. One or two of these may be all you can maintain because close friendships require a lot of time together and in-

depth sharing, risking and listening.

3. One or two *intimate friends.* Perhaps you will not be able to maintain more than one. This is the person you can share anything and everything with and still feel loved and accepted. This person mediates God's love to you better than anyone else. All the warts and wrinkles get worked out here in the safety of a loving relationship. This is the person who knows you best.

4. A *speaking relationship with your Ex.* You need the ability to communicate for the sake of the children whom you both still parent. It affects your support structure in that, if you cannot communicate, you have a greatly increased burden to bear.

5. Close ties with your *spiritual support structure.* Be part of a prayer group. Call on persons who have the gift of intercession. Know your name is being brought daily before the throne of grace. Share together in a ministry of mutual prayer support.

6. Close ties with your *pastor and/or staff.* You need the counsel they have to offer as well as their encouragement. You need them to hold you accountable. You need their guidance. They are your primary source of information and spiritual instruction. Even if you are not counseling with your pastor, you need to be checking in every so often to give an up-date on how things are going.

7. Someone to *disciple* you, especially if you are a new Christian or young in the faith. This is a very vulnerable time in your faith journey and you need to be sure you are well-grounded. Deal with your doubts and questions, especially if your faith is new or shaky. The loss of a mate through death or divorce is a trauma that can send aftershocks throughout all of your life.

8. Your *family.* Here you may need to assess what is available to you from your family, and then act on what you believe you need. In some cases family members may not be a good support base. A lot depends on your prior relationships and on their availability and willingness.

9. Your *extended family.* The same is true here as with your immediate family; however, there may be key relatives who can be of great help.

10. A *singles group.* If your church does not have a group, there may be one in a church near by. You can let your pastor know your need in going so as not to undermine your

relationship with your home church. Caution: Make sure it is going to be a support group and not an added burden. Be very careful of non-Christian singles groups for many of these will not share your values and can work against you. There are worse things than being lonely.

11. *Other single parents and/or Christian single-parent groups.* Getting with them can be a tremendous support. Some of them will have been at it for quite a while and can help you on your journey. Such a group can be of great value. If you don't find one, get help in starting one.

12. *Winners* to associate with. This is not meant to be judgmental or uncaring, but let's face it. You are coming out of a painful time in your life and you don't need to sit around with a group of people intent only on licking their wounds. You need people who have been hurt but who are seeking healing and recovery. I call these winners. Maybe they haven't won yet but they are heading in the right direction.

13. New source discoveries. Be open to attending a divorce recovery group, a Christian parenting workshop, or other similar groups. Become aware of what is being offered. A lot will be on dual parenting but you still can glean the basics you need. Some of it will be painful for you because you are a single parent, but go anyway. Learn all you can.

14. *Professional help.* Your pastor can help you determine what may be needed. Don't say you cannot afford it if you need it. *Find a way.* Watch the ads about Christian groups having speakers from the helping fields, and attend, get acquainted and find out what professional help is available. This can be an inexpensive way of finding out who is available and determining how well this person may be able to help you.

15. An *emergency network.* Who can you call in the middle of the night if you have an anxiety attack, if you get sick, if one of the children gets sick, if your car breaks down, etc.? These need to be pre-arranged relationships you can rely on.

WHAT IS AVAILABLE TO YOU?

First, assess whatever support structure you already have going for you. Note what is already in place, how well it is working and what *strengths* are there.

Second, prioritize your needs and begin working on what should be added. Divide all your needs into *A*s, *B*s and *C*s. *A* is an immediate, important need; *B* means not quite as important and you can take a little more time to work on it; and *C* means it is something you could benefit from but it can wait until you get other things going. Then begin working immediately on the A group.

Third, sit down with your pastor and/or staff and discuss the list you have made. Ask them, "Am I seeing myself as you see me? Do you see areas I am missing? How would you evaluate my assessment of my needs? Do you have someone who might be able to disciple me? Do you know of groups where I may find help? Is the church planning any new programs I need to know about?"

Fourth, go to your pastor with a list of questions and ask all of them, even the ones you feel may sound foolish. "Can you help me understand what the Bible says about divorce? I need to be able to help my children understand what the Bible teaches about it. Can you help me? I think I see a problem with my five-year-old. Can you help me identify it? I am thinking about getting some counseling. Can you refer me to someone? I am having a hard time managing my finances. Is there someone you know who might help me? I need to find child care so I can go back to work. Do you know of a place I can trust?"

Have your pastor clarify with you the church's stand on divorce. If the church has no clear-cut, stated policy, ask what most members believe and why.

Fifth, now that you have listed what you need in terms of support persons, begin a list of those who may be available, the ones you want to contact. Know what you want from them and the kind of contract you are willing to make. Not everyone will be able to fit in. Some may not want to. Be prepared for this. Be prepared to do some negotiating. You are asking persons to give of themselves and in turn you will need to give of yourself.

Sixth, once you have completed your list, make a plan of action and then begin working on your plan. For example, you are going to sit down with a close friend and explore the possibility of that person becoming an intimate friend. You need to share what you would like to have happen between you and would she be open to such a relationship developing? If so, make plans for spending the time together needed for such a relationship to develop.

Seventh, talk yourself through any fears or reluctance in building the support structure you need. You are worth loving and you are seeking persons to share love and support. You are offering yourself just as you are asking them to share themselves with you.

Let the Holy Spirit guide you and open doors for you, but don't just sit around waiting for people to fall into your life. Make it happen.

Eighth, celebrate each victory and feel the strength of your additional support network as it builds. Thank God every day for each of them. They are His special gifts to you. They are His way of putting His arms around you and giving you the hugs He has for you, of expressing His love and concern for you. When you squeeze them back, you are saying "thank you" to Him and to them.

ADJUSTING YOUR RELATIONSHIPS AS YOU JOURNEY

You have taken charge of your own support structure and this is as it should be. If you discover it's time to shift gears to meet certain needs better, do it. If you would like to add another close relationship, do it. If you find an acquaintance is draining you and you want the time for another closer relationship, break something off or at least cut back. Be up front about it. Don't manipulate. Be open and honest. This may not have been your style in the past but it must be now. If a relationship has to be altered, alter it.

Changing or terminating a relationship is never easy but at times it is necessary, especially during a hurting time in your life. Just remember that all of life is dealing with relationships and you are setting a pattern you want to have last. The Golden Rule is far from trite—it is a perfect example of how best to treat others.

You don't want to have to change any more relationships than necessary; that's why you have to pray a lot for spiritual leading in establishing your relationships in the first place.

FOR THE REST OF YOUR LIFE

Never be without a personal support system the rest of your life. It may be in constant flux, but have one. Some folks in it will come and go; others will be there as long as you both shall live. Your needs will shift along with the stages of your journey, but you will always need your support group. It's your life and you owe it to Him to live it at the fullest possible level. To do this you need a network of support for every aspect of that life. This is why He has given you more than five billion others to relate to. This is why the Holy Spirit is within you: You are never left on your own (John 14:15-17).

Δ

TAKING ACTION: SUPPORT NEEDS

Think your way through the items listed below, and then make as honest an evaluation as you can, taking the following steps.

1. First, assess the level at which you think your needs are being met. Check the appropriate column: Excellent, Adequate, Fair, Poor or Non-existent. Then prioritize them into *A*s, *B*s and *C*s.

Support	Excellent	Adequate	Fair	Poor	None
(1) Acquaintances	___	___	___	___	___
(2) Friends	___	___	___	___	___
(3) Close friends	___	___	___	___	___
(4) Intimate friends	___	___	___	___	___
(5) Pastor/staff	___	___	___	___	___
(6) Prayer partners	___	___	___	___	___
(7) Family	___	___	___	___	___
(8) Extended family	___	___	___	___	___
(9) Discipling/Bible study	___	___	___	___	___
(10) Skills development	___	___	___	___	___
(11) Programs on special needs	___	___	___	___	___
(12) Professional help	___	___	___	___	___

2. Describe your plan of action in caring for the *A*s.
3. What will you do with the *B*s?
4. How will you care for the *C*s?

6

WHO'S DRIVING?

The first frame of the cartoon shows an eggshell breaking as a tiny beak emerges. In the second frame a tiny chick breaks free. The third frame shows it standing on wobbly legs, surveying the world into which it had just come. The last frame shows the chick crawling back into the shell, trying to replace the broken off piece.

Divorce or death of a spouse will introduce you, too, to a world you may not want to face; however, there is another world some find equally difficult. That is the inner world.

You can liken your personality to an onion (no offense meant) with its many layers. If you peel away enough of them, you eventually come to the center. Over the years you have built up layers of encrustations around your inner self for protection. Well, somewhere, deep down inside, is that true self, that "me" you have been protecting from whatever you perceived as threatening. There may be so many layers you really don't even know what is inside.

YOUR INNER WORLD

Unlike the chick in the cartoon, it is the *inner* world you are afraid to explore. You pull away a few layers in an attempt to see what is down inside, then quickly retreat to the safety of not looking any deeper lest you find something you cannot accept.

I remember hearing John Powell tell of a woman who felt that way. She commented about his book, *Why Am I Afraid to Tell You Who I Am?* "What can I do about me if you decide I am not what you want me to be?" He included her comments in his book. "This is me; I can only be me. What if it is not good enough for you?"[1]

Your fear of being rejected may be so intense that you find it difficult to disclose your true self, even in a trusted relationship. Like Adam in the Garden, you try to hide when God approaches, as if He didn't know already.

Your fear of looking inside means you probably are keeping others at arm's length so they cannot look inside, either. Some people avoid eye contact for fear others may see inside them. Few of us feel as comfortable with ourselves as we could, but some are so crippled they would rather "die" than be known. You can measure your level of self-esteem by the discomfort you feel when you're with people who intimidate you.

Understanding your self-esteem needs will disclose how you relate to God, others, and yourself. I have four children: one by birth, one by adoption, and two by marriage. There is one I had difficulty relating to. Can you guess which one? It had nothing to do with how we came to be related. It is the child which reminds me most of myself. I did not feel comfortable being me, so I was saying in effect to him, "I don't want you to be like me because I am not okay." What I could not accept in myself I rejected in him. I wanted him to be better, so I was on his back endlessly trying to steer him away from being like me. It was as though I were saying, "You are going to be different if it kills us both!"

But he wanted to be like me. I was his hero so the more I put pressure on him, the more he tried to be exactly like me hoping to relieve the pressure. What a vicious cycle.

The only way it could end was for me to recognize it's okay to be me and it's okay for him to be him. By learning to accept myself I could also accept him. Acceptance begins within. See what I mean by "putting our stuff on our children"?

Some of us have so little self-esteem we feel we have to reach up to touch bottom, and we have spent a lifetime accumulating the data we feel confirms our perceptions of ourselves. We have stored up every lousy memory and every failure, and certainly can rehearse a long list of personal sins. We feel like debating Paul when he calls himself the "chief of sinners." (Paul's use of "chief of sinners" is a testimony, not a theological reality. Each person can say it of himself as well.) We obviously have self-esteem needs, but just how many and what to do about them is another matter altogether.

WHERE TO BEGIN

Much of your problem is based on how you perceived your past so you need to begin there. What was it really like? How did you fit into your family? What went on between Mother and you? How about between Dad and you? Was it as you remember it between you and your sister(s)/brother(s)? What were you like as a child?

Check things out with your parents, other members of the family, and trusted relatives. There are lots of questions you can ask them to get a clearer picture of how it was, especially if you see only cloudy images. It can be as simple as saying, "I remember my fifth birthday when . . . Is that what really happened?"

Seeing it through the eyes of another sometimes can clarify and/or confirm it for you. Don't be afraid to ask. If you are checking out a painful experience, let the person know you recognize it was painful and you are not opening up old wounds just to do it; you are searching for an understanding of your past and need him to help you. You may be helping him, too.

My younger brother has been a newspaper editor/publisher for quite a while. From time to time he writes about an incident from our childhood as he remembers it. I find myself reading the column and asking, "What family did he grow up in? That's not the way it happened." But then I remember that things look different from the bottom of the pile than they do from the top, and being older, I was usually on top.

Checking things out helps you see and accept things as they really were rather than as you perceived them then. In working with a woman who had been molested by her father as a young teenager, I discovered her perception was she had somehow done something wrong and this was her father's way of punishing her. As an adult she was able to go back over those experiences with her father and confront him with her feelings of self-blame. It was not her fault her father had molested her. He was able to help her put the blame where it belonged and to ask her forgiveness. This did not solve all her problems but it certainly brought them more in line with reality.

You have so many ways of compensating for the past when you do not understand it or have not made peace with it. The person who is a perfectionist is trying to hide a perceived imperfection. The procrastinator is seeking to thumb a nose at all the pressure imposed in the past. The manipulator is still reacting to having been manipulated. The slob may still be reacting to having been raised under sterile home conditions.

The key here is reacting. Because of low self-esteem, you are not free to act, only to react. Your inability to make your peace with the past enslaves you to it.

MOVING TOWARD ACCEPTANCE

You cannot change a single thing that happened in your past. You may have gone over it a million times in your mind, but it always comes out the same because that is how it happened. You can come to understand it more fully, though, especially if you had misunderstood it. By finding out what did happen and why, you move a lot closer to accepting it.

Acceptance isn't saying it was okay; acceptance is saying it did happen and now you can deal with it as it was. Acceptance is seeing your true place in the family system. It is seeing the role you adopted in that system and how you lived it out. You discover why you perceive yourself as you do. You also see how the others related to you and why. When it is all put together and you see the big picture, you can accept it as *being your past.* Now you can begin to move from there and see the present based on that past.

DEALING WITH THE PAST

The major hurdle in dealing with the past is your lack of self-acceptance. Only after a good level has been achieved can you truly be at peace. You have done nothing that cannot be forgiven, especially by your Lord. You may retort, "But if you knew what I have done, you wouldn't say that. You would have to say it applies to most sins but not mine."

My problem in agreeing with what you say is that I would have to discredit what God says in His Word about cleansing us from all sins (1 John 1:7). If there were any exceptions, He would have been aware of them. He says *all;* He means *all;* His blood covered *all.* So you need not be concerned about whether your worst sin is included; rather, you need to claim the truth of God's Word and allow His grace to be applied fully to that offense.

Then you need to allow the Holy Spirit to bring your memory bank into line with what God's grace has already done. The past is *past* so far as God is concerned. If your past is present, it is because you have chosen to make it present. That way you can spend your time and energy living in the past and and that protects you from having to face the present.

One day, while counseling a depressed woman in a church I was serving, I asked her to describe her average day. What she described, and how she described it, was enough to depress anyone.

Then I asked her to imagine what her day might be like if she were no longer depressed. She started off slowly, then soon found herself getting into it. She was doing quite well until she started talking about her husband and her marriage. Right in the middle of her description she suddenly stopped, stared at me, and said, "I just now realized . . . I don't want to lose my depression because then I would have to be a real wife and take better care of my husband's needs." Sometimes keeping our past present is a way of escape.

Memories never truly heal until you are willing to surrender them to the one who bought them with the price of His cross. By being healed I don't mean they are forgotten. I mean they are dealt with in His grace so they lose their crippling hold on you. You can live free of their entanglement. Through the Holy Spirit you can move into His life "more abundantly" (John 10:10 KJV). Letting go is no small task, but you must. Let the past be the past.

ACCEPTING THE PRESENT

You are who you are. This is all the you there is. You can change your body weight and make some alterations to its shape, but very little beyond that. You'll never be taller; you may get shorter; in all probability you will keep right on growing older, reaching the years you dread. Nobody is perfect. No body is perfect. You don't have to be perfect to be loved. You don't even have to be good looking. You don't have to apologize for being you. You may not be the best you that you can be yet, but you are "okay." (*Okay* is a technical term in transactional analysis. It doesn't mean sinless; it means worth loving, accepting and knowing.) You can accept all your givens—skeletal shape, basic features, feet, hands, color of eyes, and so on—and make your peace with them.

If you lost your mate in death, you are a widow or a widower, and it certainly has changed your life—but it has not altered your value. If grace has been at work in your life, you may be all the richer from having gone through such a trauma. You didn't ask for it, but as a result of working through it, and by His grace, you are a stronger, more capable, more grateful human being.

If you are divorcing or already divorced, this does not make you a loser. To be sure, this is not where you wanted or expected to be, but this is where you are. Your worth has not been diminished just because someone decided he did not want to spend the rest of his life with you. Others may put a label on you. You may not be able to prevent that, but you can refuse to put any on yourself except, "This is me and I am worth loving. God says so!"

You are also a single parent. Better yet, you are a parent who happens to be single. You didn't plan to be a single parent, but this means you get to choose which TV dinner to cook tonight, and you get to fix the popcorn the way you like it. The label on your home reads, "Christ is the Head of this house and love is the language spoken here."

Your past is a prelude to your present, but it will affect it only to the degree you allow. The enemy's plan is to keep you living in it. As long as you are controlled by the past you are unable to live fully in the present. Yet the only moment you can live is this very one. What went before is gone; what is ahead is not yet here. This moment needs to be God's and God's alone, and you must free it from the past by surrendering it to Him.

You are more than your past. In fact, you are more than your past, present and future combined. Each of these elements is still a part of you, but the whole is more than the sum of the parts. As a Christian you are eternal. What God has done, is doing, and will yet do for you, He does in real time so this moment is the one for you to zero in on.

Whatever else you may believe about yourself in your struggle for self-esteem, *know that you are worth loving*. He has placed people in your life who can see your true worth. If you allow them to get to know you and relate adequately with you, they will love you and will allow you to love them. Each one who loves you reinforces the fact that you are worth loving. You take more of a risk with some than with others, but positive reinforcement comes, and that helps prepare you to handle the negatives.

In building your self-esteem, you don't try to change those around you. This is impossible, anyway. The only one you can change is you, and this is the only one you need to change. It would be nice if those around you were nicer, but you can't control that. You control how you react to what they toss your way. Your Ex will have a hard time wiping his feet on you if you are standing up rather than lying down wearing the sweatshirt that says in big letters, "Wipe here!" A good level of self-esteem doesn't assure you everyone will love you or even like you, but it does determine how you will deal with hurt and rejection.

ALLOWING YOURSELF TO BE LOVED

The cartoon of the chick unwilling to face the world and the illustration of the onion both tell you of a major problem involved in allowing yourself to be loved. The real you is hidden inside, and for you to be loved the shell has to be broken or the layers peeled away. This means becoming vulnerable. Your self-esteem must be built up to where you are willing to risk the closeness you are made for. You have to feel that you are known and loved by another.

For this to happen you must put yourself where it can happen, right in the middle of a growing relationship. You must allow yourself to become vulnerable, opening yourself to the potential for hurt and disappointment, but at the same time for love and caring. This involves an openness to being close to someone. You need it, but you also must want it. That means you must make a decision.

To let another person in means to peel back the layers so you can be known to that person, to share feelings. Your feelings are more than what you think; they are a part of the real you. To know them is to know you. There are a lot of single parents, but when others learn how you feel about being one, they begin to know the real you, and they learn of your uniqueness.

The peeling allows you to receive into your real self the gift the other is giving. You receive him and his gift as he receives you and yours. You each need what the other has to offer. This giving and receiving builds intimacy between you. This is what you long for, to be one, as Christ and the Father are one.

Your fears can threaten you the most here. Not only are you vulnerable, but also the deeper the exposure, the deeper the hurt if you are rejected. If you sing, "No one loves me, this I know; for my fears they tell me so," you have to realize this tune isn't based on God's Word. It is based in human experience. It is so easy to equate feelings with reality. They are real, all right, but only because you have made them real. Fears and phobias develop as a reaction to things we do not want to deal with. We create these pathological fears in order to "justify" our not relating.

Opening yourself up to another person creates a fear at times of being absorbed by that person, and of you ending up the loser. This fear may have dominated your marriage. A lesser fear is that the other person may gain some sort of control over you that will diminish you. You may feel you have never been what you need to be, so any blending with another will weaken your potential. You may fail to recognize that this fear is spiritual as well as emotional. Getting closer to God involves the same process.

The shell, the layers, give a false sense of being in control and able to terminate a relationship at will. Yet there may not be a relationship if it is only shell to shell. Any real closeness must involve shared control and the taking on of vulnerability in order to achieve intimacy. The chick in the shell may feel protected but it has shut out closeness, intimacy and love. It will be alone, and lonely.

LETTING GO OF YOUR FEARS

The full impact of 1 John 4:18 is this: The opposite of loving is fear. You cannot love someone you fear. John puts it this way: "There is no fear in love; perfect love drives out all fear. So then, love has not been made perfect in anyone who is afraid, because fear has to do with punishment." *Perfect* here means mature, complete, grown up or realized. It implies that fear is associated with the child within you while love means you have grown up. These fears are the major block to your self-esteem and to need-fulfillment.

John is saying that in order to move into maturity and to receive love you must first open your heart and let go of your fears. You are not capable of holding to both love and fear at the same time. I like to think of it as being on a continuum like this:

Fear **1 2 3 4 5 6 7 8 9 10** Love

Figure B

In moving toward love, you must of necessity move away from the fear of rejection or disappointment. The joy of loving is to love no matter what may result, without any strings attached. When you know who you are and what you have to give, you can be fully open to an intimate relationship with another person without fear of being controlled, diminished or threatened. The self-esteem goal is to love maturely and completely, beyond the fear of rejection or, as John expresses it, the fear of being found wanting on the day of God's judgment. If you take Matthew 25 seriously, you know that the ultimate judgment is found to be unloving. You are commanded by the Lord—and Judge—to love one another (John 13:34,35).

Where would you place yourself on the continuum above? Take a good look at it and put an *X* at your spot. What lies to the left of your *X* indicates the journey you already have made into maturity. That which lies to the right is where you need to go, gaining new ground daily in your walk with Him. To move toward Him is to move out of the old into the new, out of the inner child's control into the freedom of His Spirit's control. No one is totally free in life; all are controlled by someone, something. To be controlled by the Spirit is the only true freedom available. To get a broad biblical view of this concept, read chapters 6 through 8 of Romans.

RISKING CLOSENESS

You are made for relating at the deepest levels with God, others and your true self, and you are restless within your spirit until this can be achieved. Your raised self-esteem level allows you to move into such levels of relating and is also built on those levels of relating. As you learn to love and be loved, the real you can risk more closeness and involvement. At the same time, as you take that risk, the real you emerges more. In reality, the greatest risk is *not* risking. It's not like you are standing on a street corner, opening your arms to an unknown world and saying, "Y'all come." You are relating to a trusted friend with whom you have developed a growing relationship, guided and empowered by His Holy Spirit.

The fear of rejection within your level of self-esteem was born of the inner child of the past. That child perceived earlier rejections that led to self-rejection. He believes that if the layers of the onion are peeled away, a self that is not worth accepting will be revealed. But as the layers are peeled away, the true self is seen as being very much worth loving. The adult learns what the child did not know in his experience, that he was loved, but in ways he did not understand. Or, that if he truly was not loved, it was because those people in his life did not know how to love, not because he was unlovable.

GIVING OF YOURSELF

Your level of self-esteem determines what you have to give, how you give and to whom. Coming through a divorce or the death of a mate may greatly diminish your ability to give, what you give and to whom it is given, but more important, what you *believe* you have to give. At this point in your life, your major focus of giving needs to be your children. It is amazing how this giving can be affected without your being aware of it. Your esteem may be so low you see yourself as worthless, and you act worthless, especially with your children.

Submerged in all of this, though, is the unique, wonderful person you are and all you have to give. Being so down on yourself, you concentrate only on what you think you need to receive. You feel that to give right now is beyond you. The tragedy is that you do have it to give, but because you are all wrapped up in your own need, you cannot see the need of your children. Yet no matter what has happened to you, you still have the true you to give. It is a beautiful gift, and it is the gift your children need from you.

No, it is not a perfect parent. You cannot become a perfect parent any more than you can be a perfect person, but you will be what they need you to be and that is the gift you can give them. God is within you to touch them through you. The gift He will give through you is life-giving; you are His partner in giving it, and it will be more than adequate for their real needs. You need to recognize this, get your head together, and concentrate on giving it. Once they are grown and on their own you will have time for a "pity party" for yourself because of what has happened to you, if you so choose, but right now none of you can afford that luxury.

HEALING YOUR MEMORIES

A damaged self-esteem level usually has its roots deep in the traumas of early life. These are added to by later traumas accumulate along your journey. You may be reeling beneath their load. The last thing I would ever want to do is to underestimate your load, or give you the feeling that I think it is some small thing so you should just "shake it off and get going." Your traumas may have been so damaging that you will struggle with them the rest of your life. My heart goes out to you, and my prayer for you is that in time, through the healing graces your Heavenly Father makes available, genuine healing will be realized in your life whether it takes years or can be dealt with in chapters.

Problems like desertion, rejection, incest and child abuse are not the norm for most of us, thank the Lord. Yet I do *know what God can do for you if you've had such an experience,* and am fully convinced of the reality of a *special grace* that can make miraculous changes. This special grace is available to every victim, as is the power-filled presence of His Spirit. My own traumas did not come into focus until I was well into my thirties. Healing was not present until my forties. What I am writing is more for those whose background was less traumatic than some—others may require more time and more specialized care—but the principles shared apply to us all.

Some years ago I preached a series of sermons on a hymn, "Christ Be With Me," written by an ancient saint. It speaks of Christ *above* me, *within* me, *before* me, *beneath* me—and *behind* me. In the message on the theme, "Christ behind me," I spoke of the Christ who walks with us back through our past and helps us understand what happened to us and why. I discussed His presence with us during those traumas, as well as how He perceived them as we were going through them. I was not prepared for the response on the part of the congregation. All thirteen of those messages were taped for shut-ins and any others who wanted copies. The requests for the tape of this message exceeded all the others combined! The realization that Jesus was there, even though we hadn't become Christians yet, that He cared about what had happened to us, that seeing it through His eyes could actually make a difference in us apparently touched a deep need in many people. I related how He had forgiven and cleansed our past, and that He understood how we felt about that past. Yet these thoughts all were overshadowed by one greater thought. It was this: *When Jesus Christ died for us, He bought our past. It now belongs to Him* by virtue of His cross, and He is within us to handle it for us as part of His gift to us.

You can surrender your past to Him. You need carry the load no more. He has freed you to live in Him, for Him, and by Him in the present. This freedom is His gift of love to you. He is in you, living out His life through you. You can be more than a conqueror through Him who loves you. (Romans 8:37. Read Ephesians 1:3-23.)

WOULDN'T IT BE NICE TO FORGET?

The culture we live in educates us away from pain and thus away from reality. So much of this has been "baptized" into what we call the "Christian life." If it is, it is spelled with a small *c*. Trying to forget your past and its pain is not where your energies need to go. You need to use those energies to accept His grace, appropriate His strength, and live fully in the present. The past isn't your problem now. Your problem is living for Him in the present. If you still need to forget the past, you have not dealt with it in the light of the cross and His grace. You're looking for the easy way out. You want to be free of that with which you alone must wrestle.

Paul tried to change his past and his present only to be rebuffed by the Spirit. He writes of this in 2 Corinthians 12:7-10. His past helped make him what he became. Your "thorn" may be your divorce, or it may be your past. "Lord, take it away!" may be your cry. Suppose He did take it all away. What would be the results in your life? How would you learn the full lessons of His grace? How would your life be tempered, hardened, matured, completed? How would your self-esteem be perfected? How would you learn to grow?

Can you, like Paul, pray that in God's love you may learn all that His grace can teach? Can you learn to see His hand in all your days? Can you learn to surrender to the fact that He "works for good with those who love Him, those whom he has called according to His purpose"? This is something to think about. (Paul's full testimony is found in Philippians 3 and 4.)

△

TAKING ACTION:
SELF-ESTEEM NEEDS

1. Evaluate your self-esteem, and then list your top five needs.

2. How can you best go about meeting these basic self-esteem needs?

3. As pointed out, fear is a major self-esteem blocker. What role does fear play in the significant relationships in your life?

4. What is lacking in your self-esteem that would account for this level of fear?

5. What can you do to eliminate this lack and reduce your level of fear?

6. In dealing with your past, is there an area in which you still have a great deal of difficulty forgiving yourself?

7. How does God regard this particular aspect of your past?

8. Are you still struggling with forgiveness for someone in your past?

9. When you are among God's people for worship and fellowship, how do you believe they perceive you?

10. Do you sense the presence of an inner block when it comes to accepting His forgiveness for your past?

11. At this stage on your life's journey, how would you characterize the present moment?

12. What does your response to question 11 tell you about you?

At the end of the book you will find a list of helps in working on your level of self-esteem. Select one that interests you and begin reading it along with the remainder of this book. (I like to read several books at a time.) This helps sharpen the focus on your specific needs. You may want to begin with one of the selections by John Powell. Zero in first on what you consider your major need.

7

SHARING THE JOURNEY

The local disk jockey was chattering on as the last strains of a new release were dying away. The record would become a hit. It spoke of people needing people. His comments included, "I guess it has a message for those who need people, but some of us don't."

I wanted to stop my car, find a phone, call him and ask, "What world do you live in? Everyone needs someone. We are *social beings.*"

IN HIS IMAGE

We are social/relational beings because we are fashioned in God's image. When God said in Genesis 2:18 that it was not good for a person (man) to be alone, He was not simply referring to a marriage relationship; rather, He was stating our basic social need. God is a relational being. The triune godhead related within itself to Father, Son and Holy Spirit before we came along, and all of us, single or married, young or old, are relational beings as well. (In Genesis 1:26, where we read: "Then God said, 'And now we will make human beings; they will be like us,' " we see the "plural of majesty." It lends itself to the New Testament revelation of the triune God.) We need people to share life with.

You need other people—in good measure—for the meeting of your basic social needs, and they need you. We assist each other in the process of maturing, finding life and growing, and we impart to one another what could never be found outside these relationships.

The contemporary emphasis in our culture on individualism may rob you of your understanding of corporate life. Both the Old and New Testaments stress the corporate aspects rather than a rugged individualism. It is true you enter your new life in Christ

73

based on your own individual decision; however, once in, "we are all members together" as Paul states in Ephesians 4:25. By your relationship with God in Christ you are now a living part of the bride of Christ. God has called you to fellowship with His Son because that is what you need most. He calls you to relationship.

On a very practical level, though, I want you to take a good, solid look at those to whom you relate most and the *reasons* you relate to those you have chosen. The how and why tell you a great deal about what is happening inside you socially and emotionally.

HOW YOU RELATE TO OTHERS

Some people are very distant in how they relate. They do not allow themselves to get close, to take any risks, or to reveal much of themselves. They relate guardedly out of fear of loss.

Others relate very closely, jumping right in and attaching an "emotional umbilical cord" so they can suck the relationship dry. When they have drained off all the other person can give, they detach and find another as soon as possible.

Some people relate by going along with whatever is asked, never making any demands lest the other person break it off. They feel powerless to say or do much else—they want to keep the relationship at all costs.

Still others relate only when things go their way, manipulating the other to meet their own need.

You may find it easy to identify these types in relationships you have witnessed. They are all self-destructive—they do not meet real needs but are borne out of perceived or neurotic needs. A neurotic need is a normal need that has become crazily exaggerated. It usually signals the fact the inner child of the past missed out on something and now is seeking to compensate for it. Strange as it may seem, the child usually seeks to fulfill these needs through actions that guarantee they will *not* be met.

THE KEY TO YOUR CHOICES

You select the persons you wish to relate to for definite reasons, though you may not be conscious of those reasons. Reflect back on the relationships of your life, and if you can isolate some of those specific choices, it will lead you to more self-understanding and awareness. For example, when you make friends only with persons you can easily manipulate and control, it reveals your own deep, inner fear of being controlled. When you seek friendships with persons who control and manipulate you, your deep, inner need may be to be controlled. You may resent being controlled, but it is easier for you than the responsibility of making decisions.

It is important that you see how you cultivate relationships that will compensate for what you perceive as a deficiency. The man who is 6'8" has a friend 5'2" because he hates being tall and sees being shorter as more normal. His friend may wish to be taller—that might meet his need for self-acceptance.

The lack of self-acceptance is the key. The opposite of self-acceptance is self-hate and self-rejection. Christians are good at this. In many circles self-rejection has been made a "virtue" of sorts.

It is true, and biblically sound, that you have been called to "deny" yourself. Jesus calls you to this daily if you are to follow Him. But what does self-denial mean? It does not mean to deny the reality of who you are. Jesus did not regard His existence as non-existence, and he does not expect you to. Self-denial means to put yourself second to Him and to put others' needs ahead of your own. John said, "He must become more important while I become less important (John 3:30). In Philippians 2:4 Paul calls you to "look out for one another's interests, not just for your own." To deny yourself is to say, "Lord, not my will but Yours. I subject all my desires and needs to Your will for my life today.

WHY YOU RELATE TO OTHERS

Bringing all this home to where you live, as a single parent, you need to look back and assess why you made the marriage choice you did. Was yours a deficiency style choice? Did you base your decision on a deep, inner need you did not fully understand? Did you marry a perceived opposite? Here's an example.

"Ms. Shopping Spree" started dating "Mr. Penny Pincher." She felt safe with him because he could save, pass up a bargain, and even enjoy life without tripping from one shopping mall to another. His bumper sticker didn't read, "Born to shop." A few months after their marriage she woke up one morning to discover lumps in the mattress where he had squirreled away not only his first dollar but also his first nickel and dime. It was agony to get him to part with money to pay overdue bills. Instead of helping her control her impulsive spending, he resented her spending anything, even on household needs. What she thought was going to meet her need left her with an even deeper one. Her impulsiveness led her to hide her purchases and she resented having to sneak to the malls and shops. This made her inner compulsiveness ten times worse. The relationship was doomed from the start since neither wanted to change.

Because you are a social being you need to relate, but all your inner needs combine to determine why you relate as you do. When you do not understand your inner needs, or you deny them, or worse yet, exaggerate them, you tend to get into relationships that increase those needs. You want someone who can meet your needs and who will allow you to give of yourself in meeting those of others.

A caution: You cannot experience healthy growth without relationships, but some of those relationships may be so destructive you cannot handle them. Others may be draining and you do not need them. Still others may be necessary due to family connections and you will need to change them. It is up to you to take responsibility for all your relationships and make them as need-satisfying as possible.

The journey you are making into the maturing process of wholeness involves social interaction—people—and thank God it does. Who wants to walk the valleys alone or absorb a breathtaking scene from a mountaintop without sharing it with someone? Social choices, for the most part, are up to you and you can decide how you will relate to your those you have chosen. Concentrate on this.

You will bump up against a lot of people, both those who choose to love you and those who do not. How you react to them is determined by what is inside you. How you allow them to affect or destroy you is a decision you must make. Your growth is in the balance. Remember what Joshua said about following the Lord? It wasn't, "I will serve Him *if* . . . " It was, "We will serve." (Joshua 24:15). Your decision will be based on what is in your heart.

DANGERS TO AVOID

The **first** danger we will consider in regard to social interaction is *isolation,* the danger of not socializing at all. How easy it is to do this when you have lost your mate. You are hurting, and it is easier to stay home by yourself. A brief time is needed at first but letting it go on too long will establish a dangerous pattern for you.

Social interaction does not mean dating. It is simply being with people, especially around the church and family. You need the healing they can bring. I like what Jesus did when He raised Lazarus from the grave in John 11. Lazarus stood in the opening to the tomb, still clothed in his grave wrappings. Jesus turned to the family and told them to "unwrap him." He invited them to participate in Lazarus' coming forth (John 11:43,44).

God will use people in your life to help "unwrap" you from your pain and loneliness.

The **second** danger is that of *manipulating* people. Since you are a worthwhile human being, it is all right for you to come to another and say, "I am feeling lonely. Could we get together for a couple of hours Wednesday? I need someone to talk with." That's a legitimate need and it has been stated right up front for you both to deal with.

On the other hand, if, because you are afraid to be honest, you manipulate someone into spending time with you, that is destructive to you and to the other person. You actually manipulate others because of your low view of yourself, but too often, the other person eventually feels it is because of your low view of him.

Not everyone is going to respond to your social needs as you may like, and you will fail others the same way. There can be some risk in any request for another's time and energies, but a good relationship can be built on trust and openness. If you tend to manipulate others, take a good look inside yourself and get in touch with your needs and fears.

A very prevalent **third** danger is that you will *load your needs onto your children*. This is extremely difficult for the children, who may now need to cling to you because of their loss. They cannot understand this kind of burden, much less handle it.

You need to understand that in your pain you tend to regress, and the inner child takes over for the time span of the regression. But in *their* pain, your children need your fully functioning adult with its caring, wisdom and resilience. (*Adult* in transactional analysis terms, refers to that thinking part of the personality that is able to reason, project, conclude, and test ideas against reality.) In time this is what you need from yourself, also. If you cling to them in response to your need, you cannot help them.

The **fourth** danger is *using people*. I spoke earlier of attaching one's emotional umbilical cord to others for the purpose of meeting one's own needs. This is a perfect example of using people. When your thought is only of your own need, you discard a person who has nothing more to give. What really counts for you is what you get out of the relationship. Sound crass? It is, and it happens all too frequently.

People who use people tend to put all the responsibility for themselves on others. They are selfish to the max. It's important for you to discern if any of that lies in your way of relating. If so, you have some work to do to put an end to it.

Let me cite **two more** dangers. **One** is to *deny your real need* of others and to try and go it alone. In our culture, men are more prone to do this. Men consider women's going to others for help as weakness. To the contrary, openness in the face of need requires strength many men do not have. One of the secrets to feminine longevity is that women learn to share, and they avoid many of the ills men fall victim to. Keeping to oneself may be a perceived strength but in reality it is a hidden weakness.

The **other** danger is in remaining *too narrow* in your relationships. Do all your friends look and act alike? Will that stretch you, help you grow? It may seem safe, but life needs more than safety. I once met a man who bragged that he had never tipped his sailboat over in all his years of sailing. How dull. He never tested its capabilities—or his. This was not some million-dollar job but a single masted sixteen-footer that wouldn't sink on a small lake. He didn't sail for fun. He sailed to prove his self-control. Add some depth and variety to your life, some fun. Don't miss out on all the wonderful varieties of people God has fashioned.

BROADENING YOUR CIRCLE

Gathering friends is like gathering diamonds and this is exactly what people can be in your life. A disintegrating marriage and a divorce may have closed you in, cut you off, but now it is time to begin adding to your life what you may never have had before. Friendships are true treasures. The investment is worth it.

A circle of friends will always have to be limited, but for most introverts the tendency is to make the circle too small. Some extroverted types may let their circles become too large and unwieldy. Each person must carefully determine what he needs and then build lasting, meaningful relationships within those parameters. You can add some for fun and relaxation, some for study and discovery, others for prayer partners and spiritual quests, still others for activities and adventures. *You cannot meet the full need of any other one person nor can any one person meet your full need.* So go ahead — stretch, and broaden.

In your twenties and thirties, doing and acquiring may seem important, but when you hit your forties and fifties the need for people will become apparent. In the final analysis, relationships are where it is at. Be just as intentional in planning for people as you are in committing to relationships.

WHAT ABOUT THE FAMILY?

Not all of us have been blessed with a loving, caring, supportive family to relate to. If yours is, thank the Lord for it every day. You have been richly blessed.

Yet, what of those whose families are not loving or supportive? That is a tough one. The "help" some families give, nobody needs. A lot of the answer lies within you and where you are coming from. Some families are too possessive, domineering or distant, and you will have to determine the appropriate degree of sharing.

Relating too closely or too often with them at this time may be detrimental to your own well-being and to that of the children. This is no easy matter. One single parent I know has loving parents but they wanted her back in their home, living under their roof, under their control. They wanted to raise their grandchildren and to continue raising their daughter as before she married and left home. They could not understand her reluctance to move back. Financially she was having a rough time, and the adjustments were difficult for the children, but they needed their independence from the grandparents. No, her parents did not understand. Yes, they did take it personally and felt rejected. Her explanations seemed to fall on deaf ears, but she made what she believed to be the right choice under the circumstances and for that time in her life. Knowing her situation I applauded her decision — and understood her pain.

Good communication with your family is essential no matter what decision is made about socializing. Loving confrontation may be needed at times. You may need to remain apart temporarily. Share clearly and carefully what is happening. Be open about your needs, expressing the hope of altering things later on. Parents' feelings are important. However, be prepared. No amount of explaining is adequate in some situations. If that is the case with you, you will have to live with it. Your first responsibility must be to your children and to your own well-being, and that is *not* being selfish.

MY WISH FOR YOU

I would covet for you a family that is loving, supportive and confrontational, depending on your need. I would want them to give you the freedom to do as you feel led for the sake of the children and your own emotional health. I would want them to be there for you as needed, but never possessive or demanding. I would want you to know their unconditional love. I would want them to relate to you as your Heavenly Father would direct. Is this asking too much of them? I hope not, for your sake. I pray not.

In turn, I would hope for you to be loving, supportive and confrontationally encouraging toward them. I would want you to give them the freedom not to understand fully how you feel. I would want you to allow them to enjoy their grandchildren and get to know them. I would not want you to be resentful or demanding. I would want you to share with them your unconditional love. I would want you to relate to them as your Heavenly Father would direct. Is this asking too much of you? I hope not, for their sakes. I pray not.

Let me pray for you and for them:

"Father, this is not an easy time for any of these, Your children. Grandparents, single parents and children all struggle to know what is the right thing to do. Above all else, help them maintain the relationships all of them need so much. No matter what may happen between them, no matter what struggles they have to face, knit them together in a bond of love that will always be to Your glory and to their joy. I ask this for all of them in Jesus' name. Amen."

Δ

TAKING ACTION: SOCIAL NEEDS

1. How would you characterize your style of relating?

2. What basic needs do your relationships meet for you?

3. How do you feel about your relating style?

4. In what style does your family relate to you and your children?

5. What is your plan to make the style of relating to your family more need-satisfying?

8

AVOIDING A DETOUR

We live in a sexually frustrated culture. Sex is used to sell everything from cars to toothpaste. It is used to promote sporting events and flower shows. It forms the basis of the "soaps," movies, art and literature. You are confronted by it on billboards and magazine covers. Still, most people fail to realize that behind all this is an impotent culture. That is why sex can be so easily exploited. In our impotence we want to give the appearance that all is well, that we can handle our one-night stands, and that the only reason for any sense of guilt is that a frustrated church has taught us since the Dark Ages that sex is bad.

Sexual impotence is more than having difficulty in functioning. When you understand the real meaning of relating sexually, you realize that a person can function at will and still be sexually impotent, or that a person can function sexually and still be frigid. Frigidity can be a psychological game or it can be due to a physical malfunction. What I need to stress at this point is the fact that few in our culture are well-adjusted sexually. Cultures exploit their weaknesses, not their strengths, and impotence is a symptom of a deeper, relational emptiness, thus the need for a cover-up. If we actually were as well adjusted as we pretend, we would not exploit sex, nor would we tolerate others exploiting it.

ASSESSING THE EFFECTS OF YOUR PAST

Whenever trouble begins in a marriage relationship, one of the first areas to show signs of it is usually that of sexual functioning. The tensions between you cause you to distance yourselves from one another, and this always affects the sexual. On the other hand, some marriages are in trouble from the beginning because of a lack of adequate sexual functioning. This is more the case today with couples in their later forties and older since most of them entered marriage during a pretty uptight time in society, when minds and mouths were closed both in education and in the church. An un-relaxed home during that time was taken for granted.

Yet when you rightly understand your sexuality, you recognize that it is one of the primary areas in which you act out the total of what is deep within you as a person. In other words, any and all levels of emotional and spiritual dysfunctioning are brought to bear on the sexual. The demand of the sexual is for intimacy, sharing and giving, but the dysfunction will not allow for a healthy relationship. You are pushed toward either impotence/frigidity, or pseudo-intimacy, which is sex without love, caring or tenderness. Either extreme is self-destructive.

WHAT IS TAKING PLACE

Acting out your emotions sexually, in a moment of surrender and self-giving that has no equal, expresses an inward commitment and decision and provides one of the deepest moments of bonding known to human experience. In this bonding you take into the self the life-giving gift of your partner, and you share with your partner your life-giving gift of self. In this moment of true intimacy each is a co-creator and, at times, a procreator. Paul likens it to a symbol of the relationship that occurs between the Father and the Son, and between Christ and His Church (Ephesians 5:23-33). A oneness is born, and there is bonding in that oneness.

Sexuality cannot be understood merely in terms of maleness versus femaleness. Nor can you talk of sex in merely physical or psychological terms. You need to see it as a total expression, involving spirit, body, mind, emotions and volition. You need to recognize how all these things within the person are bonded with the partner.

The bonding remains a mystery even to those who experience it. It reaches its fullest expression in a loving, caring, committed, intentional marriage relationship. What needs to be noted, though, is that it occurs to some degree in every sexual relationship. The writer of Proverbs understood this and cautioned his son accordingly (Proverbs 7:24-27). The example was in visiting a prostitute. What happens between them leaves both forever changed. They have given something to each other that cannot be taken back.

SOMETHING YOU NEED TO UNDERSTAND

The Bible is very specific in what it says about sexual relationships outside marriage, as well as within. Sexual relationships apart from marriage are not to be. It is as plain as that. Sexual relationships are to be within marriage. They are to be need-satisfying for both participants, each having control of the other's body. If they choose to refrain from marital relations, it is to be for a spiritual purpose. After the completion of that spiritual exercise, the relationship is to be resumed fully. Paul is explicit about this. God made it natural for the relationship and expects it to be natural within that relationship (1 Corinthians 7:3-5).

Why would God set the standards He did, especially with regard to a non-marriage relationship? Let me make something very clear at this point.

**The reason sex outside the marriage covenant
is wrong is not simply that God says so.
Sex outside the marriage covenant is wrong
in and of itself—that is why God says it is.**

God is not just making the rules; He is announcing the very nature of your sexuality and thus is seeking to protect you from yourself. Critics say people have guilt over premarital and extramarital affairs only because the church has preconditioned them to feel guilty. It's not that simple. What makes it wrong is that, as a human being, you are made for loving relationships and for sexual bonding. Without an adequate foundation within the marriage covenant, you are not equipped to handle the implications of that bonding. God understands this, thus He put up the parameters that would spare you your own self-destruction. When you violate these parameters, the results become evident in the breaking down of the very fabric that was designed to hold things together. Most people see these as restrictions, as if God were some celestial party-pooper bent on robbing you of all your fun. On the contrary, He is literally saving you from yourself, for your true self.

A HARD WORD

I am a sexual being and so are you. But at this stage in your life sex is not what you need, especially if it is masking a deeper need. When someone is overweight you say he needs to go on a diet. Is that what he really needs? Or does he need to alter his lifestyle, understand his compulsion for over-eating, and get his intake under control? Sex can be a way of making up for what you believe is lacking in your self-worth or of buying what you perceive you could never get otherwise. Maybe you believe your body is the only asset you have in finding love. What you need now is a chance to find closeness, understanding, support and encouragement as a person, not as a body. You need a chance to put your life in order so you can achieve your goals and fulfill your purpose. Sex may bring you temporary physical closeness to another warm body, or a fleeting sense of well-being, but it can also launch you into a premature relationship that will not meet your need. It can short-circuit your plans, and it can land you right into the middle of a self-destructiveness you need to avoid at all costs.

Nor do you need an intense relationship that could lead to a new marriage. How can you be ready for a new relationship when you haven't had time to assess the one you just left, or the one that was taken from you? You are in pain and the last thing you need right now is more pain. Looking through pain does not allow you to judge anyone accurately, much less a prospective new marriage partner. Pain can be like an alcoholic haze: You see what you want to see. And who is to say at this point that remarriage is the way for you to go, anyway?

RECREATIONAL ASPECTS OF SEX

There is a recreational aspect to sex, and the present culture certainly plays on that theme. One of the curses of the AIDS scare for many is the fact it has forced them to consider the implications of recreational sex. Within the marriage covenant, sex does have its recreational aspects as any vibrant couple well understands; however, this cannot be divorced from the bonding aspect. We tell ourselves it can be, and many seek to live as if it were, but the reality of it does not change. Just because it may not "bother" someone does not mean it has not bonded them. In time a price will be paid.

Not long ago a joke went around about Moses coming down from Mount Sinai and saying to the people, "I have good news and bad news. The good news is I talked God down to only Ten Commandments. The bad news is He is holding firm to adultery."

In human nature there is a lust for "free love" but God recognizes no such thing as free love. True love is not interested in being free of its object—it wants to build a relationship.

A LOVING WORD

The hardest thing in all the world to deal with is a broken relationship. Any sexual bonding that has taken place complicates it even further. This is one of the hidden traumas of divorce, and it often results in a tremendous amount of anger that oozes out over a long period of time. Premarital or extramarital relationships make it worse yet.

We human beings have mastered the art of digging deep holes for ourselves, but I want you to know there is a grace available that can fill them in. God's restorative and transforming powers are beyond your imagination. He is able, willing and ready to forgive. It is yours for the asking; it is yours for the accepting. (Sexual sins are difficult to deal with because of the pathological guilt connected with them. This tends to overshadow the real guilt — which God forgives. The pathological exists only in our minds and is the result of our own creating.)

The difference between your normal sex drive and what the Lord experienced is the fact that His was not complicated or exaggerated by a lot of garbage being carried around inside. He was a normal human being and He can understand you and your struggles. Hebrews 2:14-18 tells you this. However, since He did not yield to the temptation, He knows the way through it and can lead you so you won't end up on a detour. He can keep you from settling for sex when it is something else you really need. He can keep you from settling for what seems good because He has promised the best. He has no intention whatever of limiting your freedoms, only of protecting you from hurt. He desires to fence out what you do not need at this time in order to preserve you for that which you do need: love, caring, support, encouragement, understanding and closeness.

SOME INSIGHTS

What would sex do for you at this stage in your life? Is there something deeper you really need? How should you view sex right now? Among most people you may know sex is just sex; how can you put it in its proper perspective when you're not sure how to see it? How do you have a meaningful relationship without sex being a part of it? How do you identify what you thought was a sexual need but what may be trapping you in a bonding you are unaware of? What do you do with a drive that won't quit?

In making your assessment, let me share a few points that may assist you.

First, even if your sexual relating has to be on hold for awhile, you, yourself, do not have to be, and life does not have to be.

Second, your sexual desire is God-given, but your body does not know when you are married and when you aren't. Yesterday you were married, today you are divorced, tomorrow you may still be divorced, but your body is still the same and has the same hungers. What makes the difference is the mind and the will. Don't turn the decision over to the emotions for they will sin bravely and worry about repenting some other time.

Third, sex is a celebration of a covenant relationship, and that is not where you are at this stage in your journey.

Fourth, you have a need for closeness but this can be met without sex being a part of it. Right now sex actually would be a detriment.

Fifth, sex is often a means of barter in our culture. Many people "buy" closeness at the price of a sexual encounter, but this is self-destructive.

Sixth, you don't need to play any games. Be cautious, because even Christian groups have singles around (and some who are not single) who will offer to care for your physical needs with "no strings attached." There are *always* strings attached in relating sexually.

Seventh, be aware of the danger of creating a false or pseudo-intimacy through sex. In all probability you would end up with another broken relationship to deal with. Who needs that?

Eighth, you need to be relating at the deepest levels possible to avoid any further tragedy for you and your children. You cannot risk another failure by settling for less than a fully covenantal relationship.

Ninth, your goal is to build true intimacy and part of the price of true intimacy is a solid foundation for its covenant. It is one thing to be betrayed but still another thing to betray yourself.

Tenth, an impotent culture cannot understand real love so it substitutes sex and calls it love. Yet sex is a normal part of a loving marital relationship in which both are fully open to the bonding it affords. Nothing less will meet your real need.

AVOIDING SEXUAL ENTRAPMENTS

The time to set your personal limits is before entering a new relationship. Rehearse ahead of time what you want to say and why you want to say it. When you are ten degrees shy of the boiling point is no time to ask yourself, "How far do I want to go?" By allowing things to reach 202° in the first place, you may leave your partner rightly angry. You can get a bad burn from a lot less than 202° (your 10° below boiling). Set meaningful limits within the parameters of your life's purpose and goal. Once set, they are easier to keep.

Becoming sexual in a nonmarital relationship bonds you in ways you cannot fully understand until you are involved in it. A sense of obligation develops, and a sense of having been trapped. How do you back out now? How much easier it would have been to end the relationship if you hadn't allowed the sexual to creep in. On the other hand, the sexual aspect may be so fulfilling you unwisely close your eyes to all the rest, even though there are warning signs all over the place. Many couples have become sexually active so early in their relationship that little else has been built into it to hold it together. This is how the sexual entraps you. Once you are committed, it's hard to get out, even when you want to. When do you take the time to discover who you are so you stop making poor, hasty choices?

If sex is the price of a relationship then you know you do not need that relationship. When one who professes to love you asks for sex out of sequence, watch out. You probably have one selfish person on your hands. The inner child of the past has discovered some wonderful feelings he wants to experience as often as possible. That child will sell his birthright for those feelings any time—and he can get pretty demanding if not downright mean when he is denied. One sign of maturity is an ability to postpone gratification until a more meaningful time. Why not hold out for the best? It's your life and well-being you are opting for, and it also includes your walk with the Lord.

HOW SEX WORKS BEST

First, it is a fulfillment of a love relationship. The love expressed within this relationship has pledged itself in a covenant of marriage.

Second, it is a celebration of that love relationship and all that goes into it to make it what it is. What the partners experience physically is a symbol of what they are feeling emotionally, volitionally and spiritually.

Third, it is a uniting of two genuine lovers in becoming one just as Christ is one with His Church. Not only would these two be willing to give their all for each other, but they do it daily in the little deaths and resurrections they experience in becoming one. The symbols of their relating are a towel and a wash basin as they sub-mit themselves to one another's need. John 13:3-5 sets the example for this. (See also Ephesians 5:21.)

Fourth, it is in celebration of God's unique and wonderful gift to them of each other. What they are making of their relationship is their gift to Him and to each other.

Fifth, they are "writing a book" together entitled *The Joy of Loving,* and "The Joy of Sex" is only one of its many chapters.

SOME THOUGHTS AND QUESTIONS TO NOTE

Here is a set of questions and thoughts for you to ponder as you consider this aspect of your life, especially for the here-and-now.

1. Is it okay with you that you are the gender you are?

2. Can you affirm your own opposite side? As a male I have a feminine side, the part of me that listens best and can empathize with others. If you are a woman, can you con-front and discipline? Can you affirm your masculine side?

3. What does it mean to you to be a sexual being? Is it easier for you to think of yourself in non-sexual terms?

4. What to you is the ideal woman or ideal man? Who are the role models you choose? Are you trying to be someone other than who you are?

5. Do you consider yourself to be free of major sexual hang-ups? Do you consider your level of functioning in the past as normal, or less than normal? In your marriage, would it have been okay with you to have done without sex?

6. Are you free to give yourself to a cherished partner in ways you consider normal levels of functioning?

7. Do you see the connection between a covenant relation-ship and sexual functioning that leads to bonding? Does this concept make sense to you?

8. Have you decided to wait until marriage for any sexual in-volvement in your future? If so, why? If not, why not?

9. Do you have the inner freedom to wait until a cherished covenant relationship has been established? If not, are you willing to get help in achieving such freedom?

10. Do you have a sense of being in control of your life so you can make the decisions you feel you need to make? If not, are you willing to seek the necessary help in order to gain such a level of control?

IF YOU NEED PROFESSIONAL HELP

We live in an addictive society, and some people are addicted to sex as others are to alcohol or drugs. Support groups are available for those people. If this is your problem, get the help you need before you get your life so off center you destroy all meaningful relationships. It is an addiction and must be treated as such.

If, in the past, you experienced serious levels of dysfunctioning, you need professional help. If it was a problem in an earlier relationship, it probably would carry over into any other one.

If, in the past, you were unable to give of yourself sexually in a marriage relationship, don't assume it was all because of your partner. Your inability to give comes from within. You may choose not to give; that is a different matter. If you did not have the freedom of choice but were forced by your own inner hang-ups, you need help. Be honest with yourself in assessing your need. A few good books may prove helpful. Some pastoral counseling may benefit you, also. God intended sex to be enjoyed fully by all His children in their marriage. Get help.

You may not plan to remarry, but you still need to understand yourself, to be free to say yes to any relationship the Lord may bring into your life. Don't close yourself to full understanding. Be free to be the very best you that you can be.

A FURTHER WORD OF ENCOURAGEMENT

This will be a major area of struggle for you as a single parent in today's world, first because of your own libido, and then because of the pressures surrounding you. I know it will not be easy but you can make it a lot easier on yourself by setting your limits ahead of time, by being true to yourself, and by allowing His grace to assist you in all your battles. There are better answers than cold showers and eating oranges. These are found in having a clear purpose and a good understanding of what your real needs are, and by building relationships that are designed to help you achieve these goals rather than your being detoured for an evening or for a lifetime.[1]

Δ

TAKING ACTION:
SEXUAL NEEDS

Respond to the following for a better understanding of where you are on this issue.

1. How well were things going sexually in your marriage?

2. What was your sexual experience prior to your marriage?

3. As a teenager what kinds of feelings did you have about yourself and your sexuality?

4. How do you feel about relating to persons of the opposite sex?

5. What values do you ascribe to your sexuality?

6. What difficulties did you encounter in becoming sexually active in your marriage?

7. How well do you feel you adjusted?

8. Was lovemaking what you expected?

9. What did lovemaking mean to you?

10. How painful is it for you to go back over the past memories?

11. Was there an extramarital affair during your marriage?

12. What role did sex play in your total marriage relationship?

13. On a scale of zero to ten, how would you rate your ability to function as a sexual partner during your marriage?

14. When it comes to your views/attitudes regarding sex, do you consider these to be normal?

The markets, both secular and religious, are flooded with works on sexuality and sexual functioning. Most secular works need to be read with discernment and selectivity for they usually omit the spiritual dimensions and the element of covenantal love. On the other hand, many religious works aren't practical enough and/or carry heavy biases. Few discover the meaning God wants for you. Select carefully and read with discernment. See the end of this book for titles to assist you.

9

WHAT IF YOU GET STUCK?

We live in an age when, besides meeting a real need, getting professional help can be a fad. It shouldn't be looked at this way, though, because there are times when this kind of help can change a life, even save one. Most single parents cannot afford the luxury of a private therapist, but I want you to assess this area carefully and prayerfully as you examine your own needs.

Suppose your mate died in an accident two years ago and you are still having an extremely difficult time handling it. For you it is as if it happened yesterday. You still have nightmares. His clothes still hang in the closet, and in the daytime you look for him in the next room. The thought of him not being there wracks you with deep, uncontrollable sobs, and you find yourself in a daze a lot of the time. You may still be wearing your wedding band and talking and thinking in terms of "we" and "us." These tell you you're denying the reality of your loss.

Taking care of the children is a burden because of the load you carry inside. It seems they are being raised in spite of you, not because of you. You want to reach out to them but something inside hurts too much. If this is you, you have a major problem, and you need professional help.

TWO KINDS OF DENIAL

Or maybe divorce is your situation and you are like one single parent in a group I led who spoke of his eighteen-year struggle. He got stuck in the process. Another man in that same group wanted out of his marriage so badly it appeared he worked through his loss as if the marriage had never been. For him it seemed to be, "Here

91

today, gone tomorrow." Reactions to the death of a spouse or to a divorce can be as varied as the persons going through it. The men mentioned were each stuck in a different form of denial. It is easier for us to recognize denial when, like the first man, the person has been stuck in the process for years. "Instantaneous recovery" is a form of denial that is harder to spot, but may prove to be more serious in the long run. Someone who is stuck in the process deals with it over and over again. The other tends to run away, and may get involved later in marriage after marriage as part of his denial.

Most people who have been betrayed in their marriage get stuck in the recovery process and live in the denial stage for some time. Anger is part of this denial.

On the other hand, the betrayer may jump immediately to another relationship as his method of denial, never dealing with the first situation or even facing it. No one goes through divorce without having an enormous amount of homework to do. This takes time.

SOMETHING YOU NEED

If you have lost your mate, you need a solid understanding of what this has done to you and how you can be in control of your today and all your tomorrows. How easy it would be to put your pain into your relationship with your children, or to swallow your pain and have it ooze out through your pores into all your other relationships and not even be aware of it. You need help in getting unstuck if too much time is elapsing between the stages of recovery and growth. However, if you are becoming stronger, you know you are working through it and His grace is in control in your life.

Joyce, in her late twenties, was left with two small children when her husband was killed on the job. The couple had just begun to see some light at the end of the financial tunnel. Although his long hours had put a strain on their relationship, it looked as if they finally would realize some of their dreams.

Then tragedy struck. The first thing Joyce did was thrust herself on the Lord, and her nominal faith grew by leaps and bounds. Family and friends rallied around her for support and encouragement. She took an active role in the family business. She sensed the children's needs and put them ahead of her own. It was tough for her but she did it by His grace, and she turned her pain into peace by maturing in meaningful ways. If the Lord were to bring someone new into her life after these years of widowhood, she would be ready.

CHECKING THINGS OUT

You can check with your parents and a few trusted friends on how well they see you doing, and they can give you much needed feedback. The worse you are, the harder it will be for them to share with you because your dysfunctioning will keep them at arm's length. But ask them anyway, and then allow them to be honest in their assessment.

You can arrange for a session or two with a therapist as well. I remember one widow who sat down with me after making it through her first year. She asked me to help her evaluate her recovery process. She had made some great strides but felt she was coming through it too slowly. I was able to help her see where she was doing well, where she was avoiding change, and where she was still denying her loss. One or two sessions was all she needed. Later, she was thankful she had come.

How do you know when you need professional help? Some might respond to that question by saying, "If you have to ask, the answer is obvious." I think a better way to answer it, though, would be to assess honestly just how comfortable you are with how far you have come. For example, say you were widowed a year ago. You have been at this process since, and see evidence of working through your pain. You get out, mix well at church, care for yourself and your children, and you feel pretty much in control again. You are making good progress.

On the other hand, if the pain is not more manageable now, if your feelings are not more under control, or your days easier to handle, if the needs of the children are not easier to meet, you need some help.

As to those who go through a divorce, I think every one of them owes it to himself (or herself) and the children to sit down with a professional counselor and examine what happened and why. They each also need to be willing to make recommended changes. Remember, the hardest thing in all the world for us human beings to deal with is a broken relationship. If you do not profit by some understanding and self-awareness, you will carry your pain with you into all your other relationships, the rest of your life.

Carol did not want her divorce and worked hard to prevent it. She kept every counseling appointment, even when her mate did not. Yet when it came to working on her part in the marriage relationship, she balked. "I don't need to change," she said. "He's the one who is tired of the relationship. I'm the one staying home with our children, keeping the house, and being faithful to my vows."

The divorce happened. Carol had a load of bitterness to contend with but she laid all the blame on her husband. Now, some four years later, she is in another marriage—and back in counseling at the new husband's urging. She never dealt with her part in the first marriage. She is doing no better in the present one. It is "always" due to the other person's lack of change. (If you use "always" and "never" when talking about your spouse, it's a good clue that you need change.) If she had responded to professional help at the time of her divorce, she probably would have been able to avoid this new problem. If she refuses to deal with it this time, she may well continue a lifetime pattern of such avoidance.

Whenever you are in doubt, or when you feel there may be an unresolved problem, you need to seek professional help as early as possible. The Lord has given other people skills that can assist you in your self-awareness and growth. You need to see these skills as gifts from Him for your healing.

WHERE TO GET PROFESSIONAL HELP

As a general rule, my first referral is to a pastoral counselor. We are spiritual beings, so the spiritual has to be a part of anyone's therapy, especially for the Christian. Secular therapists may be very skilled, but they usually are unable to help you with your spiritual needs.

When I say pastoral counselor I mean a pastor who has had special training as a therapist. Any pastor is free to counsel and to call himself a pastoral counselor. But this does not mean he is skilled in the art of counseling. Even those who have had training need the spiritual gifts of mercy and exhortation. If your pastor is a qualified counselor, you probably won't have to look any further for an effective therapist. If he is not, he at least should be able to help you evaluate your need, and then you can ask him for a referral to another pastoral counselor he knows and trusts.

If you need more than what a pastoral counselor can give you, the next step is to consider a clinical psychologist. You pastor should be able to make the referral for you here, too. He also can work along with the clinical psychologist as part of your on-going therapy. A clinical psychologist is a doctor who specializes in psychological help and counsel and has a Ph.D., but does not have a medical background.

Similar help may be obtained through a psychiatric social worker in clinical practice. This person will have had training in psychological problems and works from a general knowledge of psychiatry but will not have a medical background. If in private practice, he will have a master's degree in social work, or its equivalent, and will be licensed by the state.

A psychiatrist is a medical doctor who has had additional training in psychiatry. Besides being in private practice, he usually is involved in hospitalizations, either as the admitting doctor or as a treatment doctor within an institution.

You could benefit a great deal from working with a combination of pastoral counselor, clinical psychologist and psychiatric social worker. If your background includes incest or child abuse, you may need to work with a psychiatrist.

When dealing with family matters or your relationship with the children, you may also be served well by a marriage, family and/or child therapist. In most states such therapists are licensed.

WHAT YOU DON'T NEED

Not all Christian therapists are good, nor are they always Christian in their therapy. Not all non-Christian therapists are bad, nor are they unsympathetic to your personal faith. Discernment is needed. Make your decision carefully and prayerfully. One of the sharpest, most loving therapists I know is not yet a Christian; however, every person I have referred to him has become better adjusted and stronger as a result of his work. I consider him a trusted friend. When he has a client with serious spiritual hang-ups, he refers them to me. We work in partnership for the well-being of the counselee.

Don't pick a Christian therapist just because he is a Christian, and don't reject a therapist merely because he is not a Christian. Do avoid anyone who is antagonistic to your faith, though. He will not help you. He does not necessarily have to share your faith, but he must be willing to allow you to hold it, because it is central to your healing and growth. Unfortunately, some therapists are committed to challenging Christian faith, and they feel they have failed if they haven't knocked the props out from under you. You don't need one like that.

On the other hand, some pastoral therapists can be a hidden threat. Their faith may be more in their techniques and in themselves than in the Lord. You don't need them, either.

Nor do you need a pastoral counselor who is not trained in counseling skills. You are at a vulnerable point in your life and you don't want matters made worse. A friend of mine, going through a major crisis in her life, was so desperate she verged on committing suicide. She had been away from the church and involved in a cult, so she sought the help of a pastor she had known earlier. Her cries for help were met with a proposition. He tried to seduce her. Fortunately, she did find real help in time, but now she carries the scar of that cruel betrayal.

Another thing you don't need is a quick fix. This is not to say that God is limited and cannot do things instantaneously; however, therapy involves working *through* pain, not escaping or evading it. Popping aspirin for every little ache is a symptom of our preoccupation with escapism, but we must remember that pain has a legitimate function. God promised to see us through the "valley of the shadow of death." You need to discover the cause of your pain, especially when it is spiritual and emotional. To escape the pain prematurely may mean missing the lessons it must teach. You need those lessons to get to full healing.

You also don't need a therapist who is unwilling to commit to your therapy. It is costing you a lot of money unless you have exceptional insurance, but it could cost you even more if he is in it only for the money. If you ever go to a therapist who is not a help to you, you don't have to stay. You are free to find one who will meet your need.

Finally, you don't need a pseudo-solution. James warns us about giving people pseudo-solutions, which would be like telling a starving person, "God bless you; I'll pray for you." A hurting person needs more than that. You need all the healing that God's therapeutic process can afford, but take heart—in most instances He will not give you pat answers or false solutions. He loves you too much to do that.[1]

TO GET RESULTS

No matter who you go to for help, much depends on you: your

level of honesty and your willingness to make necessary changes. There is no instant solution. Meaningful changes come about only through meaningful work done in the therapeutic process. Good results can be seen even with mediocre therapy if you work hard at it, but the best therapist in the world cannot get you anywhere if you leave it all up to him. The agreement between you and your therapist calls for both of you to give your best. You need someone who will walk all the way with you through your pain and help you find the way out.

So first, *know that the therapist is committed to your well-being.* You do not have to prove yourself; just be yourself. The first session can be the beginning of real change if your therapist is committed to you and you go committed to the process and willing to reveal what is troubling you.

Any good therapist is first of all a trained, active listener, feeding back to you, for your insight, what he is hearing. He will challenge you to listen to your true self. And he can reflect back to you what you are really saying so you can hear it yourself, maybe for the first time.

Know that the therapist is there to confront you as needed. If you are playing the blame game or merely dumping on yourself, he will challenge you regarding this behavior. You are seeking to get well, not to get confirmation of your innocence or guilt for the past. Therapy is not to prove that you are right and your Ex is wrong. It is for your healing and progressing toward wholeness. The goals of good therapy parallel Paul's experience in Philippians 3:12-14.

Promise yourself to stay with it as long as needed. I know it costs time, energy and money, but you are not doing it for the therapist; you are doing it for *you.* If you are on a limited income and/or have no insurance, find a therapist who is willing to work on a sliding scale. Be open about your financial needs.

If you quit prematurely and find you need to return, then do so. If you are honest with yourself, you will sense when it is time to terminate the therapy and your therapist will concur. Most therapists have more clients than they can handle anyway, and they will not keep you on unduly long.

Prepare to share your feelings. How you feel about what has happened is more important than what actually has happened. The facts will always be what they are but feelings can change. The little child within you has a story to tell and it is all about feelings.

Get them out. Share them. Come to understand them and deal with them.

Do your homework. If the therapist makes a reading or other homework assignment (such as contacting someone about something), do it. The more you can do in between sessions, the more it will add to your growth and healing. If no assignments are made, ask, "What can I do between sessions to aid my progress?" Reading in the right areas can move things along at a better pace and can help you know where to probe next. If you have questions for the next session, jot them down and take them with you.

Take charge of your own healing. Discuss with your therapist how you feel you are doing, how he is doing, and what concerns you may have about the entire process. Invest well in your own recovery and growth. Expect to make progress. If you feel you are not, or are slipping back, share this with your therapist. At times the approach may need altering or the tempo may need changing.

Keep yourself moving ahead. Count any regression as temporary and get growing again. Right from the start discuss your expectations, fears, goals and progress. Keep everything right up front. Remember, what is emerging in all this is the real you. Start being that real you in the therapeutic relationship.

Anticipate a miracle. Too many of us have lost the sense of the miracle of expectation. We don't expect the Lord to totally change us so we don't get changed. Therapy isn't just to recover. It isn't just to heal an emotional broken leg so you can walk again. It is to learn to "mount up with wings as eagles" and go where you've never been before. It is to expect the miracle of His full grace in your life allowing God to work in and through you. Try on your new wings.

You are not just investing in your present; you are investing in your forever. It does not end here. It is a means to an end. Christian hope sees in three directions: (1) understanding your eternal value to Him in your past; (2) becoming aware of your true worth in Him right here and now; and (3) realizing all He has for your tomorrows (Romans 8:18; 1 Corinthians 2:9; Ephesians 1:3).

You do not want to limit God's grace or His power. He wants you whole, and for the first time in all your years that is exactly what you want. If He could perform the miracle of making creation out of chaos, just think what He can make out of you. God will step back, take a long, loving look at His work in you, and say, "It is good!"

Δ

TAKING ACTION:
NEEDING OUTSIDE HELP

Ask yourself and answer the following questions to assess your present needs.

1. What scares me most about where I am now in my life?
2. How would it help if I sat down and discussed this fear with a professional counselor?
3. Who do I know who has benefited from therapy?
4. Who could help me best, a pastoral counselor, a marriage and family therapist, a clinical psychologist, or a psychiatrist?
5. Do I know of someone who can help me or will I need a referral?
6. What about going to my pastor for help in finding a referral?
7. What resources do I have to pay for such help?
8. What do I hope to gain through therapy?
9. How would I like to see my life change?
10. What will I do if I discover the children need therapy?
11. What are my personal goals for myself and my family in terms of needed changes?
12. Can these be achieved without outside help?
13. What is my plan of action?
14. How will all this benefit me and the children?

10

CHANGING DIRECTIONS

In 1 Timothy Paul encourages the young church not to regard a widow as being a true widow unless she is sixty or older. They expected she would remarry if she was under sixty (1 Timothy 5:9,14). Of course things were a lot different in Paul's day, but now most widows under sixty do remarry—as do many over that age. I have friends who served on different mission fields, met in retirement, fell in love, and married—well into their seventies. Today's longer life span might influence Paul to revise his admonition to read seventy-five or eighty, who knows?

The point is, the remarriage question for widows or widowers in our culture is purely personal with a few family problems thrown in. Remarriage for those re-singled by divorce is another matter.

INTERPRETING SCRIPTURE

Here you have to come to grips with both how to interpret the divorce passages in the New Testament, and how your denomination, local church, friends and family interpret them. My first word of caution is to encourage you to work them through for yourself and make your decision truly on your own. Make it through study, prayer and counseling, and a good level of self-awareness. Allowing others to decide for you can result in a heavy load later on. Some people want to make decisions which are binding on others, without going through adequate examination of all that is involved, simply because it fits themselves.

As Christians we often have a difficult time dealing with divorce—because we haven't dealt adequately with marriage. We think one or two premarital sessions guarantees that couples are ready for marriage. Yet the divorce rate in Christian circles is about the same as in others, showing how serious the matter is. Jesus' views, with the exclusionary clause for unfaithfulness, may be found in Matthew 5:31,32 and 19:1-12. Paul's teaching is in 1 Corinthians 7:1-16.

God granted the privilege of divorce because there are some relationships that get off on the wrong foot right from the start, and will never make it. Our culture got away from family arranged marriages to freedom of choice some time ago, but we have failed to tell our youth the difference between being in love and being in heat. Not only have many young people plopped into bed before saying, "I do," but they are also into bed before they say, "I love you." Some never even take a serious look at the other person first. This does not justify divorce; it only complicates it.

You must work through both the biblical materials and the peer pressure. In all good conscience, you and your Lord can be in agreement on what you think and what you do. Let the Spirit guide you into the full truth of what He has for you. There is no hard, fast rule regarding remarriage—but neither is there a blanket permission for everyone to do just as they please. Some who have every right to remarry shouldn't. They are not ready nor will they ever be. Others may be ready but still shouldn't.

DEALING WITH PARENTAL INJUNCTIONS

Parental injunctions can be positive or negative. Negative ones are based on prejudice such as "only losers get divorced." The inner child of the past gets hooked by these every time, so the adult within us has to free himself of them in order to make meaningful decisions on the basis of the Spirit's leading.

I heard one voice loud and clear in my own past: "Nice persons don't get divorced. Anyone who does should never marry again. God will never condone it." Maybe you heard something similar.

When I test it, reality soon tells me some very nice people do get divorced; some of them should and do marry again; and God obviously does bless some remarriages, even blended families. So what are you to do about those parental injunctions? You need to understand them and update them, if needed, but make your decisions on other bases. These I will outline as the chapter progresses.

RESPONDING TO YOUR FAITH COMMUNITY

One basis you should consider carefully is your faith community. To be reconciled is extremely important. If your views of remarriage are not in agreement, you have a real problem, especially if you are from a Catholic or conservative background that does not allow remarriage. (Some will if the biblical mandate of unfaithfulness has been met. Others will not, even then.)[1]

Changing faith communities, which you may feel is appropriate, usually isn't the best answer to this dilemma. Confronting it in love and working it through with your community is. Leaving should be the last resort, and separation should be due to the prompting of the Holy Spirit, not your desires. Self-understanding is essential, and your motive must be above reproach. Your pastor and those of your faith community will work with you on this.

I need to share with you now on a more emotional level in terms of preparation for or refraining from remarriage. I see lots of people who have settled the biblical matter, but then jump into remarriage when they really should not, or at least they should postpone it.

DISCERNING WHY YOU WANT TO REMARRY

Why do you want to remarry? I mean beyond the obvious desire for someone to share the rest of your life with or someone to care for you in your old age, what are your reasons? You need to know them and understand them.

You need to identify why you married in the first place and, if divorced, why your marriage did not work out. What did that prior relationship mean to you? What need did it meet? Why did you remain in it as you did? You need to understand every aspect of it so you can take care of whatever unfinished business may be left in it. It is difficult dealing with a broken relationship, and that's what a divorce is. If you do not understand how and why it ended as it did, you will be prone to repeat it.

If you have lost your mate through death, you still need to know why you want to remarry. Need is a very real part of it, but need alone is not enough. Your need can disguise a lack of self-love which makes remarriage necessary for you because you are afraid to face life alone. The basic reason must be one of love for that significant other as well as love for yourself.

Whether you lost your mate through death or divorce, be sure you aren't marrying someone who only reminds you of your previous mate. That relationship is now over and gone except in memories. Let the new person be himself, not a ghost of someone else. This is a new relationship with a new person, so let it be new for you, too. Similarities are bound to be present in any close, loving relationship, but no two can be exactly alike. You must accept him just for who he actually is.

FINDING THE RIGHT ONE

To identify a person as being the right one for you, you must understand who you are, what your needs and gifts are, and what that other person has to offer in response to your needs. You must understand who that other person is, what his real needs are and what you have to give. There must also be a love that draws the two of you into a desire to become one and to spend the rest of your lives sharing that love relationship. That does not come overnight. It takes time working together and learning to read each other.

When you love yourself and care about what the future holds, you can spot the "availables" who do not fit your needs. It is obvious, that is, until the love bug bites. Then you are sixteen all over again, and so is your judgment. You see traits that will later drive you up the wall and out the door, but right now you say, "Isn't he wonderful?" You're just sure it'll work. You'll change him. It'll be okay in time. Sound familiar?

Knowing who you are, though, allows you the inner freedom to decide for the true self, not the neurotic self. In working with singles groups I have seen many people seek the same kind of relationship they had before, and they renew all their problems and weaknesses. Over 40 percent of all second marriages end in divorce—among church members as well as anyone else.

Need can make you do strange things. Evidence of this is found in the numbers of second marriages that don't make it. Those who remarry for the right reasons work harder at it—their investment in it is greater. Those who remarry for the wrong reasons tend to bail out quickly, knowing the pain of a protracted bad relationship. God will not lead you into a remarriage for the wrong reasons. That's of your doing. How often do you work against yourself when you react only out of need?

KNOWING GOD'S LEADING IN THE MATTER

About the only people I meet who feel their marriages were not in God's will are those who want out of them. Most everyone else feels He is in it, or at least He was in the beginning. How could God make so many mistakes? And some very obvious ones. Either God isn't the world's best matchmaker or a lot of His children have deluded themselves. I have a sneaky suspicion it is the latter.

First, God leads best those who are in fellowship with Him. This is no easy matter in an affair of the heart. Perhaps there is no single decision more fraught with emotional entanglements than this one. You need to be sure of His leading. I often joke with my workshop participants about one person's approach to remarriage. He simply said, "Lord, if you have no objection, I'll take this one!" If the Lord did have an objection, how would this person know it?

Second, God leads best when you are truly open to His leading. All of us have our pockets of resistance—Peter found his in the dream God sent him before he went to Cornelius' home. You perceive yourself as being open—until the right button gets pushed. Mate selection is that button for many. God had better be able to get through to you early in the relationship before you close your mind to any change. He can break through at any point if allowed, but His love for you does not permit Him to violate your will. You need to recognize this fact and thus make sure you do have His leading.

Third, God leads best when your intentions in the new relationship are to glorify Him. Paul states very clearly in Corinthians that you are to "marry in the Lord." He means you are to marry someone who is also in the Lord. To glorify Him in your relationship begins here, but it also includes everything else about the relationship. Marrying a fellow Christian forms a basis on which you can build.

There is always someone who will tell their story of an exception to the rule. It is easy to justify a relationship you really want for yourself. But I have to caution you about who is doing the leading in this matter for He will not violate His Word. Many have not worked out, as you know.

The point is, this is your life. You need to glorify Him and to find the right person with whom to share, therefore trust Him. Trust His method and His choice for you. You will need His leading every moment of every day, so make sure you have it. A good relationship has to be built on many forms of intimacy, sharing and things in common. If you plan to remarry, I encourage you as a couple to work on it by using a book like the Clinebell's *The Intimate*

Marriage. (See the resource list in the back of this book.)

ON AN EMOTIONAL LEVEL

Marry the one you fall "hopelessly in love" with, and no one else. The second time around can be great, for you are not the immature person you were when you first married. You have changed; life has changed. But being in love is still the same. The bells, flashing lights, stars in the eyes and pre-ceremony jitters will all be there unless the inner child of the past got lost somewhere along the way. Marry for love, and only for love. Even if you are eighty, marry for love. Life is too precious to marry for any lesser motive (such as convenience, or having someone care for you in your old age, or fear of being alone, or wanting someone for the children). Some of the loneliest people I know are married.

Please do not marry for the children. You will do them a great disservice if you think it is for their sakes. You will not be the happy parent they need if that is your reason. God commanded us to love one another for a purpose, and the choice of a marriage partner must fit into that command. Children can survive a lot of things, but a parental relationship with no real love in it is a very difficult one for them.

CONCERNING THE CHILDREN

The new mate must be one who will fit into the family constellation, so do include the children and their needs in the new relationship.

No one will fit right without some whittling. Any new mate, stepping into a ready-made family relationship, will face some adjustment and struggle, but a whole lot of good, honest give and take will help. This is true for both parents and children. Stepparenting has its built-in difficulties as well as joys. They need to be worked on well in advance and then continuously during the life of the family relationship. None of us are perfect parents, and stepparenting is even harder.

The well-being of the children needs to be a part of your decision-making process, but not the only factor. Helping you see the big picture is where the Spirit's guidance can serve you best. If you have to do a lot of whittling to get someone to fit, there may not be much left, and maybe you'd better take a closer look at the total relationship.

Now you need to get down to the nitty-gritty of the matter. You have the right to happiness. You have the right to remarry even if the children are opposed to your choice. They will be grown and gone someday, and then who will you have? I hear you and I understand where you are coming from. You have rights—so do they. You have needs—so do they. You may even have to put your basic needs first and go ahead with your plans anyway, but that is usually when the children are old enough to handle it or to be on their own. Otherwise, work through these questions regarding them.

1. *How do the children fit into the big picture?* Does this relationship truly include them, or are they just along for the ride? Be honest. If you have not discussed it with them, you do not know. They don't fit in just because you say they do; they fit in because they believe they do.

2. *How do they perceive the new relationship?* You know how you perceive it, but if they are young, they will tend to tell you what they think you want to hear, not necessarily how it really is. You can judge it better by how they act when the new person is present and how they relate to that person. Marriage may be a concept they do not fully understand. When the new mate moves in and sleeps where Daddy used to sleep, what will they think? Life looks very different from their perspective.

3. *How do they feel about it?* Children have feelings but this does not mean they understand them, and they often cannot verbalize them. You will need to help them express their feelings, which are bound to be ambivalent no matter how great a new relationship is. Good lines of communication are of vital importance during these times. Try to think like your child does by asking yourself, *If I were five and a half, and my mother were remarrying, and I were getting a new father, a new location, a new home, etc., what would I be going through deep, down inside?* This will often give you clues as to what questions to ask to help your children find the answers they need.

4. *What role do they have in the decision?* It is your decision. Do not expect them to handle it. They need you to help them see that what you are doing is okay.

5. *How are they being prepared for the transition?* You are in love with your future mate and are more than ready for the change, but they are not. They need help to be ready. Help them understand what is happening, why and what it means to them. Answer these questions—

even if they don't ask them: What does it mean to have a stepparent? What does it mean to have two fathers? It isn't enough just to tell them how to address your new mate; they need to know how to relate.

6. *How are they to be helped through their shattered assumptions and delusions?* They believed that, no matter what happened, their parents would always be there for them. But the parents divorced. Then they believed that, in spite of the divorce, their parents would one day get back together. Or, now one parent is dead. In either case, they are facing a new situation that is destroying their earlier assumptions. They are faced with a real live "Humpty Dumpty" situation. How are they to put the pieces of life back together again?

7. *What are the gains and losses for them?* What will they actually be gaining through the new relationship? What you may perceive as gains may be seen as losses by them. What will they actually be losing? Will it move them farther away from the other parent? Will they have to share their mother with other children? In your flight to seize your new gains you may be ignorant of what is happening with them.

8. *What are their fears, questions, doubts, expectations?* These need to be dealt with, one at a time. Their fears of loss; their questions of what is expected of them; their doubts about fitting in; their concern about where it may all end up. Children of all ages are loaded with questions that can boggle your mind, but they need an opportunity to share them and to receive honest, open answers.

9. *If there is to be a move, how will it affect them?* Many times a new marriage involves a geographic move. Will this mean changing schools, leaving friends, finding a new church, living in another part of town? Have they been adequately prepared for such a major shift?

10. *How will they be helped to adjust?* Getting into the new relationship is only the beginning for everyone. The work of adjusting lies ahead and the children have more adjustments to make than the adults. They are coming through a time in which, from their perspective, their entire world has been challenged and they have experienced a trauma which is beyond their control. The new couple will have each other, but how can the children best be helped in this area? They need a level of support, encouragement and help that few of them get.

11. *Are they accepting it just for you?* Children usually are a lot smarter than they are credited for being, and they seem to know intuitively what is expected of them. They may go along with a new relationship out of loyalty to you, but at the same time build up some pretty negative feelings about the whole thing without even knowing it. These feelings may ooze out, especially during their teen years. You need to be prepared to help them understand their feelings.

12. *What about their former loyalties?* If their parent was taken from them by death, what should be their loyalty to the memory of that cherished person? Are they living with a ghost? Will they feel they are being disloyal by loving a new parent? Or, though you divorced your mate, they did not divorce their father. They never will, even if they were treated badly or were rejected by him. He is inside them; he is a part of them. You must understand that this loyalty is present with them and probably always will be. How will you help them handle it in light of the new relationship? Is it okay for them to love both? How are they to relate now to their natural father?

13. *How is the timing of the remarriage for them?* We all work through our pain of loss at different speeds. Some children rebound faster than others. You may be ready for a new step, but have they had the time they need to process the whole matter and to accept it and adjust? Who will help them understand the timing? Changes can be handled a lot easier if the timing is right.

14. *How can this be a win-win situation?* Is it possible for everyone in this situation to win? What is the commitment of each adult to the family aspect? What will you do to turn obstacles into opportunities? How can you best create a win-win situation?

15. *Are any behavioral problems evident?* Is there any acting out against the relationship? If so, why? Who is helping the children understand their behavior? Some acting out is to be expected as emotions are worked through. How are these to be perceived and handled? How are the children to be helped?

16. *Can the children see God in the decision?* It is important that God not be blamed for the new relationship. By being told God is in this, the children could now transfer their hurt and anger to Him for allowing it to take place. Or do they see the new relationship as a gift to them from Him? How do the children understand His part in it?

It is no easy task to bring children on board so they are a vital part of the new relationship. There is so much going for you, but not necessarily for them without real intent and commitment on your part. We parents do a lot of assuming, and this can lead to real trouble. If you want to know where they are in their processing of all this, ask, then help them answer. But don't put your hoped-for answers on them.

HELPING THEM UNDERSTAND

Children may not always ask the right questions or they may not put them in ways you can understand. One may ask, "Will you always love me?" when he really wants to know how he fits into the new relationship. In this case, a simple "Of course I will" does not suffice. A better response could be, "Are you wondering how Mommy is going to love you now that she has a new husband to love, too?" This can open up a lot of other questions that, in time, can restore a sense of safety in the relationship for the child. Before responding, ask yourself, *What am I really being asked?* and then speak to that level.

During major transitions you need to spend a lot of time reasoning, explaining and sharing with your children because they often do not understand where you are coming from. They observe all that is going on around them, but they are not very good interpreters of what it means or why. If you say, "I want you to know what is happening and why it is this way and what it means," it will help the child's understanding. Also, you will establish a way of relating that he will cherish. Of course, you need to reason with him at his level of understanding, but he also can surprise you with what he does grasp. Most of us err in assuming children understand less than they actually do.

Perhaps the most difficult thing for adults at this stage is not to expect from children what they want from them, but rather to discover what the children are really feeling inside. You want so much to have your marriage work. You want it to be great for the children. You want it to be for God's glory. It can work, but it requires a lot of work to make it work. It can be great for the children, but it has to be made great. To do this requires a lot of listening, sharing, explaining, groping and struggling together.

I remember so well sitting down with my oldest son and seeing my remarriage through his eyes. He shared it with me when he was twenty-eight, some fifteen years after the fact. It had been difficult for him. At the time I thought we had touched all the bases and he understood what was happening and why, but I found out he needed more time with me in preparation. He went along with it because he thought I wanted him to, and he kept his thoughts and feelings to himself. Those thoughts and feelings had rumbled around inside him all these years. They could have been cared for so easily if only I had taken the time to ask myself, *What is he experiencing? What does he need to know about what I am experiencing?*

Children will reach their acceptance level of the new relationship in their own time and way, but it must be with your help, and it may take years. Thank God for the romantic elements in the new relationship. They will carry the adults a long way and will spill over to the children. However, what brings them along best is the understanding, communication, sharing and caring that allows them to feel they are a vital part of the new relationship.

When Donna and I were saying our vows, the minister asked, "Do you take this woman to be your lawfully wedded wife?" Our youngest daughter, then almost six, said, "We do!"

Δ

TAKING ACTION: REMARRIAGE

Reflect on the chapter you have just read, and respond to the following for a perception check.

1. I want to remarry/not remarry because:

2. I believe God is in this decision because:

3. (If you plan to remarry) I believe the children are ready because:

4. Some ways I plan to work with the children on a continuing basis are:

5. Some problems I will need to work on are:

6. Some things they will need from me during the transition are:

7. What I anticipate happening during the transition is:

8. My family thinks my decision is:

9. My close friends think:

10. My Christian community thinks:

11. The person I plan to marry has the following qualities to share with my children:

12. I believe we can work together to meet the children's needs because:

Write out how you believe this family will have progressed when you have been remarried for five years. After completing that, add a page for ten years, then one for fifteen or until all the children are grown and on their own. Visualize where your hopes, dreams, prayers and goals are going to take you. Get in mind a clear picture of where your family is to go and how it is to get there. Let your faith carry you into the full realization of what God has for you.

Part II

CONVERSATIONS ON
SINGLE PARENTING

An in-depth look at the problems and potentials

11

TAKING YOUR SINGLE-PARENT INVENTORY

Let's begin with something so obvious you actually may have overlooked it. You had shared your parenting, but now you have entered new territory. Never having sailed this ocean before, you could easily assume that certain out-of-the-ordinary things happen because you are now a single parent. You may be saying, "If I were part of a parent team, these things would not be happening." This may or may not be true; however, how are you to know?

You need to keep the following questions in mind throughout all your assessing of what is happening. What part of it is common to all parenting? What is due to your being a single parent? This will lead you to discover five basic things about your situation:

1. Some things are normal to *all* parenting.
2. Some are normal to all *single* parenting.
3. Some are *exaggerated* because of the complications of single parenting.
4. Some are *lessened* because of single parenting.
5. Some will be *unique* to you because you are who you are. The parenting configuration has nothing to do with it.

Now all you have to do is assess correctly which is which and what to do about each.

Single parenting does differ at times from dual parenting; however, parenting is not easy for anyone, single or not. This is a major reason you need good, solid information to equip you for your task. That most people do not have this information is obvious by the scars they bear from their parenting attempts. Get with a roomful of parents, propose a problem for them to solve, and listen to how each would handle it. The solutions run from the extremes of *A* to *Z,* with lots of milder ideas in between.

Let me share with you two scenarios from real life. The first is a mother who tells her four-year-old she can ride her trike on the front sidewalk but not to go around the corner. Mother can watch from the window. The child goes outside to ride and the mother returns to the dishes at the kitchen window. The child rides back and forth. Mother gets engrossed in her thoughts.

A little later, Mother looks out the window and cannot see the child. Mother goes out front to check, but Daughter and trike are both missing. Now Mother is concerned and starts down the sidewalk in the direction the child was last seen headed. Unknown to Mother, not only has Daughter rounded the corner, which took her out of view, but she also has peddled on down the sidewalk to investigate the big, wide world of her neighborhood.

Not seeing her child in that direction, Mother quickly retreats and heads the opposite way. The child is still nowhere to be found. Mother is now frantic and heads back home with heart pounding and blood racing. Her fears are in full control. Then, just as she reaches the front yard, there, from the opposite direction, comes Daughter, peddling for all she is worth, heading home from her new adventure—discovering the wider world down the block.

Running over to her, Mother yanks her off the trike, spanks her bottom, and screams, "Don't you ever do that to me again!"

The mother hid her fear beneath her anger, which has exploded in a display that shatters the child's excitement of new discoveries. A much-needed lesson on obedience and safety has been replaced by fear for the child. On top of all this, a great opportunity for true communication between mother and child has been lost.

Scenario two: a large discount store where Mother and her three-year-old son are shopping. Mother stops to look at some fabric, and Son, told to wait nearby, gets bored standing among the bolts of cloth and wanders off to another, more interesting department. It isn't long before it dawns on Mother that they have become separated. Expecting him to be around the first corner, she walks over only to discover he is not in sight nor does he respond to her call. She begins to walk quickly, her eyes searching each aisle, her fears increasing with every step. Then she spots a familiar blonde head bobbing up and down in another aisle. They meet at the end. Sure enough, she had found her prodigal looking for the way back. She drops to one knee, gives him a big hug of reassurance, then pushes him back so their eyes can meet. Taking his face in her hands she gently tells him, "When Mommy couldn't find you I was afraid you were lost until I saw you and knew you were okay. Let's not get separated like this again because it makes me feel frightened, okay?" He nods a reassuring assent.

Think of the lessons that child learns: *My mother cares for me. She's frightened when I am missing and she can't find me. She hunts for me because she cares about my safety. I don't want her to have bad feelings, so I won't wander off and make her feel that way.*

At the same time he is now free to say, "But Mommy, I wanted to see the toys." This allows her to get in touch with his feelings. He is also free to tell her, "I couldn't find you, and I was afraid."

She can help him understand his feelings at being separated by saying, "If I were you, I would have been feeling afraid, too."

Both would be learning; both would be sharing. See the beautiful experience they are having together? Look at the lines of communication these two have begun to establish for the future as well as for the present.

GOOD PARENTING SKILLS

Parenting is an art to be developed, not scientific facts to be proven. To learn good parenting skills, you first must know what they are and why you need them. Your discoveries will help you to:

1. assess your present skills;
2. affirm your strengths;
3. identify your weaknesses;
4. sharpen your skills;
5. add new skills as you need them.

You want your children to have what they need from you, especially now because you fear what your single-parent situation may do to them. Thus, gleaning good information is an absolute must.

In the scenarios mentioned above, how easily can you identify with the mother who yanked her daughter off the bike and applied "the board of education to the seat of learning"? But what was the child learning? Discipline must not be for the parent's benefit, a vehicle for you to vent your negative emotions; it has to be helpful for the child. Good parenting requires lots of learning on your part, no matter how wonderful your own parents were or how skilled they may have become. Your children will have to do their share of learning if they are to parent your future grandchildren as well as you will be able to do by that time. Why do people become expert grandparents when they weren't expert parents? Two reasons: (1) By the time they become grandparents their self-esteem level has risen to where they are less intimidated by parenting; and (2) they have continued to acquire and develop new insights and skills.

What I want you to know now is this. Good parenting skills must always be in the process of being sharpened. Using them has a way of wearing the edge off them. A knife has to be resharpened now and then to be kept at its best. So will your parenting skills. The use of some skills will be common with each child, but some will need to be more specialized. One of your children may be more of a challenge than the others. As they each grow and enter new stages of their own development, your old skills may no longer serve effectively. You do not live in the child's world of school, peers, pressures, dreams or fears, and you may feel you have been left too far behind to understand him. Good parenting does not come naturally — it takes intentionality and commitment.

The two parts of this book sum up my concerns: (1) that you know who you are as a person so you may be free to become a good parent; and (2) that you know good parenting skills, know what your children need from you, and have the ability to meet those needs. Every significant change in you — your self-discovery and your parenting skills — will mean significant changes for them. You want your children to know themselves at a much younger age than you were when you made that discovery so they can mature more easily than you did. You want to acquire the best possible parenting skills, for their needs, and for the future parenting of their own children. All this can glorify God and be a joy to them and to you.

Throughout the remainder of this book I want to share with you some things I have discovered about parenting, especially single parenting. It is in no way all you need to know, though, so I will guide you to sources I have found helpful and have tested in groups and conferences, in one-to-one counseling situations, and in my own life and ministry. No single volume can tell it all — there are too many areas of specialization. You have to pick and choose once you get beyond the generalities. This allows you to assess your family needs, and then move in a specialized way toward meeting them. Please understand me when I say this: God has given you the natural instincts, intuition and inner guidance to be the parent your children need you to be. These will all come to the surface if you are open to doing your part, which is to deal with your own unfinished business from the past that gets in the way. Books on parenting skills will be of little help unless you get yourself under control. When you do, you will open the door of your own true potential for good parenting.

WHAT YOU NEED TO KNOW ABOUT PARENTING

What you have learned already about parenting can be great or it can be totally inadequate, even harmful. Before we can learn good parenting skills, sometimes much must be unlearned. We too often fail in this area. We accept the old data, act it out, then squirm because of the results. At least, the skills you may have learned from your past need to be updated and affirmed as valid before you use them. You need that confirmation to know you are on track.

The following questions will help you determine in which areas you need to improve your parenting skills or acquire some new ones. Study the list and react to it from your own perspective. I share it out of my concern for your parenting skills, and for the sake of those children you are parenting.

1. *How much do you know about how children develop at each stage of their journey through childhood?* How are you to know what a child needs at five years of age if you do not remember your own childhood at five? (And how many of us do?) How can you meet the real needs of that child if you are not aware of them? In all fairness to the child, you must know not only what he needs at five, but also how to go about meeting those needs. If parents knew this intuitively, we would not be reaping the results we see in our society, world and church. Approaching parenting on the basis of our own experience is how the sins of the parents get put on the children. Very few of us are adequately prepared for parenting and we all need lots of help. The book by Dorothy Briggs, *Your Child's Self-Esteem,*[1] is one of the most helpful. In fact, in her summary of its contents, she lists what a child needs in each stage of his development.

2. *What are the basic needs of children and at what stages*

in their development should these needs be met? Parenting is the most sensitive and important task we have, yet where is our Ph.D. for it? What is the extent of your training for such a task? In our culture so much of parenting is based on *our* needs, *our* convenience, *our* lifestyles. In our society today there is a sense in which children are not really wanted—they tend to cramp our styles. This all-too-popular attitude makes our understanding of our children's basic needs, and our task of effective parenting, all the more difficult.

3. *What problems should you watch for and how can you evaluate them when they are observed?* Parenting involves an awful lot of problem-solving, to say the least. What problem areas should you be watching for in children at ages two, three, four or five? Without this knowledge, something which arises at age five that should have been dealt with at age three can be damaging to the child. You need to know, not only so the situation can be anticipated, but also so you can act adequately and appropriately at the proper time. Problems are always worse when misunderstood or misinterpreted. Knowledge will give you the ability to spot them and diagnose them, and know-how will help you prescribe solutions for resolving them.

4. *What are the stages of spiritual development?* Biblical concepts need to be taught at various levels and in various ways depending on the child's stage of development. Abstract concepts which can be grasped at one stage may be totally meaningless at an earlier one. When you know the stages of faith development, you can assist your children more adequately and appropriately. You are concerned that they come to Christ at an age in their lives when they will understand the meaning of their decision and the decision will stick. When is that likely to be and why? Nothing is more important to you as a Christian parent than having your child grow spiritually as needed and be able to come to Christ at the appropriate moment.

5. *What are the stages of moral development?* It is important to you that your child learn right from wrong, of course, yet how much do you understand of this developmental process? What does your child grasp at three or five or seven? Many of us put on our children adult concepts of morality which they cannot even understand, much less identify with. Much of what they do learn is caught from observing us in action.

Peers also exert a great influence on them. How do you teach them ahead of time to handle the moral dilemmas they will encounter? How do they grow up with the ability to say no to a "joint" when they have not yet learned a good level of self-discipline? When will they be able not only to say no to things but also to understand *why?* You may be able to drum into them some responses identical to yours, but when can they learn the things that will uphold their own morals best when you are not around?

6. *What are the stages of emotional development?* One of your major tasks is to lead your children in their emotional development so they can be fully alive, fully six-year-old mature at six years of age. What does a mature six-year-old look and act like emotionally? Can you assess their progress? Are you aware enough of what it involves? Many people have been so stunted emotionally as children that their development has been delayed or frustrated. Jesus warns us about "offending" one of these little ones, and to stunt their emotional growth is to offend them greatly. It may even destroy them.

You need to know how children develop emotionally, also how to assist their progress. You can do this by knowing what to look for at each stage of their emotional development. Fads come and go, and as a result children often get pushed here and there too soon, too fast. By understanding good emotional development, you can free your child so he can express natural interests and abilities rather than having imposed ones due to a parental need.

7. *What are the stages of physical development?* In order to assist your child in every area, you must consider his physical development carefully. Take for example the most awkward age ever invented: junior high. These early teen years are fraught with spurts of growth in the midst of prolonged periods of puberty and adolescence. When teens' bodies are showing signs of maturing and their voices are changing, their emotions go crazy. So do their feelings of self-worth. Today it seems they might make it to adulthood; tomorrow they are only a few steps removed from infancy. What is happening? What is normal and what is not? If you don't know, how are you to assist your child through it all?

8. *What are the stages of intellectual development?* Remember the commercial that said, "A mind is a terrible thing to waste"? It is. Not many of us have ever been pushed

anywhere near our potential in intellectual development. But does this mean reading at three years of age? What are the stages involved and what constitutes good parenting skills at this level? You need to know.

My father was forced to leave home at twelve and work to help support his mother along with caring for himself. He learned a skill as a design machinist and finally put his tools aside at age ninety. However, I never saw him read a book other than his Bible and a daily devotional. Books were not a part of our home life when I was growing up. As a result I found learning difficult. It seemed foreign. I wasn't sure how it would fit in. Learning a trade seemed more like the way to go. In time this was updated and books became some of my best friends. As a result of this updating our children have had a different experience. Our oldest son is an independent trucker, hauling from coast to coast. Last time we visited I asked him what he was reading when he got off the road and during layovers. In addition to his Bible study and Christian reading he was going back and rekindling his love of Homer, whom he discovered while he was in high school. Right now he is reading *The Iliad.*

9. *What are the stages of social development?* You are a social being, having been made in God's image; however, how you socialize, and when, is a taught/learned concept. Much of it is caught as you observe your family and others in your ever-expanding social world. But how well you are able to develop socially depends a great deal on the help you get along the way. What stages of social development did you go through as you grew from childhood into adulthood and what social skills have you acquired? Parents need to be skilled in this if the child's development is to be mature and gregarious.

I grew up in a family where we children seldom brought friends home because our parents never had any. Their example made us unsure about how to have friends, and we questioned what to do with them when we did. School is a social time but many of your socializing patterns are set long before you get there. To become well-balanced, children need help and encouragement. It doesn't just happen. One reason peer pressure is so strong for many of them is that they have not learned good social skills and they fear rejection by their peers. Will your child be influenced or will he do the influencing?

10. *What are the stages of sexual development?* This may be the

hardest for you to feel comfortable with, but you need to face it. The sexual education of your children should not be left to school or church or peers or anyone other than yourself. The others can assist, but the main responsibility has to be yours. This is such a critical developmental area and they need to hear it first from you. No one in their lives is more important than you, their parent. No part of their lives will present a greater mystery or a greater potential for joy or problems.

One day, when our oldest daughter was around fourteen and we had just finished the evening meal, she turned to us and asked, "What do people do on their honeymoon?"

Mother started clearing the table and I started to answer with general comments like, "It's a time for getting adjusted to being together twenty-four hours a day," and, "It's learning the likes and dislikes of each other and of sharing affection in deep, meaningful ways."

When I paused after a few moments, she looked me in the eye and replied, "Okay, now that we've gotten that out of the way, tell me, what do they really do?"[2]

11. *What are the stages of personality development?* My mother was a very coercive parent in that she could reach a decibel in her commands that left no doubt in your mind as to what was expected. She started softly and built with each repetition, but when she reached that certain decibel you knew life and limb were now on the line. It was time to move. She could have saved a lot of time, energy and vocal strain by merely starting off at that crucial decibel. I had learned over the years it wasn't necessary to move until it was reached, so I waited and kept doing whatever I was doing.

She has been in Heaven for many years now but I still hear her. Only now I scream at myself, "Get that work out!" My adult tells me to do it *now* so I can feel relaxed and free of guilt, but the little child of the past has learned to procrastinate until he hears that decibel. It usually comes a couple of days before the work is due. This process always leaves behind a residue of guilt—what loving child puts his mother through such agony? See how it works? The inner child grew up in reaction to who his parents were and how they related. The child is reacting, not acting.

This is an excellent time to read Missildine's book, *Your Inner Child of the Past.* (See the resource list at the end of this book.) You can readily see what happens when you are a permissive parent, overcoercive, perfectionist, neglectful, rejecting, abusive, restrictive or hypochondriacal, versus fair and balanced? Your children grow up in reaction to you and your style of parenting.

You can serve your children best if you understand their skill development so you can challenge them in meaningful ways and not put too much on them too soon or not enough too late. Just because it seemed to work for you in growing up doesn't mean it is what your children need. Some good reading in this area will assist.

Along with this is the need for you to understand their attitudinal development as you help them react and act appropriately toward their Lord, themselves and the world around them. You pass your prejudices and delusions along to them without even realizing it. They pick up your values — or lack of them. In so many ways they are carbon copies of you because you are such a strong influence on them. One day you overhear your little girl "disciplining" her dolls who have been naughty, and all of a sudden it dawns on you, you are listening to you. She is mimicking you. You hear it first-hand.

PARENTING YOURSELF

As you develop good parenting skills, apply them first to parenting yourself. You will love your children as you love yourself. Maybe that's the problem! The "monkeys" you allow to remain on your back are the same ones you tend to put on theirs. Because my mother was overcoercive with me, if I do not do something about it, I will be overcoercive with my children. Her voice is in me and how easily I can mimic it to my children, making them hate it as I did. Or, I can get the help that was not available to my mother in that day, and I can change the pattern so my children will have what they truly need from me. I need to do this for my sake and theirs.

You help them learn good parenting by allowing them to bump up against you and your parenting of yourself as well as of them. Good parenting always involves give and take, the ability to change and adjust, the ability to say you are sorry when you are wrong, the ability to be human, and always the ability to ask for help when it is needed. It helps to know that in a child's perception you do not have to be perfect, only adequate; not always right, only honest.

YOUR INVENTORY OF PARENTING NEEDS

What has been listed above involves long-range planning, lots of reading, study, research, comparisons and diligence in seeking to be your best — in short, lots of hard work throughout the entire parenting process. For your immediate assessment, here are some things to think about. In fact, you can begin to act on them right now. Rate yourself on the following skills:

1. How well are you able to help your children with their feelings, especially their negative ones?

2. How good are you at listening to them and hearing them out before you jump in to correct, explain or cut them off?

3. How well are you doing at helping them assess any feelings of self-blame for the divorce or their parent's death?

4. In what ways are you able to help them enhance their self-esteem? Do they see you working on yours?

5. How much effort are you putting into enhancing your parenting skills, or are you content to go along with what you now have?

6. How well do you function under emergency conditions? Do you give the children the feeling you might cave in?

7. Can you trust them, even when they may have demonstrated a lack of trustworthiness?

8. Can you get and keep your stuff under control so you are not dumping on them?

9. Are you willing and able to call for help when you believe it's needed, no matter what others may think?

10. Are your expectations of the children realistic or are you expecting too much of them in order to lighten your load?

12. Are you aware of the present stage of each of your children's development so you can knowledgeably assist him through it toward full maturity?

13. Are you working together with intentionality on family unity?

14. Are you providing the spiritual leadership needed in your family at this time?

15. Are you alert to the problems typical to this time in the children's lives and journeys?

Nobody said parenting was easy. Maybe nobody told you it would be this hard, either. But the good news is: You only have to parent one day at a time, get though one experience at a time. And the best news is, He is in it with you, all the way!

Δ

TAKING ACTION:
YOUR PARENTING INVENTORY

1. On this scale of 0 to 10, circle the number that indicates where you see yourself in terms of your parenting skills:

   0   1   2   3   4   5   6   7   8   9   10

   Poor   Fair   Average   Good   Excellent

2. Within the next six months you anticipate increasing your skills so you will be at the following point on the scale:

   0   1   2   3   4   5   6   7   8   9   10

   Poor   Fair   Average   Good   Excellent

3. By one year from now you anticipate increasing your skills so you will be at the following on the scale:

   0   1   2   3   4   5   6   7   8   9   10

   Poor   Fair   Average   Good   Excellent

4. Write your plan of action to increase your parenting skills in the following areas:

   Spiritual

   Moral

   Emotional

   Physical

   Intellectual

   Social

   Sexual

   Personality

   Attitudinal

5. Write the name of each of your children at the top of a separate column on a sheet of paper. In the space below the name, list what you see as the major needs at this stage of the child's development. Examine the list and target those needs for which you want to improve your skill. Rearrange the list, making the top priority any areas you feel reflect emergencies within your family.

RESHAPING YOUR FAMILY

Think of the choices and options available to you as a single-parent family. Whatever you had before has been interrupted by the death of a mate or by divorce. This has altered the family in many ways so you must put it together on a different basis; you must reshape it.

How would you like it to be? How does it need to be to meet the needs of all? These are critical concerns as you reshape your family.

A FOUR-FOLD PURPOSE

As a family you each have a four-fold purpose toward every member—parent toward child, child toward parent, and child toward child. **First,** you are to assist each other to *know and love the Lord* with all your being. This is your primary responsibility. **Second,** you are to assist each other to *know and love others,* beginning with those relationships within the immediate family, then reaching out to the extended family, friends and strangers. **Third,** You are each to assist the other to *love, accept and respect himself* as a special creation of God. This self-love forms the basis for all other loves. **Fourth,** you are to assist each other to *respect, enjoy, care for, enhance and preserve the world* which surrounds you, God's creation. Each person is to live fully, freely, responsibly within that world. Genesis 1 and 2 set forth the four-fold purpose of life in our God-other-self-creation relationship. Jesus affirmed the first three aspects in John 15:11-17. Couple this with Matthew 22:34-40. Paul expresses the same thought in Galatians 5:14.

When you think of it, this is an overwhelming task. You are overseeing the development of a life in every aspect. You are preparing that person to move out from the family cluster into a world in which he will form another family cluster and begin the process all over again. On and on it goes, and where it stops you already know— in God's Forever Family, soon to be united in glory. Your purpose is to be a faithful part of that process and a creative contributor to its final result.

WHERE WERE YOU BEFORE?

The first phase of the assessment should be a comparison of where the family was (prior to the divorce or the death of your mate) with where it is now. I know there can be a lot of pain in making such an assessment; however, it also can be a healing time as you realize how stable things may be at present in spite of the changes. Look for strengths in it as you go.

Before		Now
_____	Residence	_____
_____	Style of living	_____
_____	Resources	_____
_____	Location	_____
_____	Schools	_____
_____	Bedroom	_____
_____	Plans	_____
_____	Major needs	_____
_____	Concerns	_____
_____	Sense of well-being	_____
_____	Happiness	_____

Figure E

Consider the impact on each of your children, and on yourself, of the areas listed above, and Ask yourself three questions. **First:** *What was good, right, meaningful and need-satisfying about it before?* Hold to these elements. They do not need changing. They are the pillars on which the new will be built. **Second:** *What needs to be changed?* **Third:** *What was never there before that needs to be added?* As you determine what needs to change and what needs to be added, you can begin to plan for these changes.

Even though I teach family life, I still read widely, attend lectures and workshops in search of what is new, better, wiser and more soundly Christian when it comes to understanding. Family life is a practice, not a science, and "practice makes perfect" — well, almost. You need to change as your knowledge of family life expands and deepens. You owe it to the Lord to discover the best practices and incorporate the best styles of relating in your family.

BUILDING A SOLID FOUNDATION

Resources are listed in the back of this book to assist you in areas where you may have a concern. By using what they offer, you can build the solid foundation your family needs no matter how many are in it or what your background experiences have been. For some situations, such as child abuse, incest, abandonment and neglect, you definitely will need professional help. But along with that help the child still will need all you can provide for his well-being. God wants you to be whole, and to enjoy a whole family. His powers to transform, heal, renew and change are limited only to your appropriating. Know also that His desire for you and your family is greater than any you could ever have. Why settle for a good family when you can have a great one?

A faulty foundation has been the ruin of many a tall building that looks great. In time a shift of the foundation rendered it useless, even dangerous. In our lives our faith in Christ is a firm foundation. He never shifts. He never fails. He is the only foundation on which we can build with absolute assurance.

You cannot make a decision for your child to put his faith in Christ, but you can see that he receives all the instruction and encouragement he needs, and you can provide the environment in which he can make the decision for himself.

The only way to come to God is through Christ, but there are many ways to come to Christ. What is important is to whom you come, not how you get there. For a guide to receiving Christ yourself, if you never have, or to introducing your child to Him, see "Would You Like to Know God Personally" in the back of this book.

The Holy Spirit's Role

Once you have received Christ, the Holy Spirit is forever within you, but He will not violate your will and force you to be the kind of parent you should be. You are co-creators, and you must accept His help. He does the working but you do the willing. Add your true potential released by the Spirit to your acquisition of new parenting skills through your study and the result can be a parent your child will bless Heaven for.

I remember hearing the story of a farmer who was complimented by a friend. "You and God have done a super job in creating an outstanding farm. Look at that acreage. Look at the quality of those crops."

The farmer reflected on what had been said, then added this observation. "You're right, it is a beautiful farm. And you are also right, God and I did it together. But you should have seen this place when God had it all to Himself!"

You and God are partners in raising the children He gave you. One day you will be able to look back and marvel at all they have become. But just think how they might have turned out if you had to do it all on your own without Him.

To many families in our culture, the pressures and temptations that come from without prove destructive. For the Christian family, though, direction and motivation come from within due to the presence and leading of the Holy Spirit. This means standing against the prevailing culture. It means setting your own standards and keeping them regardless of what others may be doing.

This is no easy task, especially when your children are a part of that other culture just as you are. For you to select a higher standard and to follow a higher calling does not mean they will share your motivation or intensity. But what you need to be following is nothing less than God's call to the higher.

What motivates you to obey this higher calling is your love for the Lord coupled with your love for the children and for yourself. When you share it with your children, they can sense that same calling. This is His calling you are obeying, and He alone knows best.

Fruit of the Spirit

The key to a solid family foundation is understanding and living out the fruit of the Spirit as described in Galatians 5:22,23. These are the qualities to strive for in family life as in all other relationships. The Spirit is the producer of this fruit, so the manifestation in your lives depends totally on His working within each of you. This is the source of the family's true joy and accomplishment.

1. *Love*. The quality of relating to one another, to God, and to others outside the family, also to yourself. It is relating in need-satisfying ways that are both dependable and accountable. You manifest to one another His love for every

one of you.

2. *Joy*. An inner state of being built on His forgiveness of all your sins and His transforming of your life through His grace. His presence within you gives you a fountain of inexhaustible grace, which allows you to know your eternal relationship with Him. With this comes an inner state of well-being that cannot be diminished by what lies outside. You are His and He is yours no matter what.

3. *Peace*. Your peace. You are now one with the Father, one with others, and one with yourself. Forgiven and free. Nothing can separate you from Him. You are secure in His love and grace, as Romans 8 points out so powerfully.

4. *Patience*. How the children relate does not prove your value or your parenting skills. How life goes does not tell your true worth as a person. Knowing you are lovable and you are loved allows you to relax, and you can be patient because you don't have to prove anything. You are free to zero in on what your children need from you.

5. *Kindness*. Your inner freedom provided by His grace allows you to be kind to each of the children, even to the one who reminds you most of yourself. It is okay for that child to be as he is. You are learning acceptance and this allows you to relate compassionately.

6. *Goodness*. In all of your relating there is a sense of the eternal values in mind. You are to relate as God relates to you and seeks to relate to others through you. God is at work, and goodness prevails. Thus the true purpose of the relationship will be fulfilled.

7. *Faithfulness*. Jesus is the same yesterday, today and forever, and your love can be just as faithful. Unlike His, your love will have ebb and flow, but it will always be there. This is demonstrated to each child by the faithfulness of your presence and your giving to him of yourself.

8. *Humility*. You do not have to be all things to all your children all the time. But you do need to know your utter dependence on God for all things at all times. When your children sense this in you, they can be secure. True humility is not to debase the self nor to exalt the self, but rather to be right on target.

9. *Self-control*. Nothing is scarier to a child than a parent out of control. Putting yourself in God's control allows you to be in control of yourself in the face of adversity or frustration. You are able to provide family controls. You

know that the one within is greater than anything without and you are controlled from the inside out.

Put yourself in your children's shoes and feel what family life is like when the fruit of the Spirit is present. The Christian family cannot be without it if there is to be a real sense of well-being.

SETTING LIMITS

Having laid your solid foundation, you are now ready to begin reshaping your family. This will necessarily involve some limits, and for the Christian family, that means Christian limits. There is a fence beyond which you will not go, and within that safe enclosure are limits as to how you relate to one another. One can be a Christian and not act Christian. Limits have to do with both.

As a single parent the only limits you are really in charge of are those you set in your own home while the children are with you. You can ask for cooperation from your Ex for the sake of the children. This may not be forthcoming, but ask anyway.

By limits I mean bed and wake-up times, mealtimes, rest times, getting-home times, rewards and discipline, and a general schedule for each child.

Once these limits are established and working within family life, there arises a sense of safety, dependability, accountability and routine. The children need to know what is expected of them, and when, and what they can expect. They need limits—and they want them, even when they are testing them, and you, all the way to the limit. Hang in there. Their well-being is at stake. Even those families your children claim have no limits ("they get to do whatever they want") have limits of some sort. The main purpose for limits is to assist your children in learning to put limits on themselves. To give in is to confuse them and leave them unable to accomplish that.

Dr. James Dobson, on his radio program, "Focus on the Family," told of an experiment with school children in which the fence surrounding the play yard was removed. Those in charge observed that the children clustered near the center of the yard, away from the edges. When the fence was replaced, the children returned to their normal routine and played freely, some at the fence, others on it, others pushing against it—but all safely within it.

As an adult you construct your own fences because you understand that you need limits, too. Your children are just learning what they need and they look to you to assist them. In time they will come to realize there is no such thing as absolute freedom for anyone. Each has limits imposed, whether by society or by self or both. What you are presenting to your children are meaningful limits that secure safety and enjoyment, and God's blessings for your family. By knowing what He wills, you can truly raise them in His way.

BUILDING A HEALTHY FAMILY

Healthy families, whether single- or dual-parented, do not just happen, they are made. Although there are myths to the opposite, some single-parent families are healthier than many of the dual-parent ones. In reality, many families will never become healthy, but the number of parents available is not the issue.

Some of the best work published on the family is by Dolores Curran.[1] Everything she has to say in *Traits of a Healthy Family* applies equally to single-parent families as to those with two parents. In fact, it applies to everything from a one-parent, one-child family to blended families with lots of parents running around among scads of children, and every family in our culture needs to hear it. Her research has drawn family practitioners from many fields into a synthesis we all can benefit from.

Some of her observations, gathered under the topic, "Fifteen Traits Commonly Found in Healthy Families by Those Who Work With Them," are:

they *teach respect* for one another;

they develop a sense of *trust;*

they have a sense of *play* and *humor;*

they exhibit a sense of *shared responsibility;*

they teach a sense of *right* and *wrong;*

they value *rituals* and *traditions;*

they have a *shared religious core;*

they respect the *privacy* of one another;

they value *service to others;* and

they admit to the need for and *seek help* with problems.[2]

A healthy single family is one in which each of the elements cited above is an established part of the relationship. Each family will differ in the degree to which these elements are present; however, every family must include all of them in good measure if needs are to be met. To slight any element is to weaken the fabric of the family. To overdo in any area is to strain the relationship.

What is a healthy family to you? Determine the degree to which each of these elements must be present to meet your needs. Assess the need of each individual and begin there. Just because the present style meets your need as the parent does not mean it will meet the needs of your children. Look at it in terms of their needs; then, through give and take, hammer out what would be best for all. This is how the family process works. All for one and one for all.

SETTING FAMILY GOALS

One of the joys of my life was building a new home from the ground up. This involved selecting a plan and starting at ground level, then making those plans become a reality. It was a lot of hard work, but we were all kept going by the need for its completion and by the satisfaction of knowing what it would mean when done.

Scripture says: "Except the LORD build the house, they labor in vain that build it" (Psalm 127:1, KJV). Dr. Curran outlines a structure for your family. Using her research, plan what your family needs to be. Guided by the Spirit, adapt these plans to your individual needs. Then you make them a reality.

Write out family goals and refer to them often. This allows you to measure progress. As soon as the children can comprehend, share these with them. You will be building a healthy family in which you can live out your commitment to one another and to Him.

If, during your building process, you discover that your family needs some changing, then let the changes begin with you. You can change. This is what grace is all about. If you had known how to change your children, they already would be perfect. But as you change it is marvelous what happens to them. **One,** they do change in response to your changes. **Two,** when you change you see them in a new light—and their need for change suddenly has lessened. Your perception of them and their need has changed.

Sometimes major results can come about through minor changes. A single father I once worked with had two small girls and a live-in housekeeper. His profession involved long hours, and the serving of the evening meal, which was held for his arrival, could range anywhere between 6 and 8:30 P.M. The housekeeper would plan for 6 and he got there "when he could." The children were kept waiting so "they could eat with Daddy." This was their special time together; however, it usually resulted in tears and disappointment for everyone concerned. He felt guilty for keeping everyone waiting; the girls felt guilty for being angry about so long a wait; the housekeeper felt guilty for feeling angry over having to put up with the whole mess. (Do you know what peas look like that have been kept warm for two and a half hours?)

Finally, an agreement was reached. The father would come home at 6 and have dinner with the girls each evening on schedule. They could count on it. They agreed that if he needed to go back to the office after dinner, they would understand and give him that freedom. The dinner hour was transformed by the change. Everyone was relaxed (and the peas looked like peas, not green raisins). The evenings were less tense and the children much happier. School work picked up, their rooms became neater, discipline problems lessened. The change he could and did make brought forth many other changes he had been unable to effect before, changes the girls now willingly made on their own. Incidentally, he was so encouraged by the changes in the girls, he made it possible to get his work done by the dinner hour and did not return to the office. You can change you; you need to begin there.

Without having definite goals to work toward, though, the family is left to drift or be driven by circumstances and situations. With goals you have targets to aim at and work for, increasing the possibility of your family becoming what you want it to be. There is real intentionality in this. Paul tells about "pressing toward the mark . . . " The mark is the goal and the pressing is the only way it can be achieved. Remember, healthy families are *made*.

REACHING FOR YOUR GOALS

First, name your goals and write them down. Make sure they are measurable.

Second, prioritize them. You need to do this for yourself since your family is different from every other one.

Third, assess available resources that can help you achieve your goals.

Fourth, determine what help you may need in additional resources or training.

Fifth, evaluate your progress; get feedback from all involved.

Sixth, celebrate your victories along the way so you can encourage one another to hang in there for the long haul.

Seventh, re-evaluate your goals regularly to make sure they are adequate; they may need revising. Be sure they are reachable.

Some goals are easily obtainable with little effort on your part. Others may be like pulling teeth. A few may require long-term investment before any real measurable results can be noted. Knowing all this tells you to keep the big picture in mind and to keep pressing on in the right direction.

WHAT YOUR FAMILY CAN BE LIKE

Shaping your family life is like going for the gold in an Olympic event—the end result is worth the investment. Your family is made up of the most precious people you know, loving, caring and committed to moving toward wholeness. You are concerned about the growth and well-being of every member, to the glory of God and the joy of each one. All the rest is behind you. Now you need to envision the family that can be, not the one that was. Rejoice in what it is and in the one who is transforming it and you.

When you arrive at all your family is going to become, what will it look like? Dream about it with me for a moment. You have all the gifts necessary to meet the needs of your children. You will goof sometimes, but not in any way that cannot be understood or forgiven. You will not always know the right thing to do or say, but most of the time you will. You will not always exercise the best judgment, but you will most of the time. Most of your concerns for the children will melt away into fulfillments that will gladden your heart and soul. You will rely on God's grace and it will never fail you no matter what. Being the parent of your children will be a great source of joy and personal pride for you. You will look back and see where you and God have done a great job in caring for them. It will have been worth it all.

Δ

TAKING ACTION: FAMILY NEEDS

1. Reflect on the research cited in Dr. Curran's book, *Traits of a Healthy Family*. On a scale of 0 (meaning the *worst*) to 10 (the *greatest*), how would you rate your family on the items cited?

   Write your evaluations below in these three steps (all three of these observations are important in the shaping of your family):

Before = What was your family like before the divorce or death?

Now = How are things in your family today?

Future = What is your goal in this area as you plan your family's future?

	Before	Now	Future
Shows mutual respect	_____	_____	_____
Has a sense of play and humor	_____	_____	_____
Shares responsibility	_____	_____	_____
Teaches right and wrong	_____	_____	_____
Observes rituals and traditions	_____	_____	_____
Shares religious core	_____	_____	_____
Respects privacy	_____	_____	_____
Is committed to service to others	_____	_____	_____
Seeks help when needed	_____	_____	_____

2. How would you rate your family in regard to fulfilling its 4-fold purpose?
3. How would you evaluate the spiritual foundation upon which your family is built?
4. Which fruit of the Spirit does your family need to concentrate more on expressing?
5. As you review your evaluations, what are your top five priorities for action?
6. You anticipate the most difficulty in which area?
7. Does anything seem to be missing in your family's foundation?
8. What limits seem to work best within your family?
9. In what ways might *you* change that would take pressure off the children and allow more changes for them?

13

GROWING YOUR FAMILY

Your family is God's gift to you; what you do with it is your gift to Him. A family needs to be fashioned to go in a given direction, and you are the co-creator with Him in its fashioning. With intentionality and commitment, you can form a profile that will be rewarding for each member of your family. So I want you to sit back, take a good hard look at each one, and do some serious thinking about all of them.

First, diagram your family constellation according to Figure C below. For example, if your family consisted of you and four children, your diagram would look something like this:

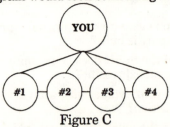

Figure C

Put in the name of each child in birth order, starting on the left with the oldest. Place the birth date under each name.

EVALUATIONS

The following list applies to each member of your family. Beginning with yourself and moving through the children, from the oldest to the youngest, give thought to each category as it applies to that person. See how much you know about each one, his position within the family and his needs. This can be a rich time of getting in touch with all you know and feel about each child. It also may be your first real, in-depth assessment. Enjoy the experience!

1. *Name.* Why was that name selected, and does it have any special meaning?

2. *Birth position* (of the child). What is the span between this child and others in the family?

3. *Strengths and weaknesses.* This is your perception as to how the child is doing. Note especially if there are more strengths than weaknesses.

4. *Personality style.* Even small infants display certain characteristics such as an ability to entertain themselves versus needing attention. How do you see this child's personality developing?

5. *Physical characteristics.* Noting features, body style, height, and so on, allows you to describe each child physically. Include a few thoughts on how his physical characteristics blend with the rest of the children in your family.

6. *Abilities/talents/gifts/interests.* What have you observed with this child? Each is unique, yet there is usually some blending because of family influence and environment. Look for the unique qualities in each.

7. *Behavioral traits/problems.* Each child tends to act and react in certain ways that may distinguish him from the rest of the family. Some areas will overlap. Note behavioral problems and how each child interacts with the whole.

8. *Close relationships.* How each child seems to relate with you and with other family members. Chart each child's safe orbit of relating. Note also those the child may not relate closely with and why.

9. *Your key concerns.* Each child gives you certain concerns due to his development, family position or style of relating. Note these concerns and why you feel you have them.

10. *Skills.* List both basic skills you observe in the child and any skills unique to the family constellation. Children are more than peas in a pod, and their uniqueness often exhibits itself through their skills.

11. *Support structure.* Each child develops a safety zone. He may go to a brother or sister for support when in need, rather than to you. One may cling to you and ignore the others. How does your Ex fit into this for each of them?

12. *Development rate.* Each will have a separate rate and may be at, ahead or behind level. Each will be all of these in dif-

ferent ways and times. Try to establish a norm and rate each on that basis rather than rating them against each other. Note any major differences.

13. *Communication style.* In large families younger children tend to have a more immature way of communicating while older children tend to be more verbal. See each one individually in terms of style and abilities.

14. *Affection style/level.* Is the child affectionate? How well and in what ways is this demonstrated? Is it expressed selectively or generally? Does the child have problems displaying it toward other siblings, adults, or anyone in particular?

15. *Limitations.* Each has limitations but may not have any of the same ones as the others. Note each child's limitations and how he interacts with the others in the family.

16. *Verbal skills.* What are the skills of each at his present age level? How do these add or detract from family communication levels? How does each fit into the family whole?

17. *Learning skills.* Rate of speed is a part of this but not the whole. How does each child stack up in terms of skills and learning abilities? "Slow" may not be as important as noting the end result. Some are slow but thorough, and have lasting powers of concentration.

18. *Athletic abilities.* This includes coordination, dexterity and skills. Interest may not be high in a given area but what about abilities?

19. *Friendships.* How well are friendships made, maintained and repaired? What type of friends does the child tend to select? How do his friends relate to the family constellation?

20. *Place in extended family.* This may depend more on the attitude of extended family members toward the child than on the child's part. How does each fit into this extended whole? Is it a comfortable fit or is it one-sided? Does the child seem content with the fit?

21. *Place in family mix.* Some children seem to get out of step and never really appear to fit in. With others the fit is natural. Does the child seem to fit in well, take a rightful place, find ways of expressing his individuality and appear to be a comfortable part of the whole?

22. *Sense of humor.* This does not mean being the family tease or agitator. Does the child have the ability to laugh at himself, to laugh freely with others rather than at, and to initiate laughter within the family?

23. *Spiritual interest.* Does the child ask questions and show general curiosity in spiritual matters? How well is he able to pray? How would you evaluate his personal relationship with the Lord and his concern for spiritual matters?

24. *Giving/caring/sharing level.* Is the child able to give of himself? How does he express his care when a sibling is in pain? How well does he share his things? How does he show his care and concern for you?

25. *Your intuition.* What do you sense about this child that isn't brought out by the other points? Is there some need that hasn't been included?

Write a paragraph in response to each item listed and keep it in a separate book of memories for each one. Let your child see at a later time how you saw him fitting into the family constellation.

YOUR EXTENDED FAMILY

On the basis of what you have written in response to the above questions, what do you see in ways that the children and you could benefit from an extended family? The primary source of the family's support is within itself—each other. But you need to add to this through your extended family.

Make another diagram, like this one, and include your and your Ex's parents and grandparents.

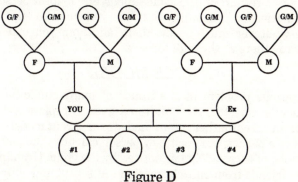

Figure D

Add to this significant aunts, uncles, cousins, adopted relatives and so forth to complete the extended family picture. In your assessment of each child, indicate those people in the extended family diagram with which the child has meaningful ties, is a favorite, or where there may be problems in relating. You may wish to use the following designations:

Meaningful ties: **+ + + + + +**   Problems between: **x x x x x**

Favorite: **o o o o o o o**   Distant: **. . . . . . .**

Some people grow up in an immediate family with little or no contact with other relatives. I shared with you earlier how I grew up in an extended family. Yong, a student from Shanghai who lived with us for two years, had more "Aunties" and "Uncles" than we could keep track of. Asian families do not have clearly defined boundaries as we may. And when the Bible speaks of the family, it means each and all such concepts. In a literal sense, the concept behind the word is more Oriental than Western.

If your family lives a thousand miles away, why not include some adopted grandparents as part of your extended family? You share with the children who these people are and who their own natural grandparents are, and then you allow the children the opportunity to have "grandparents" here and there both, as needed. You can do the same with "aunts" and "uncles." Each adds more richness to your life and to the lives of your children.

You can find resources also in church family and friends, other single-parent families, dual-parent families and individuals. Your resources for support and encouragement are as many and as varied as you make them. You can build a support structure that includes affirmers and encouragers, emergency sitters, professional resources, activities resources, spiritual supporters, helpful persons and just plain friends. You build whatever you need to support you through whatever must be faced. In addition, you can be this resource to others as they are for you.

A ROLE MODEL

A serious problem in the minds of many single parents is having a role model in the children's lives to replace a deceased parent or an absent father (or an inadequate parent model). No one can replace a parent, but each new person can offer the child a role model. None of these will go unnoticed by the child. Grandparents, relatives, friends from church, teachers at school and church, and others can all provide modeling for your children. Select the ones you believe will be best and cultivate them into lasting relationships.

Help the children see what you want them to emulate. They will make their own choices in time, but right now the need for exposure to good role models is a major reason to develop an extended family. This is all part of reshaping your family into one you are proud to call your own. Let it be an exciting time for all of you.

BROADENING EXPERIENCES

Families tend to build on things the parents experienced when they were growing up. If the parents grew up in a sedate family with very little outside activity, they tend to create a similar family structure. Yet, out there is a big, broad world filled with lots of things just waiting to be explored. As a Christian you do have to make meaningful choices for the influencing of your children, but there is still a breadth of experiences available.

As a single parent on a limited budget, you can divide these between those that are free, those that cost a little and those you may need to budget for, eliminating the ones that are out of the question. It is amazing how many activities are low cost or free. It may take a little transportation or a lunch out; however, the event will be well worth the effort.

List all the things you would like your children to experience between now and the time each is on his own. At what age would it be best to start with each? For example, you want to expose your child to different forms of music including classical, country, ethnic, and so on, in addition to what the child will select himself on radio, records and tapes. When and how do you start?

I enjoy opera. I discovered it in college through a Saturday radio program. Neither my wife nor my children will listen beyond three measures before threatening to leave the room or the car. Not all experiences will prove to be winners. But I tried! I still listen, but this is not a shared experience. What is important is knowing your children have been exposed to life and have been allowed the freedom to make their own choices based on a wide exposure.

RETURNING POINTS

Along with broadening experiences, you will be giving your children meaningful memories that will become "returning points" for them. These memories will draw them, and you, back to center in on what really counts most for each of you, the family. What does this best are the memories you share in common. Now, if you never plan a thing and just go about living together, some of these will happen naturally. There may be a few or a lot. But this is so important to their future, and yours, that it needs to be approached with intentionality and purposefulness. Don't allow it to just happen.

Make it happen. These returning points are so important that they become cherished possessions.

RITUALS AND TRADITIONS

As you plan, I want to give you some suggestions that will provide meaningful memories for your family.

Recall from your past what was meaningful to you, and in order to create similar rituals and traditions for your children, the first question you ask is, *What do I want my child to remember when this event is over?* The second is, *How can I make that memory a reality?* Then you plan.

One thing I remember from my own childhood was a Saturday night tradition. We gathered in the sitting room around the radio and listened to comedies while we ate ice cream. We all laughed at Jack Benny and Rochester, Fred Allen, and one of my favorites, "Can You Top This?" A listener would send in a joke which was read, then each panel member would tell one in the same category while the laugh meter determined a winner. As I write this I can still see each one in the room, feel the warmth, taste the ice cream, and, much to my children's dismay, remember some of the jokes. When my children came along the radio was replaced by the TV and with it, something was lost. Another approach has to be created for TV, such as watching and then discussing a special program or a carefully chosen video tape. Many Christian book stores rent Bible stories and other films for small children on up. Give your evening together lots of meaning.

Mealtimes are rituals. I mean more than the youngest spilling milk so you can get it over with and get on with the meal. They are comforting, stabilizing times for things like family dialoging, storytelling, praying and sharing concerns for members of the extended family, but they are not times for problem-solving, such as trying to determine why school is not going better. This can be taken care of privately with the child in question. Mealtimes are to be fun times, family times, celebration times, relaxed times.

Once in a while an evening meal can also involve the best china, cloth napkins and candlelight, as though you are entertaining, but it's just for you and the children. Why save the best for company when the best company is your family?

During my pastoring, there were few mealtimes when the phone did not ring. But I was also a father, so I made sure the phone conversations were short unless it was an emergency. You can do the same; offer to call back. This may be the only time in the day when all of your family can be together. Do not allow the telephone to control it. Treat all those calls as interruptions. Your family time is important — guard it jealously.

Traditions are ways you celebrate birthdays, anniversaries, holidays like Thanksgiving, Christmas, New Year's Day, Easter and July 4th. They are the big important annual observances. Other times of remembrance can be Memorial Day and family reunions.

Along with these come Hallmark days such as Mother's Day and Father's Day. Children's Day tends to be minimized because most parents see every day as theirs. My suggestion is you make them all equally important. Mom gets breakfast in bed on Mother's Day, Dad on Father's Day, and the children on Children's Day.

Since you are a single parent no one will be around to remind your children that this Sunday is Mother's Day. If grandparents are not available to put in a word for you, do it yourself. Children need reminding and they would feel bad if they forgot and then found out from others what day they had missed. This is a family day, not just your day.

They may need reminding about your birthday, too. Help them do something for you, short of telling them what and how.

On a child's birthday he should be honored, and we do it up with style. Banners, balloons, cake and ice cream, games, gifts and all the attention he deserves. We start days ahead and let it lap over, depending on how long we can all be together. At my age I would rather not have the number of years plastered all over the house, but they won't let me off the hook. Signs appear in the refrigerator, in the shower, on each mirror, under my pillow and on the back of my jacket. I have to check carefully before I leave the house!

HOLIDAYS AND HOLY DAYS

A natural for the Christian family is celebrating the special days on the church calendar. These holidays are truly holy days, and should include a time to worship as a family. Prepare the children for what is planned so they can enter into it freely and as fully as their ages will allow. Christmas is more than gifts; Easter is more than colored eggs; Thanksgiving is more than a meal. Share the meanings as well as the other elements.

For example, many Protestants do not emphasize Lent and

that is our loss. It is a marvelous teaching time, and can be a special personal or family devotional time leading up to Jesus' suffering and death, culminating in a glorious Easter celebration. What a great time for family dialoging on the meaning of your faith. David and Karen Mains have sought to help us with materials the family can use. Other sources are available as well. Make up your own if nothing else seems to fit.

In time each of the children will create his own traditions as he leaves home and marries, but you will have taught him their value. In our family we have changed the way we celebrate Christmas because it is Jesus' birthday, not ours. The children give gifts to mission projects in our name and we do the same for them but no other gifts are exchanged. It is the Lord's birthday, so we all give to the Lord's work as our special gift to Him on His day.

Last Christmas our youngest son was in Southern California and unable to get home for the holiday. Since he would not be sharing with us as in the past, he wanted to do something meaningful nonetheless. So he went through all his clothing and possessions, found extra blankets, clothes and towels, and other things he wanted to share. He put all those goodies in a large garbage bag, borrowed his roommate's motorscooter, and rode downtown to where the Street People congregate. He distributed all he had to those he could find. Later he told us, "It was my best Christmas." We know he gave away more than just "extras" for that is the way he is. One day he will share the same values with his children.

FAMILY ACTIVITIES

As children grow older and elect their own activities, the family has a real struggle in maintaining theirs. The result is each person in his own orbit with an occasional event bringing you together. This is hard on family life. Good patterns need to be cultivated early so they can be maintained as long as possible. Teen years can be stressful enough. That is no time to start building family activities.

Family fun has to involve the youngest through the oldest at a level meaningful to all. For example, a family frisbee game can do all that is necessary if it is sometimes slowed to the level of the younger children. At the same time some tosses can be over the heads of the littler ones and involve the older ones. As it shifts back and forth between these levels, the whole family has a sense of united involvement in the game. Once when our family did this, our oldest son and I collided and I broke two toes. I should have played at the younger children's level!

Design your own activities, those which you believe will work best. Here are some suggestions:

1. Crafts Night

Small children can enjoy a crafts night. Get out the paper, scissors, paste, crayons, stick-on eyes, driftwood, rocks and whatever, and go to it. It can be a time of making things for someone else, the grandparents for example. All the family can play together. Assist each of the children to develop hobbies as soon as he is old enough. Many adults still enjoy hobbies they started very young in life. These can be a source of delight for the child and a great learning experience as he gains expertise in a given area, and it will give him a distinct sense of accomplishment. Craft night can center around hobbies or it can be a time of total family involvement. We still have rocks painted with messages like, "Smile — God loves you," products of craft nights.

2. Game Night

Another might be a game night. Most every parent has endured certain children's games over and over again. The needs of the children have to be considered so hang in there, the games will mature as they do.

Learning how to be a gracious winner and a cheerful loser does not come easily to any of us, especially children. Family solidarity gets reinforced while these valuable lessons are learned.

3. Music Night

On music night everyone in the family helps, each person playing something and making his share of noise. If no instruments are available, make some. Sing, dance and play together. Don't allow recorded music to be all you have. Make your own. Tape it and play it back for all to hear. Hopefully, as all mature, so will the quality!

4. Story-telling Night

A story-telling night can be fun. Tell the stories or read them. At other times let the children do it. A story can begin with one person telling it for a few minutes, then it can be passed on to the next for him to add his part, and around the room it goes. No one knows how it will end. Let your imagination take over. Try this sitting around a bowl of popcorn on the floor in the middle of the room.

5. Entertainment Night

Your children are born entertainers if allowed to express themselves. Encouraged make believe—being able to share it with the family—is an important part of childhood. Set the stage and introduce the family players—a great time to applaud one another.

Entertainment around our house included charades, puppet shows with makeshift staging, and dress-up times. In dressing up, the children did the entertaining. Today we add games like Pictionary, where each person gets to draw and participate.

6. Family Mystery Adventure

Plan a day or a trip in which no one but you knows ahead of time where the family is going and what will be experienced. Build it up appropriately, then let it be a total surprise. The boys will tell you they knew ahead of time what it would be, but that's a way of protecting a fragile ego that thinks it has to know everything. They actually will be surprised, but you may not hear that from them.

If you feel brave enough, let the children plan a surprise day for you. You can be pretty sure it will involve something they like to do or someplace they like to go. Go, and enjoy it. They may want you out of the kitchen so they can create a surprise meal for you. There may be an awful mess to clean up after and the meal might not be "gourmet." But the point is they are doing something special for you within the limits of their capabilities. That is a special gift from them to you. Applaud it; enjoy it! A meatball and peanut butter sandwich isn't really fatal, especially when it's eaten with love.

7. Devotional Times

It is important that the devotional times you plan with the children are enjoyable. Sermons are for Sunday at church. Remember the attention span of those involved. With smaller children, prayer times need to be brief. Take the biblical injunction "Watch and pray" very literally. You can plan short prayer times to follow listening times in which each is allowed to share feelings and personal concerns. This gives each child a feeling of being heard and supported. What seems small to you may be life-threatening to them. Do not minimize their feelings or concerns but pray with them for the guidance and help they sense they need.

8. Reading/Sharing Times

An evening of reading together followed by sharing what has been read can be of enormous value. This is a great time for a Bible story with a discussion on how it applies to your lives. Spending an evening together like this seems to be a lost art in our busy lives, but I'll bet you'll find it if you turn off the TV!

Some years ago during a severe storm we lost power for three days—no lights, no heat, no TV. It was cold but glorious. We spent our evenings reading, sharing with one another and playing games by candlelight. We huddled together around the fireplace, watching the fire and talking. We treasure our memories of those few days.

9. Dinner Out

A dinner out usually means a trip to a fast-food place—the younger ones want hamburgers. Make an evening of it by going the long way around or including a trip to the park. As the children mature, the choice of eating places will change. Again the importance is the shared experience.

10. Day Trip

A Saturday trip to the beach, mountains or lake is always a great opportunity for family sharing. Let the children help with the chores in the early morning so you can relax along with them. A trip like this can be inexpensive if you pack your lunch and take along most of what you will need.

A day at a museum, park, zoo, garden, aquarium, or the like, can also be a memorable time. Most of these are inexpensive, and they have the added benefit of being educational.

11. Campout

You can camp out in the back yard with whatever equipment is available. Cook the meal over a camp stove with beans and franks as the basic menu, and make a tent or a lean-to of old blankets and rope—nothing fancy. Everyone pitches in for this family time.

12. Family Camp

Family camp should be on your list. I know most of those who attend will be from dual-parent families but don't let that keep you away. You can accomplish more with your children in a week of family camp than in months of relating at home. Last summer I spoke at a family camp in which about half of the participants were single-parent families. It was a very special time.

It takes advance planning and a lot of saving, but it can do wonders. Many of these camps make scholarships available, especially for single-parent families. Write ahead and inquire.

13. Service

A trip to a nursing home can bring new life to a shut-in, and to the family. If you don't know of someone, ask your pastor for a name. Clue the smaller children in on what to expect and what they might find. Watch the one visited come to life when he sees small children or has one crawl up into his lap. Share your feelings about it on the way home. It gives each one a sense of ministry, a sense of being needed in the life of another.

14. At the Church

Activities at the church include picnics, ice cream socials, pot-luck dinners and family nights. Encourage your church to have a lot of family gatherings. Don't stay away even if your family is the only single-parent family in the whole church. You are a family, too. Encourage any singles group to have single-parent family times.

15. School Activities

Activities your children participate in with their peers will mean a great deal to them. For this reason school activities need to be high on your list of shared times. Whenever you, as a parent, are invited, make a special effort to be there. Attend all the activities you can in support of the children. They may act embarrassed at times, but how would they feel if you showed no interest at all? Learn enough about their sports to tell the difference in scoring methods. Your expertise will increase as you observe. If you holler too loud at the umpire, the children may act as if they never knew you. That's okay. You are there and that is what counts.

One caution: It's important to allow these to be the children's activities, not your reliving some unfulfilled dream through them. Nor do they need to excel to make you look good.

Schools tend to overprogram, and choices have to be made. Discuss these with the children and make the choices together so they understand your absences. They also will know it is not due to a lack of interest. The extra-curricular activities could keep you going all day if you have two or more children. You cannot attend them all but you can talk about them and be keenly interested. The children will sense and appreciate your genuineness.

16. Vacation Times

The ages of the children often dictate what can be done and enjoyed by the whole family. A vacation can be split into a series of day trips if the family cannot afford to get away for more than that.

Some families develop a routine of returning to the same place each year. What a wonderful tradition if this is what the family wants. Others like variety. What matters most is doing something the family plans for, saves for, and enjoys together. Vacations are for a change of scenery, a change of pace, not necessarily for a rest. If some rest can be added, all the better.

When on vacation, visit a church with a style of worship different from yours. You can discuss with the children why you attend where you do, why you enjoy worshipping as you do. The Body of Christ is broad and varied. Let your children see this and learn the differences. God's people come in all sizes, shapes, colors and backgrounds. They worship Him in diverse ways and with various symbols. Let your children discover His bigness.

As you enjoy family activities, you can expose your children to a variety of music, art, literature, sports events and other experiences. Not all of these will become a part of their life patterns but some will. They will bless you later for the exposure. Why should your children grow up without ever having been to a band concert or a symphony or an art museum or on a train ride? Life is full of opportunities to discover new things and take part in new experiences.

Δ

TAKING ACTION: FAMILY GROWTH

1. Are you satisfied with how your family is growing? What encourages you most?

2. In reviewing each child's place in the extended family, did you find negative relationships needing attention?

3. What memories do you cherish most from your childhood and teen years? Why are they important to you now?

4. Dream of what memories and returning points you would like your children to have in the following areas:

   Public confession of faith

   Being baptized

   First day of school

   Becoming a teen

Joining the church
Entering junior high
Entering high school
First date
Becoming sixteen
Getting a driver's license
First job
Graduation

14

EXPERIENCING YOUR VALUES

When our oldest son was about twelve and our youngest daughter five, the following encounter took place. John was cutting a piece of cake to share with his sister as he had been told to do. As he cut, obviously not into two equal parts, he commented to his sister, "Now, Karen, the Christian thing for me to do is cut this piece of cake and share it with you. Since I'm a Christian I'm cutting it into one large piece and one small one. Since I'm a Christian and you're smaller than me, I'm going to give you first choice. This is what Jesus would do. Now, if you really want to do the Christian thing, too, you'll take the smaller piece."

Karen scooped up the larger piece and began stuffing it into her mouth before brother could grab it away.

He protested, "You didn't do the Christian thing!"

Her reply: "I'm not old enough to be a Christian yet!"

You have a value system which determines how you live your life. Part of it was derived from your background, part of it from later training and conditioning, and it may or may not be truly Christian. John's value system let him "con" his sister into giving him the bigger of the two pieces of cake. Karen's, as a five-year-old, was to grab and run, stuffing it down before it could be lost.

HOW VALUES ENTER IN

Your values are seen, not in your pronouncements, but rather in your lifestyle and ways of relating (Matthew 15:10-20). They expose what is most important to you; they show the intent of your heart and your purpose in living.

Values mold lives, establish directions, and assure destinies. They are the power building blocks out of which you fashion your life and family. They form the backbone of your very existence.

How do you use money? How do you view possessions? How do you prize relationships? How do you fashion a lifestyle for yourself? How do you give and why? How do you relate to others and allow them to relate to you? What is truth to you? How honest and dependable are you? How do you use your time and energy? How do you spend your leisure time? What sense of mission and purpose is there to your life? How do you view the worth of others? How important are peace and justice?

These questions ask: "What are your values?"

SOME AREAS TO CHALLENGE AND UP-DATE

Some of your values may prove not to be scriptural or valid and worthwhile. These you must go to work on at once. They will be "caught" by your children and will be the basis of their actions and lifestyles. Like so many other things, values are caught more than taught.

For example, I grew up in a home where "children should be seen and not heard." As a result most of my memories of the dinner table were those of me eating in silence, listening to adults talk. That became a part of my early value structure. When I examine it today, I find it drastically needs updating. Children should be seen *and* heard; they should be listened to. Jesus saw them this way and this is how He valued them. Now my value of their worth is more in keeping with His (Matthew 19:13-15).

YOUR VALUES AS A SINGLE PARENT

If you are a typical single parent, resources are scarce and you have more wants than haves. Your income may be so limited you have very little for extras, much less for splurging. This brings you face to face with what is most important to you and what you believe you cannot do without. You have lots of choices to make, maybe even some sacrifices, but what emerges clearest for you is what your values are.

All of us differ when it comes to what we may have or want. A few single parents are well off, but not many. More of them live near, at or under the recognized poverty level in our country. A few see themselves near it when they may only be crying "wolf" while others are at or below it but haven't discovered that yet. Your state of mind has a lot to do with how you perceive your situation. Our values govern and motivate us, and they tie us all together, but they need to include far more than just possessions or wishes.

I have worked with single parents from several ethnic backgrounds and with varying size families, and they all have one thing in common. They find their true values when they are faced with hardships, losses and inadequate resources. When things are going well, some values tend to be put on the back burner.

One single parent took his relationship with his two children pretty much for granted until after the divorce when he could see them only every other weekend. Suddenly the children took on new meaning in his life and in the allotment of his time. Another single parent, used to an affluent lifestyle, now found herself on a very limited income and had to spend carefully. She discovered there were lots of things she could do without and still be happy. Another man sold his sports car to buy one with more room for the kids. Before the divorce he thought it okay to cram them in just to be able to have a show car to run around in.

WHAT WE CAN DO WITHOUT

It is so easy to get lured into consumerism and get caught up in a plastic world of materialism. The airlines say, "Go now and pay later." (The local mortuary says, "Pay now, go later.") Out there are plenty of companies willing to extend you credit so you can mortgage your soul. Television will help your children want one of everything. If that doesn't do it, their peers will provide adequate pressure: "You'll be the only one in our class without one." Consumerism is making cowards of us all when it comes to saying no. We are raising a generation who have everything but meaning. "Too much good is no good," the saying goes. There's lots of truth in that.

Sometimes you must say no because you cannot afford it. Other times it is because you don't need it. You need not apologize for either. You are teaching a valuable lesson. Life is more than things, and things do not necessarily bring meaning. In fact, they often are used to provide a kind of meaning in our lives. The truth is we find meaning only in and through relationships, not things.

NEEDS VERSUS WANTS

If you want to get down to the bottom line, what you need are the basics for physical survival. All else are wants and are a result of desire, wish, demand, compensation and/or just plain selfishness. Your needs are far less than your wants—they may even be far less than you can imagine.

Circumstances may force you to cut back and to renew the meaning of your true values. Count it all joy! You are blessed in having the opportunity to re-evaluate. Take full advantage of this situation and share with your children values that really count.

When I was a small boy growing up in New England, our summer place on Cape Cod, where we spent our vacation, was the victim of a giant tidal wave. The man across the street didn't leave his home, and when the waters began to rise he pushed his wife and children up into a giant elm tree in the front yard to wait out the storm. It was a scary time for them. As they watched, their home disintegrated and was swept out to sea. All they possessed went with it. When they were finally rescued all they had left were the clothes on their backs. The man's response was he had lost only that which he couldn't keep, anyway. He had his faith, his wife and children, and the strength to begin over again. What more did he need? It may not have been all he wanted but it was all he really needed.

MAKING DO IN MEANINGFUL WAYS

Feeling bad about their children losing a parent or having to go through a divorce, many single parents are tempted to overindulge the children. This is seen as a way of compensating for the pain of their loss. First, no amount of things can ever compensate for a lost relationship. Second, adding overindulgence will only add to the total pain of the child in the long run. The pain needs to be faced and worked through, not compensated for. Using things this way is like offering them a tranquilizer they will eventually get hooked on—and then what?

You have limited resources, and that can pose a problem; however, you can learn to use those limited resources in meaningful ways that meet real needs and teach valuable lessons. A family evening does not have to involve steak and lobster to be meaningful. The most important thing is being together. A stay-at-home vacation can be meaningful if it is centered around relationships.

As a parent you do not have to provide the best of everything, nor do you have to outdo the neighbors. When you allow yourself to get caught in this trap, face it, you will always feel you come up empty. How can you compete as a single parent on your income and resources? Get out of the rut of comparisons. It can be a killer to family life and sanity. Avoid the game of "Where did you go on vacation and what did you do?" Most children will have a good time doing whatever you do if they sense you are enjoying it, too.

BUDGETING FOR SUCCESS

On a very practical level, most single parents I know need to live on a budget in order to make ends meet. A budget can be a helpful tool to assist you in achieving your goals and maintaining what is most important to you. If it is viewed as drudgery or as constraint, you will have a fight on your hands. See it as a tool and make it work for you, not against you. When the children are old enough to grasp the concept, let them in on how it works and how it helps in planning for emergencies as well as in keeping the family afloat.

This is also a great time to teach Christian stewardship, not just in giving to the Lord, but in the total use of resources. Be cautious of what attitude comes through in dealing with limited income and resources. Being surrounded by an affluent culture makes it easy to become bitter and resentful of what you do not have.

Make sure there's ample fun provided for in the budget, even though many fun times can be free. Don't construct an insane budget and allow it to rule your every move. Rather, budget for success as well as sanity. Many single parents are "too poor to borrow and too rich to beg." To borrow you almost have to prove you don't need it in the first place. Keep your credit rating as high as possible in case of an emergency. Watch the plastic. It can be too convenient. Before you know it, outgo exceeds income. Your family finances can be a major source of headaches and heartaches. Keep yourself from being trapped into guilt buying.

LIVING OUT YOUR VALUES DAY BY DAY

Christian values are for day-to-day living as well as for crisis times. The Spirit wants you to experience them on a day-by-day basis. Learning to trust Him includes when there is plenty as well as when there is little. This is what Paul is speaking about in Philippians 4:10-13. Being content is an inner state of being that is based on one's values, not on one's possessions or status. Children can come to realize a sense of contentment even though they will still want "one of everything." You help them achieve this best when you yourself are not intimidated by what you do not have.

You may have had grandparents who told you about living through "The Great Depression" and how little they had to exist on. You may have resented hearing the stories over and over again, but there is a message in them. God does provide. He always has; He always will. Your needs will be met (Philippians 3:12-21).

PRACTICING WHAT JESUS PREACHED

Stewardship for Jesus is a lifelong process of returning to the Lord what is rightfully His in ways that glorify Him. In fulfilling this concept, what you do with all you have is as important as anything you may give directly to His work. You are teaching your children a way of life, not just how to give the Lord a portion of your income and goods. God's call is for total stewardship in a total life process. All you have can be used to glorify Him. This is what stewardship is all about. It involves your use of time, energy, spiritual gifts, talents, income, possessions and your heart attitudes. You are His totally. This is what His Lordship means.

His concern is not just what you budget for the church but what you budget for rent, food, insurance, child care, clothes, fun, gifts and so on. It is a concern for the totality of life being lived "as unto Him." Your children need to see how all life fits together in Him and giving to the church and to others is only a small part of the whole. Teach the whole.

DISCOVERING WHAT MONEY CANNOT BUY

Poverty-stricken lives demand gigantic resources to compensate for their emptiness. In a poverty-stricken life, "enough" is always just a little more than you have. The need is insatiable. But in a life that has Christian values at the center, relationships and the gifts of love that come in and through these relationships are valued most. To lose sight of this is to be poverty stricken, indeed, no matter how much you have to live on. The richness of life is not in what you have to live on but rather what you have to live for. Your children need relationships, loving, caring, sharing relationships. Their true riches are to be found in those things money cannot buy. To cheat them on this truth is to point them in the wrong direction. If God enables you to move beyond your present financial status, think twice about any changes you make. What you lose in the process may be far more than you will ever gain. Invest rather in the things you need most, and none of those are material.

REJOICE IN ALL YOU HAVE

Living in a culture that has available more than you could ever consume, you are faced with tremendous temptations. It is so easy to get swept up into what is going on all around you. What makes the difference is what is going on within. If you sense a lack as a parent or are still struggling with a sense of guilt, you have little to rejoice in. You are tormented by self-doubts that knock you off balance. One way some people seek to re-establish a sense of balance is to buy things for their children and keep them so amused they never notice the imbalance. This is part of your self-deception, and it betrays your children's real needs as well.

Rejoicing in all you have does not mean you do not work to change your status or to enhance it. It means you are able to be content where you are at a given moment instead of thinking, *I will be able to be happy when I have* . . . It means being able to see God's hand in your life right now and rejoice in that relationship.

It isn't a matter of comparing yourself to the have-nots or the haves. It is a matter of seeing where you are at this moment, rejoicing in His faithfulness to you, and thanking Him for all He is and all He has done. It is to see this moment as worth living. "This is the day the Lord has made" and you are rejoicing and glad about it. Tomorrow is in His hands (Psalm 118:24; Matthew 6:25-34).

Your spiritual core tells you how to value God, others, yourself and creation, how to relate to each, and the importance of enhancing the relationship of each to the other. A faith that fails to touch you at all these levels is a faulty faith. What affects you at one level is to affect you at all. As you teach your children responsibility toward life, property and the rights of others, you enhance their abilities to relate adequately with the Lord. And as you teach them to love the Lord, you also teach them to love all those He has created and the world in which He has placed them. By looking at the big picture you discover they are all interrelated, interconnected and interdependent. Everything is synthesized into a meaningful whole because of your values as a family.

The Christian values you want to share with your children must be experienced if they are to be real. Telling them they need to be loving is not like experiencing love and loving. What is real to them is what they are able to experience personally. They bake a batch of cookies and take them to a sick neighbor, and they learn what caring is all about. It feels so good they want to do it again. It becomes a way of life.

Respect is experienced by helping them relate to different ethnic persons and groups. Tolerance can be experienced when you help them work through a bad relationship into a new friendship. Understanding can come by sitting down with another person and learning to listen to feelings. Acceptance can come through learning why some people act as they do. Sacrifice can be meaningful as they see a child without any toys enjoy one shared by them. Helping your children experience values gives them a solid basis for life.

KINGDOM VALUES

Think of all the time Jesus spent teaching values. When He said to put the Kingdom first and to allow all other things to fit into place behind that, He was giving you a value structure He wanted you to have. This, then, is what you need to pass along to your children, and through them to theirs some day. Kingdom values are eternal values for persons living in a temporary world. They are ways of saving His children from the bankruptcy of their day. They are ways of guaranteeing they will live fully and not die empty. They are ways of assuring the continuance of the Kingdom (Matthew 6:31-34).

Kingdom values involve loving Him first and foremost, then learning to love others and yourself. They teach the importance of persons and relationships, a Christian lifestyle, and how to relate to the material world so as not to destroy or devalue yourself or others. They help you understand what lasts and what doesn't. They are life savers as well as soul savers. The Sermon on the Mount in Matthew 5 through 7 is a good place to begin. It speaks to our values and happiness.

Kingdom values are not easy to live by. They are unnatural; they are supernatural. Who "turns the other cheek" in a "dog-eat-dog" culture? Who goes "the second mile" in a "me, myself and mine" culture? Who forgives "70 times 7" in a world of "rugged individualism"? Who bothers to be honest in a "finders keepers" society? Who bothers about feelings in a world of "corporate ladders" to climb? Jesus stands in stark opposition to most all that surrounds you, yet He invites you to stand with Him (Matthew 12:30; Luke 11:23). That is no simple call. In His grace He stands with you (Matthew 28:20).

Your children are living in a competitive world, in school and on the playground, that pressures them to be anything but Christian. What Jesus is calling you to live out before them is a lifestyle that is neither competitive nor self-oriented but supportive and self-less. Can you imagine their confusion? What they need from you is what Jesus gave His disciples: "You have heard it said . . . but I say to you . . ." You give them the whole story so in time they may make the right choices.

TEACHING THINGS THAT REALLY COUNT

Here are some questions that will help you think through Kingdom values, and some Scripture references that will show you the mind of God in these areas.

1. Why is it important to put the Kingdom of God and His righteousness first, and what does this mean for your life here and now? (Living out the values of a human culture, even the best, tends in the end to be destructive to the true self.)

2. What things will be added to you if you obey Him and put the things of His Kingdom first? (Matthew 6:33, all you really need!)

3. What does it mean to live a Kingdom lifestyle, and how will you know when you are doing it? (Matthew 7:24-27)

4. How is a Christian to value money, and how is it to be used? What is to be your purpose? (Matthew 6:24-34)

5. How are you to view things, and what should be their meaning in your life? (Matthew 6:19-21)

6. What values do your children need to learn, and at what ages is it best? How will you know when those values are being "caught"? One evidence will be in the children's abilities to share, be considerate of others and begin living for others. (John 15:13)

7. How can you help them experience the values you want them to learn? (Create opportunities in which they can experience their values by living them out.)

8. What is the best way to reinforce these values when your children are being taught differently in the secular world? (Study the contrasts together and discuss them.)

9. How would Jesus have you live and teach your children to live their lives? (By following His example as He lived in relationship with others.)

10. How will living your values affect your family and personal

life? (John 14:15,21; 15:1-17; 13:34,35.)

MAKING WINNING FAMILY PLANS

As a Christian, you need to think through your values and see if they really stand the test of Scripture. Values you hold that are good, scriptural and life-sustaining need to be affirmed and taught to your children. Christian values are redemptive and loving, not alienating or selfish. They work toward the common good and are not self-destructive.

List the values that are important to you and that you want to see amplified in your family life. You may want to include the following:

1. *Trust.* It is important that you have a high level of trust between you and the children, as well as helping them develop it among themselves. Much is based on this trust level. You will need to teach them what trust is, what it means to a family, the security it affords, the good feelings it engenders, and the safety it assures in interpersonal relationships. It involves giving and keeping one's word and being trustworthy. You will also need to point out what happens when it is violated and how disruptive this can be. In your family, trust is valued.

2. *Respect.* Each person knows and respects the needs of the others, especially the younger ones who are more vulnerable to manipulation. In any family children learn how to push one another's buttons, but with respect these areas remain inviolate. You protect the one under pressure. This reminds me of the day I overheard an older brother say to his sister, "I'll trade you my nickel for your dime. See? The nickel is bigger!" In your family, respect is valued.

3. *Privacy.* The children learn this as you model it for them. Many a mother has justified snooping in a daughter's diary because of what she found. "She left it out, knowing I would find it." This form of rationalizing is really destructive to a relationship. Establishing privacy—yours as well as theirs—in a family teaches every member his own worth. You are important; your feelings are important; your well-being is important. In your family, privacy is valued.

4. *Openness.* It is important for your children to know how you perceive them and what they mean to you. You are the mirror in which they catch their first glimpses of

themselves. If you are not open with them, their images will develop distortions, even without you realizing your part in it. Let them in on your feelings about them.

Also let them know when you are wrong and need to apologize. This elevates you in their eyes. They know when you're wrong, and now they know you are big enough to admit it. In your family, openness and honesty are valued.

5 *Sharing*. Including the children in the decision-making, planning processes elevates their feelings of self-worth. They do not need to know all the details, but they do need to feel included. Feeling important enough to be a part of your life will prompt them to make you a part of theirs. In your family, sharing is valued.

6. *Possessing/owning*. The children will learn to share in time; however, before they do they must learn the meaning of possessing/owning. A person cannot really share unless he first has a sense of ownership. This means one child's toy belongs to that child and permission to use it needs to come from its owner. You may have bought it for the child but when you gave it to him you relinquished all rights of ownership. You can decide how, when and why it is to be used and under what conditions, but the receiver of the gift now has ownership. It is not yours to give or lend to another. All negotiations must be made with the rightful owner. This is how life works and the lessons of ownership begin here. In your family, possession/ownership is valued.

7. *Rights*. Your child has a right to his feelings. He does not have to feel the same about things as you do. To tell him, "You shouldn't feel that way," is not uplifting. If you ask, "Why do you feel that way?" and then are able to see it through his eyes, you may feel the same as he does. He needs to know his feelings and thoughts are all right and he can own them. In your family, rights are valued.

8. *Caring*. Caring is love in action. It is God's love demonstrated. It is the most precious thing your child may ever experience—to be cared for because he is cared about. Many adults still stagger through life seeking this care because they never felt it as a child. To care for your child is to work for his total physical, spiritual, emotional, intellectual, social, sexual, nutritional and educational well-being. Here his self-worth gains a sure foundation. It also teaches him to care for you and for others, even the stranger in need. In your family, caring is valued.

9. *Forgiving.* The real lesson a child needs to learn is not that he is capable of making mistakes, sinning, or just plain goofing up — the real lesson is one of forgiveness. Of course he will fail at times and fall flat on his face, but that is not the end. He can get up and start over. He is still worthwhile, and he can be reconciled. He can be forgiven. Once forgiveness has been extended, he can go on renewed and restored. To know this at the human level makes the divine level so much more believable. The sweetest taste in all the world is forgiveness. In your family, forgiveness is valued.

10. *Approving/accepting.* How you value others determines how you relate to them. Persons you perceive as worthwhile receive your approval and acceptance. You relate to them in unconditional love. God knows their worth and you have discovered it, too. Your children need to know your approval and acceptance. They do not have to earn your love. They have it because they are worth loving just as they are. You are glad they are yours. Of all the children in the world, these are the ones you want to call your own. In your family, acceptance and approval are valued.

LOVE DOESN'T HAVE TO COME IN FANCY PACKAGES

Donna and I have a box of home-made cards, gifts, drawings, pictures and a few things hard to classify, that we have received over the years from our children. They were made with paper, paste, crayon, rocks, driftwood, odds and ends, water colors, and whatever. To us each of them is a prized possession. They are the things our children made for us at Christmas or birthday time or for Mother's Day/Father's Day, etc. Each one says, "I love you." Someday our children will have to throw them out in sorting through our stuff because we never will as long as we are alive.

Our children have notes from us and special things we made for them on special occasions in their lives. These are their treasures, our messages of love to them. All of us have special treasures we cherish. These gifts reflect our true values. Give your children the same things to cherish. These are the values that get you through a dark and lonely night, keep you zeroed in on reality when all else seems to be going insane, and keep the frail boat of your life pointed into the storm when all around you are foundering.

Some of the richest people I know are very poor in the goods of this world. The richest are those who have taken seriously what Jesus said about laying up for themselves "treasures in Heaven" and living out eternal values day by day. It is a matter of perspective, isn't it? Kingdom perspective, that is (Matthew 6:19-21).

Δ

TAKING ACTION: EXPERIENCING YOUR VALUES

1. Thinking through your values can help you clarify them and discover not only what they are but also why you have them. To help you put them in context as a Christian, respond to each of the following as it fits into your belief system. What does each of these mean to you?

1. Money	17. Worship	33. Feminity
2. Possessions	18. Friendship	34. Forgiveness
3. Acquiring things	19. Relationships	35. Love
4. Gifts/giving	20. Pleasure	36. Reward
5. Time	21. Responsibility	37. Sharing
6. Home	22. Commitment	38. Reconciliation
7. Car	23. Truthfulness	39. Apologizing
8. Clothing/fashion	24. Faithfulness	40. Accountability
9. Entertainment	25. Kindness	41. Openness
10. Food	26. Goodness	42. Secrets/Confidences
11. Recreation/hobbies	27. Tradition	43. Sharing feelings
12. Education	28. Family	44. Giving your word
13. Reading/study	29. Justice	45. Music
14. Leisure	30. Freedom	46. TV/radio
15. Service	31. Equality	47. Having fun
16. Vacation	32. Masculinity	

2. What do your values tell you about yourself and your family's life? What do they tell you about the vitality of your Christian life?

3. How do your values clash with the world around you?

4. Did you discover areas that concerned you? If so, which and why? Do any of these need to change?

5. What are you finding most difficult in terms of living out your values in the family?

15

HANDLING PROBLEMS FROM DIVORCE

Single-parent families have no priority on problems, but with either a single- or a dual-parent family, its perception of itself is crucial. If you are convinced you are a "broken" family and subject to a lot of problems because of this, that alone guarantees your seeing problems where things actually may be quite normal. You will tend to exaggerate them when otherwise you might take them in stride. How has becoming a single-parent family through a death or a divorce affected your perception? Close friends who know you and your family well can assist you with your perception check. Say to them, "This is how I think we are doing. Is this how you see us?"

HOW YOU SEE YOUR FAMILY

Years of pastoring and counseling have shown me it takes only a parent and a child to form a family, and this relationship can be whole and healthy. On the other hand, a family of ten children and two parents can be so fractured it is unable to meet the real needs of any. On Mother's Day we honor them for having the most children, but sometimes the single-parent family is much healthier.

True family is not determined by the constellation of those involved nor by blood ties. Family is a state of being in a loving, need-satisfying relationship with those bonded by marriage, birth and adoption, sharing a common essence of caring and mutual commitment. The relationship of these members depends on their perception of who they are as family, not on any external standard.

I know one healthy family in which the parent is actually the grandmother, but due to the death of her daughter and husband she is now "mother" to the three children. They are family in their perception—and that makes them family. When Jesus was told His mother and brothers were outside waiting for Him, He replied, "Who is my mother and who are my brothers but they who do the will of My Father?" Family for Him was: "Anyone who obeys the Father is mother, brother or sister to Me."

Creating a sense of family can be complicated for the single parent, especially when a divorce is involved. Little Karen lives with her mother. Every other weekend, and for a month during the summer, she lives with her father on the other side of town. This gives her two parents and two homes. When she lives with her mother she goes to bed at 8:30 sharp every evening but when with her father she is allowed to stay up until 9:30 or 10.

Her schoolteacher asked, "Karen, when do you go to bed?"

Karen's answer was complicated because of her situation. She perceives both of the above as her "family," not just the place where she spends most of her time, so she answered out of the whole.

The teacher responded, "What do you mean, you 'usually go to bed at 8:30'?"

"I do when I'm with my mother; I don't when I'm with my father."

One child can be part of a constellation that boggles the mind yet feel secure and whole. Another child can be in an obvious constellation of parents and siblings yet feel no real sense of belonging.

The most complex situation I have encountered is that of a couple who had children, divorced, each married new partners who had children, and then the new couples had children together. Later, each divorced a second time, married again, with both new mates having children by previous marriages. Family identity became a major problem for all of them.

Get in touch with your own perception as well as that of each of the children in your family. Brokenness or wholeness is determined there.

PROBLEMS YOU CAN SOLVE

In addition to your reading about normal family problems, you need to look at those common to single parenting as a result of divorce. Consider them opportunities for family growth, because they really are. The following list touches the major ones:

Visitation and/or Custody

Visitation can be worked out fairly when parents are working toward the well-being of the children. However, too often visitation becomes a tug of war, tearing the children apart. Each parent demands the letter of the law, or worse. Every exchange can end up in tears, anxiety and confusion.

Holidays and other celebrations are easier to arrange when all concerned live in the same proximity. When distance is involved, holidays may have to be alternated. This is difficult because holidays are special family times. It's no fun having to give up old traditions and rituals, especially on Christmas, Easter or birthdays.

A birthday can be celebrated a day before, a day after, or on a weekend around the time of the actual event. It can be worked out to the benefit of all, but you must put the child at the center of the consideration. He will survive the necessary adjustments as long as he can share with both parents and feel loved in the process.

How visitation is handled will set the tone for family life. It will be either an interruption and a constant source of irritation or a normal transition in which the children can shift with anticipation and spontaneity.

No visitation arrangement will be wholly acceptable to children. They want to be with both parents all the time. There is no plan that will leave them without hurts and disappointments. But parents, when you allow your stuff to get into the decision-making process, you complicate it. You can adjust a lot easier than the children can and the more adjustments you make, the fewer they will have to make. Help them by keeping things as normal and tension free as possible. They will adjust best if they feel loved and supported, and allowed to relate freely with each parent.

Know that things are not going to be as they were before, nor will you be able to achieve the ideal family arrangement, but you can still make things meaningful. This means dealing with the arrangements that have to be made and making them serve family needs. Don't just toss away your ideal; create a new, single-family ideal.

A word of caution: Don't allow yourself to get in competition with your Ex on vacations or special events. Your Ex is still part of your children's family, so be glad for every meaningful time for them whether you are a direct part of it or not.

Weekend Adjustments

It is time to spend the weekend with Father. What kind of experience is this for the child? How is it perceived by each parent? How is it handled? The children pick up on all the clues – and some that aren't even there – as they observe how parents relate to these times. *Is Mother glad to have us go? How will she get along without us being here? What does it mean to her that we are going and she is not? Will she miss us? When we return to Mother, how will this be for Father? What happens to him when we only get to see him every two weeks?*

Since these questions seldom get asked aloud, each child answers them for himself. Most of the answers will be wrong, but each will carry a bag of feelings along with it which the child will have to process.

Encourage the children to ask their questions: "When you're going to spend a weekend with your father you may have a lot of questions on how I feel about it. Let's talk about this together, okay?" Or, "I've noticed that when you come back you are very quiet and don't talk about what fun you had or what you did together. Are you afraid I don't want to hear it?"

You may be struggling with strong feelings about their visits to your Ex and what happens while they are there. There may even be justifiable concerns, but these need to be acted upon with your Ex and not with the children. They will not understand and will misinterpret at best. Help them understand what is happening so they can relate to each of you spontaneously with no need to keep a guard up.

Time With Each Parent

Children never feel they have enough time with a parent. Most parents are under some pretty difficult time constraints. You are working all day as well as keeping a home. You need time for you, time for them, and time, time, time. So, like any conscientious parent, you tell yourself, "I only have so much time I can actually spend with the children, but as long as it is quality time, all will be well." The problem with this is, children do not understand quality time. They only understand what time with a parent is.

By quality time I mean time to talk, to share, to listen, to really be present to one another. They need you when they need you, not just when you're available. You need to work at making all time together quality time. Some moments, if postponed, are lost. Quality encounters, the bedtime story and/or prayer time, the tucking in and the play time, need to take place every day.

Divided Loyalties

Your children will always love you. Never fear losing their love. But know they will always love their other parent, also. A divorce is not going to destroy their love. If one of you rejected, neglected or abused them, their love need would be a neurotic one—but it would still be there. But now that the two of you have gone separate ways, they feel split in half. When they are with you they feel loyalties first to you, then to him. When with him, they feel loyalties first to him, then to you. How are they to act now? Is it okay for them to talk of their love for their father when with you? Is it okay for them to talk of their love for you when with him?

The presence of a stepparent on the scene always complicates it even more. The child struggles with divided loyalties, and you must recognize this and assist him with them. The child may not be conscious of these, but you may be sure they are there.

"If I love Jim does that mean I'm being disloyal to Dad? Will it take away something that really belongs to Dad?"

How can children know you can give your whole heart to one person and still have a whole heart left to give another when some adults don't even know this?

The situation may also be complicated by Dad's jealousy of the child's relationship with Jim, and that could make the child feel it is not okay to love Jim, even a little. In that case the child has such a deep need to love Father and Mother that he may be afraid to allow any natural feelings for the stepparent.

You can help the child through this if you will talk about the relationships, and explore the feelings involved. Don't assume all is well just because things aren't asked or said. Know that the confusion is there. Speak to it; ask questions about it. Share your own feelings. Help the child understand what is happening. Know also that the child is reluctant to speak of these things with you, especially if he does not know how you feel about them.

I remember a time in my youth when my parents were going through a very difficult time. My mother saw to it that I heard all about her feelings as well as the details of what she assumed was taking place with my father. I remember how deeply I resented her dumping on me. I didn't want to hear what my father was doing or why. I wanted his love. I needed him. I needed to love him. What she accomplished was a deepening of the alienation between herself and me, not me and my father.

Let the Lord guide you in what to do, providing the spirit in which to do it. Your children will appreciate it one day when they look back and see what you did for them.

Extra Brothers/Sisters

If your Ex has remarried, there may be children of this new relationship and/or children brought to this new relationship by the new mate's previous marriage. It poses problems for your children, and they will need your help. It is not easy for them to see their father living with a new wife and her children while they are "visitors" to the new home on visitation excursions. They may feel like intruders into the territory of the other children. Your children feel like guests in "their" home and in "their" rooms, and are told what to do by "their" mother while listening to stories of what they did with "our" father. Put yourself in their place and try it on for size. Ouch! It hurts.

You can prepare them for the feelings they will have along with doubts about where they stand with their father. You can help them through these times of building relationships with the new stepmother and her children. At best it is a difficult time. Their world is changing faster than they can cope with. Their circuits are getting overloaded.

Shattered Assumptions

When you married, your basic assumption was it would be forever. When the children were born they assumed certain things also. One was that their parents would always be together to provide a home, and would always be there for them. Now Mother and Father are divorced and living apart. Another assumption that may have arisen during the divorce is that in time they would get back together. Now Father has remarried.

To a child the divorce becomes a time of challenge to all the basic assumptions of life. I remember one little girl who wasn't ever going to pray again because she had prayed her father would come back but he didn't. That meant to her that prayer doesn't work.

When our assumptions are shattered, what takes their place? Frustration, disappointment, anger, negative behavior, poor school work, belligerence, bad dreams, aches and pains, depression, and many others as well. Children are unaware of their basic assumptions, yet these are the building blocks of their young lives. Help them replace them.

Vivid Imaginations

"If I act badly enough, Dad's new wife will divorce him and then he'll come back to Mom." I heard that from an eight-year-old.

"If I had been better, my parents would not have divorced, so I'm going to be as good as I can so they will get back together again." That came from a six-year-old.

"In Heaven my parents will be together again and our family will be like it was." (Both had remarried.) That was shared by a twelve-year-old.

"I am scared to death my father is going to be killed because my mother told me he deserved to die for what he has done to us." This came from a nine-year-old who had been deserted by his father and was afraid he'd never see him again.

If we knew what goes on in the minds and imaginations of children, we would pause and re-examine what we are putting these children through.

Help them understand these thoughts and why they have them. They need to understand the reality of their situation.

Adjustment Anxieties

Children do not understand divorce. *Father has left home because he and Mother no longer love each other. Does this mean in time he will no longer love me? Is there a chance Mother and I will no longer live together? How can we be a family anymore if Father is no longer here?*

What does it mean to a child to have divorced parents and two residences? What if they have to vacate the family home for an apartment, a new school, a new church, new friends and new teachers? Can you imagine the anxiety level of a four- or five-year-old? Though Mother is going through her own adjustment anxieties, she cannot allow them to obscure her view of those the children are experiencing. It is an extremely difficult time for the children, and they need help.

Angry Parents Using Children as Pawns

Nothing pushes the buttons of divorcing parents faster than

threats involving the children. This is their most vulnerable point.

"If you don't get that child support payment to me by 12:03 P.M., Eastern Standard Time, you will not see the children this weekend!"

"If you try to keep me from seeing the children, I'll leave the state and then you can have fun trying to collect!"

The inner child in each of these parents is in full control; things can go from bad to worse; and all of it can get dumped on the children.

"Do you know what that father of yours has done this time?"

"Do you know how unreasonable that mother of yours is?"

The children feel like they are the ball being batted back and forth in a ping-pong game.

Angry parents see only their own anger. They are unable to assess realistically how it spills over onto others, and they fail to see what it destroys in the children. Can you imagine what a child feels like when he is used by his mother, whom he loves, against his father, whom he also loves and wants to have love him?

These differences must be settled, but not at the expense of the children. Children who get used as pawns end up not loving themselves. They feel guilty and betrayed. They may comply because they are afraid not to, but they will hate it, and that will add to their level of self-hate.

There is a better way. It involves first getting in touch with your own level of anger, discerning why it is there, and then dealing with it. Ephesians 6:4 is addressed to all parents. What happens when a child is discouraged about life? The twig is bent in a negative direction for growth. What does this mean for the child?

The CIA Syndrome

Due to the divorce there is no longer any real contact between you and your Ex. One way to find out what is going on "over there" is to turn the children, knowingly or unknowingly, into little CIA agents. "Where did your father take you this weekend? What did you do? Did anyone else go along? Did he take you to that woman's place again? Did you get to see his parents? Did they say anything about me? Did they ask how I was doing?"

You need to ask yourself what is going on inside you that you have to plant spies. Have you dealt with your divorce or are you still "in" the relationship? Why do you need to know these things? More important, why are you involving the children in your hunt for information? If it is so important to you to know what's going on, there's the telephone. Ask for yourself. You can't do that, you say? Then don't do it through the children. The children are there to share with their father, not spy on him. Do you want them reporting to him as little CIA agents about you, answering questions like: "Is your mother seeing anyone? How is she spending the money I give her for you? How much time are you spending with her parents? Do they ever criticize me? Is she as angry as ever?"

There is nothing wrong with asking questions when you have a genuine concern, but there are proper ways to go about it. The children have just returned from a weekend with their father but they need time to process the weekend, to adjust to being back home, and to sift through what did happen.

Rather than launching into a question, an affirmation is more important. "I hope you had a good time with your father."

This allows the children to take a deep breath, feel assured it was okay to have had a good time, and be able to respond spontaneously with a "Yup!"

"Share with me what you did" is okay then if the children know you are not simply prying. Celebrate with them and be thankful they had a good time. Help them love him. They need this from you.

Tearing him down will lessen yourself in their eyes and it may well turn on you in time. If you tear your Ex down with them, they will feel that one day you will tear them down too. They learn from observing how you treat those you say you no longer love.

Self-blame Feelings

Because you hold your children totally innocent of what has happened to your marriage, their reaction of blaming themselves may escape you entirely. Allow me to stress this as strongly as possible:

**Self-blame is at the root
of almost all behavior problems.**

Children blame themselves for the divorce of their parents because of their intense love and need for them. It is easier to blame oneself than to deal with anger or confusion over a divorce. As children enter adolescence their self-blame may become more repressed — but it is still present.

Don't fault the children for not understanding. They don't yet know how life works. They have a way of reasoning which adults cannot understand, but Jesus said, if we would "[become] as a little child," certain truths would become real to us. Put yourself in your child's place and ask, "How do I perceive this trauma?" Help them understand their feelings and deal with them. Don't simply reply, "How silly of you to feel responsible for your dad's leaving." Help them every time the feelings surface.

Loss-of-Love Fears

In divorce a child may perceive what has happened as a loss of love. His parent is moving out. Visitation may be every two weeks—and for a child that's a long, long time. A new fear arises, that of losing love. This the child cannot tolerate.

The child is so dependent on those he loves that he cannot process adequately what is involved in the separation. He may begin to cling. If he has been overcome by despair, he may withdraw. Withdrawing and clinging are each ways of reacting to the fear.

In either case, the child will need help in understanding what is happening and why. Mother, who is going through her own trauma, may assume the child is missing the absent parent, as she is herself, without realizing the child clings to her out of fear of losing her, also. By understanding what is happening within the child she can stop her own need for further clinging and help the child to understand he will not be losing her.

Bad Dreams

After the trauma of a divorce between parents, most children will pass through a stage of bad dreams. In divorce, dreams usually take on the form of reconciliation, but these can be "bad" in that the child can build a lot out of them. False hope is still false.

Bad dreams are scary for any child and must be seen for what they are. They are real to the child and need to be handled as being real. To suppress them, ignore, or, worse yet, dismiss them as foolish, is to rob the child of much-needed support, encouragement and compassion. Help him understand those dreams. Bad dreams are only dreams to an adult, but they are much more to a child who is still having trouble sorting out reality.

Behavioral Regressions

In the trauma of divorce, adults tend to regress to an immature state, though temporarily, and it can throw a person off balance for a while. We all react in different degrees, and we cannot say how a person should react — we can only meet him where he is. Children have similar experiences but their regressions may be more pronounced. A nine-year-old who regresses to an infantile stage is obviously identifiable. So is a pre-teen who resumes bed-wetting after ten years of being dry. But an adult who appears to be just the same outwardly when has regressed inwardly may be labeled as pretty normal. In each case it is essential to assist the child (or adult) to work through the regression and return to the previously mature level of functioning.

Acting Out

You have gone through a divorce and you have noted some obvious changes in the children. The oldest child, a boy, starts acting as though he is now the head of the family. He begins to parent you and the other children. What are his actions telling you?

The youngest child had been doing very well in school but now she is bringing home notes from the teacher telling you of poor grades and poorer performance in class. What are her actions telling you?

The middle child suddenly appears more agitated, picks more fights with the other two, and even tries to bad-mouth you a time or two. What are this child's actions telling you?

The first child may be feeling, *Dad is gone now and I need to take over and hold this family together.*

The youngest one may be feeling a loss of love and a sense of self-blame and may be punishing herself for it. She may be feeling, *My daddy left because I am no good and I am proving he was right.*

For the middle child it may be a matter of anger, frustration and hurt. This child is thinking, *My life can never again be the same, and I am angry at the world for putting me in this position.*

Each child is acting out an inner feeling. The feeling may be based on delusion, but it is so real to the child that he accepts it as reality. So understand the feeling, and speak to it. To speak only to the action is to miss the whole point. The child knows how he is acting; he does not understand why. It is his way of calling for help. See it as a cry for love. Understanding the feeling will alter the acting out.

School Problems

Most of the children's problems will manifest themselves in school since the children spend the bulk of their time outside the home there. This may also be the safest environment in which they can express their feelings. The pressures of having to perform in school may provide the catalyst which brings these other pressures to the surface.

First, know problems will be there and anticipate them, not in a negative sense, but in a sense of being forewarned.

Second, ask appropriate questions from the start without waiting for the school to intervene.

Third, ask ahead of time for the teacher's cooperation in observing the child's problems and in dealing with them. "My husband and I are going through a divorce. I want you to know this in case you see Johnny slip in his work or manifest anti-social behavior."

Fourth, touch base with the teacher from time to time and share the progress you may be observing at home. Classmates can be so cruel during these times. Can you imagine what it does to a child when he hears, "Ha, ha! Your parents are getting a divorce"? But don't be too hard on the other children when this happens. How do you react to someone you have just discovered is different?

Fifth, explore feelings with your child so they can be talked out in the safety of your love and understanding. How should a child feel when his parents divorce? Most of them assume they should feel awful. Is it supposed to make a difference in how you see life? They assume it must since everything else seems to be changing. Help them understand.

Hidden Feelings

When I remarried, my son John was my best man. That was very special to me. He took his role seriously and did an excellent job. He was thirteen at the time, but years later he shared with me how hard that had been for him. He had not let me know it because he didn't want to disappoint me. I needed to hear those feelings. I also needed to ask myself, "Where was I at that time that I did not explore more with him how he felt about my remarriage?" I assumed his enthusiasm was what it seemed on the surface. I did not probe beneath to find out.

Children sometimes have hidden feelings they themselves do not understand. They may sense something is there but not be able to isolate it and thus identify it. As parents it is our task and responsibility to explore these feelings so we can assist the children in understanding and dealing with them.

For example, a single parent I was counseling shared with me her son's problem of failing grades in school though he had once been a good student. I met with the boy to explore his feelings. Something was happening that the mother had missed. She had been dating a man who had never been married before and who had little experience with children. He had taken the boy fishing several times and this delighted the mother as she saw a relationship budding. But she was not aware that the boyfriend had let it be known he was doing this to win her attention, not because he wanted to spend time with the boy. The boy, not wanting to upset his mother, kept all this to himself. His failing grades were a way of calling for help. Once out in the open, the situation could be dealt with, and in time the boy's grades climbed back up.

Make dialoguing a part of daily family routine. Communication is a much over-worked term, but not an over-worked reality. Most of our talking is to or at, not with. Listen to your child as he expresses his feelings. Allow him to communicate them to you for your understanding. When you can feed them back to him exactly as he shared them with you, then maybe you can say, "Now I understand."

Absent Parent

In a divorce where one parent has deserted or rejected the children, they will be left with a terrible burden to bear. They will not understand, but their need for the absent parent is still there. Help them come to grips with the rejection by stressing they are not at fault. Some people simply cannot accept the responsibilities of parenting, and in their fear they abandon the role altogether.

The absence of a parent is something that most children will accept in time, but the remaining parent may not understand fully how this has affected the child. In the child's mind that missing person becomes the main focus and he may need help in integrating the experience into his life.

Competitive Parenting

Messy divorces can include a lot of competitive parenting. Each tries to outdo the other and the results are often oversubmissiveness and overindulgence. The child says, "But Dad allows us to do this when we are with him," so Mother gives in because she doesn't want to be the heavy. Or, "But Mom is going to let us get such and such," so Father has to get something of more value to outdo her.

You now feel you have to compete for the child's love. You fear losing it. You think, *Maybe he will love his father more than me.* Or, *Maybe he will want to go live with his mother.* The trap has now been set and you are in the position of wondering, *How does the child see me? Is he losing his love for me?* This is self-torture.

The real question with children in any family situation is not: Will they love their parents? The question is always: Will they love themselves? Children who learn to love themselves will love their parents, also. You give love out of what is inside you, but without self-love there is little to give.

Parental Dumping

This remains a great temptation, especially when cases have been built against one another in the process of obtaining the divorce. Too often, negative feelings get dumped onto the children.

"I'm so angry at that father of yours!"

"I wish I could get my hands on that no-good mother of yours!"

These outbursts are difficult for the children to handle. The children have exaggerated perceptions of what is happening and it frightens them. You are speaking about their mother or father whom they love and need.

There's a true friend in our community whom I have never met but whom I surely have come to depend on. Every Wednesday morning he comes by the house faithfully and picks up the garbage, hauls it away, and I never have to deal with it again. What a favor he performs.

When parents haven't been able to dump the garbage of their negative emotions at the foot of the cross so the Lord can care for them and choose rather to dump it on their children, it never goes away. The children carry it around inside them, and when they get too much it affects their relationship with the one doing the dumping. In time they want to protect themselves, and they resent the one doing the dumping. They may want to say, "Why can't you grownups be grown up and get your act together?" The entire process is very painful for them.

"I Want to Go Live With . . ."

You probably have dreaded this one since the day of the divorce. Your hidden fears told you it would come. If the child says this to manipulate you, offer to help him pack. If he calls you on it and begins packing, let him know you are open to rational discussion but you will not allow yourself to be manipulated. Let him know how this makes you feel, especially if you believe he is doing it just to get what he wants. To you, it's "cruel and unusual punishment" you don't deserve or need.

On the other hand, if the child is struggling with a deep, unmet need centering in the other parent, it may mean he should go to live with him. He may have unfinished business with his father. It may be because of his struggle to love himself. Help him resolve these even if it means he makes the move.

Don't resort to emotional pressure to keep from looking bad to your Ex. This is the child's struggle. Keep yourself out of it. Hear where he is coming from, and don't force him to make the decision alone. Be a part of it. Make it mutual for the child's sake.

Whatever you do, never threaten, "If you go live with your father, you'll never be welcome in this house again." No matter how it may hurt deep down inside, leave the door open for him to return if things don't work out. You are his parent and he loves you. You can survive his going but he may not survive if he cannot attend to this unfinished business. Keep his need as your focal point.

There are times when permission may need to be denied. Seek professional help in determining this if the request is troubling you or if the Ex is not a suitable parent. You can't allow your child to move into an abusive situation, but he does need you to be honest and objective if this is the case.

Divorces are built on the reality that partners have not been able to relate satisfactorily and meaningfully. Sometimes this is relaxed a little when they no longer have to live together. At other times it gets worse. Now that they don't have to live together, there's no longer a need to try to hold things together. For still others it is the same old thing after the divorce as before. Like trying to prove one is always right and the other always wrong or that one is a better parent than the other. This confuses the children as to what life is all about and how it should be lived.

Divorce is so common in our culture that we tend to take it in stride, but we often fail to see how it affects those involved. Studies in this area have been slow, but the Christian community is becoming alarmed at what we are now learning. Our churches have not dealt with the situation adequately and many of them have compounded the problem. We have not given the children the support they need. One of my fears is that, because their problems often involve serious financial and emotional needs, we brush them aside, not wanting to get involved. Just when these children need us the most we push them away. After all, we are a "family church" and we aren't sure how to relate to those who do not fit the normal definition of dual-parent families. "If we were to concentrate on single-parent families, someone might get the idea we condone divorce, and we certainly don't want that, do we?" So it goes.

Δ

TAKING ACTION: FAMILY PROBLEMS

1. Use the following codes in rating each of the items in the categories that follow. A = Not a problem. B = Somewhat of a problem. C = A problem. D = A serious problem. E = A critical problem.

Problem Area	Rating
1. Visitation/custody	_____
2. Holidays/celebrations	_____
3. Weekend adjustment needs	_____
4. Time with each parent	_____
5. Divided loyalties	_____
6. Extra brothers/sisters	_____
7. Shattered assumptions	_____
8. Vivid imaginations	_____
9. Adjustment anxieties	_____
10. Angry parents using children as pawns	_____
11. CIA syndrome	_____
12. Self-blame feelings	_____
13. Loss of love fears	_____
14. Bad dreams	_____

15. Behavioral regressions   ____
16. Acting out   ____
17. School problems   ____
18. Hidden feelings   ____
19. Absent parent   ____
20. Competitive parenting   ____
21. Parental dumping   ____

2. Now that you have completed the list from your perspective, go back over it and rate each item from what you believe is the perception of your Ex. Then do the same for each child. What do the results tell you about problem areas to target? Which should be first?

3. How would you feel if your child wanted to go and live with your Ex? What would you do?

16

HANDLING PROBLEMS FROM LOSS BY DEATH

If you have lost your partner in death, some of the points of the previous chapter will relate to your situation as well. However, the following are additional concerns for you and your children.

The Big Question: WHY?

The biggest question the child has to deal with is: Why? The surviving parent has the same question but the difference is, being an adult you have learned various levels of coping whereas the child has not. Both need help, to be sure, but the child needs the help that a surviving parent is not always ready or able to give.

In your grief it is easier to be in touch with your own needs than with those of your child. This increases the child's problems and questions. You may be asking yourself, "Why did this have to happen to me?" You mean it in terms of why now, why in this way, I don't need this, and what will all this mean for me?

The child may be asking it in the sense of, "Why me? What is wrong with me that this happened? Why did my father leave me?"

Asking why is natural, and can be good for both you and the child — a part of the healing — if you come to the right answers. If the child is not helped to do this, it will deepen into self-blame.

Mary Jo was thirteen when her father died of acute alcoholism. She was very close to her father, and during the last two years of his illness she did a lot to care for him. When he came home drunk in the middle of the night she would get up and make sure he got to bed. If he was covered in vomit, she would clean him up. She took the responsibility for him. She also believed with all her heart that she could *love him out of his drinking*. But his body could not take it. He was hospitalized just prior to her thirteenth birthday, and so, missed her party. He died soon afterward. She remembers very clearly standing at his casket, unable to cry, for she blamed herself for his death. "If I had loved him better I could have kept him alive."

Some twenty-seven years later as she stood at the grave of her stepfather, Mary Jo suddenly started shedding the tears she had bottled up all those years due to her self-blame. She began to realize how angry she had been at her father for drinking himself to death. Now it was coming into focus for the first time. She had blamed herself and that had resulted in her years of self-punishment. Today her life is changed totally by the truth that sets one free. But for some thirty years she lived in the pit of personal despair and depression because no one helped her understand it was *not her fault* her father died as he did.

Idealization of the Deceased Parent

One sign of self-blame is the idealization of the one who died, especially if things were not going well between the child and that parent prior to the death. At times, the worse the relationship was, the more the idealization is. Self-blame does not allow the child to pass any blame along to the deceased parent. In a healthy relationship the child can "speak the truth in love." "Dad may have had his problems but, he was my Dad and I loved him." This is healthy. The negative is recognized but the positive is freely shared.

I was asked to do the funeral of a woman who had been murdered by her husband. There were several children in this family. At the funeral home after the service, all the children and I stood at the casket as they said their final goodbyes to Mom. She had been anything but an ideal mother—she had neglected the children through her drinking and numerous affairs. The father had had it with her, and in a rage he beat her, causing her death.

As each child shared their thoughts one of the older brothers chided the youngest for crying. "She was no good; we are better off without her; she never loved us—if she had, she would have taken care of us."

With this the younger one cried all the louder as if his heart were breaking. I tried to comfort him and he looked up at me and said through his tears, "Pastor, I don't care what she was, she was my mother. I love her and I miss her."

I put my arms around him and we cried together. I could feel his tiny body pulsate with waves of pain as he recognized his little world had crumbled.

The oldest child of that family was a girl who truly loved each of them and kept the family together. She was a mother to that little one. But as long as I live, I will never forget his look of pain, his plea for understanding, and the violent rhythm of his sobs as he clung to me that day, and I pray, "Dear Lord, help the children who are in such pain. Do not let them have to face it alone."

Repression of Feelings

Can you imagine a more emotionally wrought time in the life of a child or anything more devastating for him to have to face than the death of a parent? Yet some children cannot cry or show emotion at this time. It is so difficult for them to handle that it all gets repressed. They retreat into a fantasy world of denial, bury their normal emotions and do not cry, or they react hysterically and express their emotions by inappropriate, uncontrollable laughing. How are you supposed to act when your world is falling apart?

Crying is a God-given release valve that can keep you from exploding. Well, instead of exploding, some children implode. That is, instead of letting it out, they hold it all in. The energy which would have been expressed by exploding outwardly goes inward as though it were being pulled into a black hole in outer space. And, as with a black hole, it pulls the child in after it. Outwardly it is as if nothing has happened. This is the strongest cry for help you'll hear.

If a boy has been raised not to show emotions, he may need permission to cry. His perception may be, "I surely need to be a big boy now that Dad has been killed, and big boys don't cry." His body, mind and spirit are crying, but he won't let it be seen outwardly. This inner crying may last a lifetime, and since he cannot share his pain, he will not be able to share his pleasure, either. No one will know his true feelings. He has learned too well how to repress them. You know adults like this, especially men in our culture. They may make good drill sergeants and corporate leaders, but they can also make poor husbands and lousy fathers. We live in a feeling world, and a person who is not in touch with his full range of feelings is not in touch with the real world.

Help Is Needed

The safest rule of thumb to follow is this: Know that a child going through the death of a parent has feelings he cannot handle without help. You need to be the primary source of that help. I know you are going through your own pain and may need help yourself. But, as stated previously, you have many sources available; the child's main source is you. He may have only you. Do not let this fact panic you, but do let it alert you to his need. You can be what he needs you to be just by being yourself and sharing that self with him. It means more listening than anything else, and you can do that. The fact you are listening to him is important, but more important is the fact *you* are doing the listening.

Fear of Being Close, Then Losing Again

The experience of having lost a parent can cause a child to think like this: *It is too painful to be close and to lose someone you love; so I will not get close to anyone again. Then it won't hurt so much if I lose that person, too.* It is a way of protecting the self from having to go through such a painful trauma ever again. The child may pull back from the surviving parent for this reason; he also may not be willing to form any new intimate relationships. This is an unconscious reaction but nonetheless real. While most children tend to cling to the surviving parent, this child begins moving away.

Yet once he understands what is happening and why, he can begin to adjust. He needs to see that moving away does not work, and in fact works against him since closeness is what counts most in cherished relationships, even if it runs the risk of increasing pain.

Adults often react the same way. It is a perceived form of self-protection, but it really isolates rather than protects. There is always a risk in loving someone, but the relationship that results is worth the risk. Your real needs are met in close, intimate relationships, not in playing it safe.

The Meaning of Death

What is death, anyway? What has been the child's experience with death? Remember, he is seeing it from his own perspective. Try to get inside his understanding and thus help him with it. Just because you accidentally flushed his goldfish down the toilet bowl while changing the water doesn't mean the child has dealt with death. You may have talked about it when a great-grandparent died, but that does not necessarily make it real to him, either. There is no way for a child to comprehend death as an adult might, and adults themselves have enough trouble with it.

Because of your Christian faith you stress where the person is now, he is with the Lord. But what the child struggles with is, "Why isn't my daddy here with me when I love, want and need him?" It isn't the theology he struggles with. It is the reality of having been left.

The fact that one day there will be a reunion with Father in Heaven can be a tremendous comfort for the child—in time. But at this stage he needs lots of help in understanding what death means here and now. "He will not be here to take you to your soccer game, or watch you blow out the candles on your birthday cake, or listen to you play your first piano solo, or be sitting there when you are baptized." Death has an exact meaning to each of us and you need to explore with the child what that meaning may be.

Don't hide your reactions from them. They will know. Let them observe the stages you go through, and let them go through them with you as you explain what is happening and why.

Blaming God

You never expected death to come this soon, but here it is and you and your children are right in the middle of it.

I worked with one single parent who had given up on God because He had "allowed" her husband to die. It didn't matter that her husband was driving on a winding road at high speed in a car with bald tires. He lost control on a sharp curve and plunged down a steep four-hundred-foot embankment. He was found dead at the bottom in the crumpled car. "I had asked God to watch over him and keep him safe—and God let me down."

After some twenty-five years of pastoral ministry I have concluded there is probably not a single thing that happens but what God has been blamed for it at some time by someone. When it comes to death and dying, very few let Him off the hook. It is so easy to blame God—how else is it to be understood? After all, He is in control, isn't He? He either causes it or allows it, or steps in and prevents it, doesn't He? Oh, that life were so simple.

Some dear saint (small letter *s*) will come up to your children at the funeral and try to explain, "God needed your daddy more than you so He took him home." What child wouldn't blame God for that? Who needs him more than the child does in his perception?

Or, "It was God's will." How do they know? It is so easy to say something like this rather than deal with the pain and loss and adjustment involved. We give pat answers without realizing what they may mean to the other person, especially a child.

Who doesn't blame God in one way or another? We all need scapegoats when faced with such a crushing load. But we don't stay in that position. It is important for the children to see that we move through it to a better understanding.

Be open and honest in helping your child deal with death and with blaming God. Avoid pat answers. Be biblical and up front. Death is a difficult concept for a child to grasp. If he is angry with God, help him get it out and deal with it. Show him how God does fit in, how He claims us at death as His own, where we go at the time of death, and how He comes in a special way to each of His own and leads them through it. No one cares more about you who are left at this moment in your life. No one understands your pain as He does. You are not alone and you can depend on Him totally to get you through it. He did not cause it. He does not zap away your loved ones to teach you a lesson. He loves you and all He gives is out of His love for you. If you, being sinful, know how to treat your children at these crucial moments, then how much more does your Heavenly Father know how to treat you? When it comes to death and dying, He is the only one in whom you can place ultimate and absolute trust.

Feeling Abandoned

Part of a child's anger is from feeling abandoned by someone who was an object of the child's love and devotion. Of course the child has you and others, but right now he is feeling totally abandoned. Remember it is a feeling and must be handled as such. Please don't regard it as "only a feeling," as if that lessened the load. For a child a feeling is reality and feelings can be concretized if they are fed and kept alive long enough. If the child is feeling abandoned, he is absolutely convinced he has been abandoned. What you need to do is add another feeling by allowing the child to feel your presence, love, acceptance and understanding. In time the feeling of being abandoned will dissipate, but the child is not going to be talked out of it. He needs rather to be lovingly led through it.

The best way to deal with a negative feeling is to replace it with a positive one. Feeling abandoned is so powerful for a child it can seem all-consuming. Gradually work to help the child see what he still has with you, and allow him to cling. He will let you know what is happening inside by how he acts. Talk with him. Talk, and talk some more. Keep the lines of communication open. And above all else, listen.

When a Child Gets Stuck in a Grief Stage

The stages of grief you as an adult go through are much the same as what your children go through. Yet each goes through them in his own way. Each moves from denial through acceptance and adjustment. Each child has a pace with which it is accomplished. And each, including any adult, can get stuck in denial or anger, or any other stage in the process, short of where it needs to end. This is always a danger.

Children can easily get stuck when left on their own. They need help to see the process through. A stuck parent makes it easier for the child to get stuck, too. He will conclude that this is what he is supposed to do. A child being stuck usually indicates there has been a lack of adequate help. When this is the case, it can go unnoticed; it can be excused and/or discounted; but it does not go away. It may lie dormant for a long time only to surface during or after adolescence. What you need to know is that by dealing with the entire grief process as normal and natural, the child can make a way through it that is normal and natural. Help him grieve and understand the process, and then help him move on.

General Confusion

Whenever there is a death within the church family, many resources are available to meet the needs of the surviving adult and the family. But how much attention is paid to the children? It is assumed that healing takes place in one fashion or another and life seems to go on.

A man who loses his wife in death may spend six months living in a daze of numbness and denial, then awaken one morning and ask himself, "Where have I been?" But the confusion caused by a death in the life of a child must be more like that when the Titanic, the "unsinkable," was sinking. What should never be happening is, and the child is totally unprepared for it. If ever children do not need to be left on their own, this is the time. Get them all the help they need in working through their confusion. To help a child at this point can literally save a life.

A Checklist of Behavioral Problems to Look For

1. Acting out that indicates the child is having difficulty handling the trauma.
2. Behavioral change that makes him radically different from what he was before the loss.

3. Passive and withdrawn or aggressive and hostile attitude that causes problems among the other siblings.

4. Increased or pronounced sibling rivalry.

5. Anxiety reactions such as change in appetite, sleep habits or routine.

6. Withdrawal from friends or family members, and/or evidence of depression.

7. Greatly increased or newly acquired accident proneness.

8. Chronic, unexplained illnesses.

9. Strong-willedness, belligerence, defiance that was not evident before.

10. Manipulative behavior not present before.

11. Continual denial of negative feelings about the loss.

12. Regressive behavior.

13. Inability to adjust and return to normal routine.

14. Pronounced clinging to you that does not let up or diminish in time.

15. Inability to share feelings about the deceased parent.

16. Inability to express appropriate levels of sorrow.

17. Chronic need to blame others for the loss.

18. Inability to deal with anger toward the deceased parent for leaving.

When Outside Help Is Needed

As a concerned parent you may want to find someone to work with the children just to make sure things are going well.

If the children's problems linger too long, cannot be managed with your help, or prove unreasonably disruptive to family life, you will need outside help. Your pastor or pediatrician may be able to refer you to a competent child therapist. Pray diligently for guidance in this crucial area.

Many of us are not equipped to deal in depth with such losses for our children but God has provided helpers in many forms. Let Him guide you to them.

Δ

TAKING ACTION: FAMILY PROBLEMS

Use the following codes in rating each of the items in the categories that follow. *A* = Not a problem. *B* = Somewhat of a problem. *C* = A problem. *D* = A serious problem. *E* = A critical problem.

Problem Area	Rating
1. Idealization of deceased parent	____
2. Shattered assumptions	____
3. Adjustment anxieties	____
4. Fear of loss	____
5. Bad dreams	____
6. Behavioral regressions	____
7. Acting out	____
8. School problems	____
9. Repression of feelings	____
10. Fear of closeness	____
11. Needing to take over	____
12. Separation anxiety	____
13. Meaning of death	____
14. Blaming God for the loss	____
15. Feeling abandoned	____
16. Getting stuck in the grief process	____
17. General confusion	____

Now that you've completed the list from your perspective, go back over it and rate each item from what you believe is the perception of each child. What do the results tell you of problem areas to target? Which should be first? Which ones may require professional help?

Continue to rejoice in the strengths present in your family and build on these for everyone concerned. This gives added strength to tackle some of the other ones marked "serious" or "critical." You know the Lord to be your Great Problem Solver. Let Him prove His faithfulness to you as you include Him with intentionality in your problem-solving.

17

THE TRIPLE-A FAMILY

Each family has certain things going for it, certain strengths. So does each member of the family. By strengths I mean personalities and abilities to deal with change, stress, uncertainty and pressure. Other strengths are resilience, an ability to grasp what is happening and why, and an acceptance of reality that keeps one focused on what can be.

The greater the strengths, the more risks can be taken in moving into new areas. If each of the children has made a pretty solid adjustment to the loss of a parent or to the divorce, you know there is a good level of strength to build on. On the other hand, if things are still shaky, the fewer major changes you make now, the better.

Know each child and his present potential. See him in relation to the others and to yourself. List the strengths and weaknesses of each, and affirm his strengths to him. Also examine your part in the family's strengths. Listing all these will encourage you as you see what you do have going for you and as you reach toward the family you want yours to be. Keep in mind the Triple-A Family described below as you consider the topics we'll look at in this chapter.

One thing I must caution you about as you assess your family strengths. You must realize that the family function is not to meet the total needs of any one member. No family can be all that family needs. It needs relationships beyond itself. The wise family recognizes this, and encourages and fosters the creation of other relationships.

BECOMING A TRIPLE-A FAMILY

The first **A** is for *Acceptance.* All your child has to do to be loved by you is just be. You accept him as he is, where he is. I often wonder how it is for Cliff Barrows, song leader for Billy Graham, to lead a congregation every night in singing the same gospel song, "Just As I Am," but that's the one way we can come to God, and that's the one way your children can come to you.

The second **A** is for *Approval*. Approval moves beyond acceptance. It means approving of the person the child is and is becoming. For example, your male child is very artistic. He does not do well in sports nor does he have the inclination to learn. He is more interested in drawing, painting and reading. Yet you approve of who and what he is, and you allow him the freedom to develop as he chooses. It is okay with you.

The third **A** is for *Affirmation*. This comes whenever you say to your child, "I'm glad you are you. I'm glad God gave me you. I'm proud of you." It also means to affirm his accomplishments and efforts without any strings attached or any hidden messages.

Being a Triple-A Family means your children will know where they stand and how great it is to be there. The refrigerator may look like a bulletin board of hand-made creations and achievements. It is the family's art gallery, trophy case and "warm fuzzy" collection all rolled into one.[1]

APPRECIATION OF DIFFERENCES

Take a good look at the differences you find among your children. Celebrate the differences as you appreciate the individuality of each. This may mean lots of work for you in melding these differences into a common family, but each difference is a special gift to the whole.

It is important that you yourself have been able to accept these differences. They should not matter in your ability to accept and love each child. If the differences bother you, this will become apparent to the children. Differences are those things that make each of you unique even though you are all in the same family.

Help the children accept their own differences. By learning to accept their own they can then accept those of the other family members. Self-acceptance is the basis for acceptance of others. Help them to accept the differences in each other and to appreciate oneness within the family diversity. Children tend to develop along the lines of their differences as a way of gaining individuality, but if these differences are not accepted, the family is headed for troubled waters. Smooth sailing comes through acceptance and appreciation.

IMPORTANCE OF APPROVAL

Each child lives out of his approval reserve — or he lives out of its deficit. Everyone enjoys approval — it meets our inner need of being needed. We know we count. Approval gives a child a good reserve of self-worth to draw from. The reason you shy away from giving approval is not your fear of spoiling the child as much as it is a lack of your own self-approval. Not knowing how an ample amount would feel creates fears of what it might do. Some say this would damage a child, and others buy into this idea due to a lack of insight. This perpetuates the myth. In reality, one's approval reserve has a natural overflow valve. A child cannot get enough in the form of sincere approval without making major changes in his self-perception. It flows outward from the child in the form of his approval of others.

LETTING EACH KNOW HE IS LOVED

One of the most critical misunderstandings in parenting comes from the parent knowing they love the child but somehow not getting this message through to the child. Do your son and daughter feel that love? The young child understands only what he feels. In the Old Testament, to "know" something means you feel it; you experience it; you don't just grasp it mentally. The family is where love is to be felt in good measure for the child's understanding and where every member is allowed to feel it and to share those feelings. Telling your child you love him is not enough. He really needs you to help him feel he is loved and know that you see him as worth loving. Be sure to address the feeling level.

There are really only two kinds of feelings or strokes: positive and negative. Everyone lives according to feelings and spends time collecting them. If a child does not feel he is worth receiving good strokes, he will settle for the lousy ones, but he will get some somehow. He can get negative feelings by acting up and causing trouble. He knows this will get your attention. If he feels he is worth loving, he will seek good feelings. He has no need to collect negative ones. He seeks the kind of feelings that fit into his perception of himself. The feelings he accumulates in turn reinforce this self-perception. You can detect a person's self-perception by the feelings he insists on collecting.

The way to interrupt a cycle of negative-feeling collection is to address the self-perception. What inner need causes a child to collect only the negatives? They fit his self-perception, so changing the self-perception changes the need.

TRUE SELF-WORTH

Children are not to be built up at the expense of others, though. To tell them they are the greatest by comparing them to others and putting those others down does an injustice to all concerned. You affirm your children for who and what they are, not for how they compare to someone with less abilities. Creating little egotists is not the answer. Helping children discover their true worth is.

BUILDING A MUTUAL AFFIRMATION SOCIETY

The scene is an evening meal when everyone is together and relaxed. The conversation sounds like this. "Vicki, that was an excellent report you did for your anatomy class. You ought to feel good about the grade the teacher gave you. I'm proud of the job you did.

"John, I know you have been struggling over your relationship with Danny. I am very pleased with the way you have been handling it. It shows real maturity.

"Jeff, you were quite upset earlier today when you missed out on a field trip at school. I am proud of the way you handled it and were able to get on top of it so quickly. I'm not sure I would have done as well.

"Karen, I liked the way you cleaned your room after school — and without having to be asked, too. This gave me a good feeling. I hope it does you, too."

Each is an unqualified affirmation, not, "I like this about you, but . . ."; or, "I would like this about you a lot more if . . ." This is a time for affirmation with no strings attached. If there is a "but" to be shared, do it in private.

After you have completed the circle, encourage each child to do what you just did, affirming and sharing something positive about each. Help them to keep it positive. When a child has been affirmed you may want to ask, "How does that make you feel?"

Or, if they are quite small, "If I were you that would make me feel really good. Is that how you feel?"

You can also ask each how he felt in going around the circle and sharing something positive. The family is to be a mutual affirmation society. Affirm the worth of each and be affirmed. This is great. Some people would think this is "spoiling" children, but don't be concerned about that. You "spoil" a child by giving him too much or by allowing uncontrolled freedom or by being possessive, but never by giving your love and honest affirmation.

Many times during the day children are anything but affirming of one another. They don't get many good strokes from school or playground activities, either. Their main source is probably you and you have so little time together. This affirmation experience at the evening meal can set a tone that is very important. This can make your home the child's oasis in a world of indifference.

GOOD LEVELS OF SELF-ESTEEM

In a Triple-A Family, the parent works with the children all the way along on both their faith development and their self-esteem. These fit together like hand and glove. Any lack of self-esteem on your part will hinder your helping them with theirs. On the other hand the more yours grows, the easier you can assist them. As they develop you will find them opening themselves up to God, to you, to others and to themselves. There will be lots of evidence that they feel better about being themselves.

Don't worry about what will happen if they get too much self-esteem. Do concern yourself about there being too little. Too much does not occur, because, like approval, self-esteem has within it a natural instinct that turns the flow outward as soon as a healthy level is reached. You will know how they feel about themselves as you witness how they share themselves with others. The opposite of self-love is selfishness, a form of self-hate. It occurs when the self has been turned inward on itself, and it is one way of dealing with perceived rejection. True self-worth serves others, not self. Jesus is our best example of self-love in action. Who gave more of self than He did? (See Mark 10:45.)

There are some who will label all self-esteem as wrong, or at least for the Christian. Yet self-esteem is more for the Christian than anyone for each believer has within him the Spirit of truth. Who should be in touch with reality more than the Christian person? Low self-esteem may sound quite Christian until you actually think it through. Then it becomes obviously demonic and self-destructive. Jesus had a high level of self-esteem. He was in touch with reality when He said, "I am the Way, the Truth and the Life"; "I am the Good Shepherd"; "I am the Light of the World."

Help each of your children achieve the healthiest level of self-esteem possible. Let him assist you in achieving the same for yourself. Helping each other is how love works.

COMMUNICATION – SHARING OF FEELINGS

One of the most important characteristics you will see in a Triple-A Family is true communication. For communication to be adequate and genuine, it must involve sharing feelings. Many of us were not brought up to share feelings, nor were we in marriages where feelings were shared. To do so now is a difficult matter. But, if your family is to be what you want, and the needs of you and your children are to be met, you must learn to do just that.

It is not unusual for a half-dozen people to grow up in the same home, exist for years as a family, but never come to understand each other. They are virtually strangers to one another. They may have done a lot of talking but they were never able to communicate. My parents were married for sixty years and to this day I still do not know how they *felt* about one another. I never saw any display of affection between them except for a perfunctory goodbye kiss on the cheek.

Communication lines must be established and kept open in order to maintain mutual understanding among all concerned. Every form of closeness in the family builds on your ability to communicate. Communication is far more than talking to – or at – one another. It is an ability to get inside the other, feel what that person is feeling, think what that person is thinking.

Each is encouraged to own his feelings, to share them and to explore their meaning. This leads to family congruence, transparency and openness. Out of this can come the development of a family world-view that sees a sense of responsibility toward and for the whole. This way a person's feelings cannot become so ingrown that he self-destructs when the time comes for him to leave the nest.

NURTURING, CARING AND AFFECTION

The newborn infant in your family gets all your attention because you realize how dependent he is on you at this stage of his development and survival. You nurture that child by meeting his every need. In a real sense a person never loses his need for being nurtured, but in time he is able to nurture himself. Between that beginning stage and that independent stage are a lot of other stages with varying needs for nurture. If these needs are not met in good measure, something happens, and the result of it is maladjustment, a missing of the mark in the person's development.

The Triple-A Family gives nourishment and cares about you as a person as well as caring for you. The members share affection. It is God's way of caring for you as well as sharing with you the depths of His love and care. It is the setting in which He shares with you, through others, and in concrete and practical ways, what He and life are all about.

You are a feeling person, and to experience the fullness of life you need to be in touch with all your feelings. The family is designed to do this. Family life is to be "touchy-feely" in the best sense of the word. You may think God gave you so much skin just to hold in your insides, but in reality it is the best organ your body has, and He gave it so you can pick up lots of messages of love, caring and worth — and you need those messages. The language of touch is the only one an infant understands. The little child within us never loses its need for touching.

COMMONALITY, ONENESS AND COHESIVENESS

The peas in the pod of your family are all different in many ways, yet all need certain things in common. One of these is a shared faith. Another is shared experiences. Still another is shared love. Your oneness as a family lies in the commonality of its experience in being accepted, affirmed and approved of, along with ways in which this love is expressed and enjoyed. Temperaments can be different as well as styles of relating, but what you share within your family must be equally need-satisfying and dependable if it is to bond your family and provide cohesiveness. When they are missing, or are not shared in good measure, the family lacks "stickability."

PERSONAL ENHANCEMENT OF EACH MEMBER

If major growth in learning how to live life and acquiring good people skills, as well as enhancing the self, can take place in your family, that is a definite strength. You are there to encourage your children and help them discover their full potentials. All are in the formation stages and you can challenge them along that line.

This involves life-long learning and discovering. It involves acquiring interpersonal skills. It involves full development in every area of the children's lives just as it involves "growing up into Christ."

Part of this enhancement is learning how to share family power in the decision-making processes. This kind of sharing is in preparation for being on one's own out there in the wide world. Testing things here is a lot safer than testing them out there. Trying their wings while you are there to catch them is what a family is about.

And one of the best ways to teach good decision-making is through family powwows.

FAMILY POWWOWS

The average family spends no more than five minutes a day really talking to one another. The temptation is to live touch-and-go lives. To create a true family, this tendency has to be interrupted.

Dialogue can take place during family councils or powwows — or whenever the Spirit moves.

The purpose of a family powwow is to discover how things are going among the family members and how each is relating outside the family. What are the joys and problems? What are the victories and temptations? This is a time when each is allowed to share and each is listened to. It is a time of airing family frustrations, active listening, boiling things down into manageable sizes, and exploring options in seeking solutions. Things are out in the open, and the family can go to work on resolving the issues shared.

Family decisions merit full family input, and this is the best time to teach children how to make good decisions that will solve problems.

Most teenage anger at a parent is due to his feeling of a lack of control over his life. When you make all the decisions, it's like saying, "I have all the power and you have none." His reaction is to exercise all the power he can, and you won't like his ways. Family council takes time, energy and risk — and a whole lot of prayer, but your children will receive needed valuable training.

What you need to know is that many of their noes come from feeling helpless, and it is their way of grasping a sense of power. As you share power with them in a family council situation, they feel a stronger sense of their own significance, and less need to rebel.

But do remember shared power means just that—at times you may get outvoted. It takes time and energy to share power in decision-making, but the long-range goal is to have children who are equipped to make good decisions.

Preparing your children for independence at age eighteen or soon thereafter begins as soon as they are mature enough to be part of the family council or powwow.

The family council is also where things get prayed about or where decisions are postponed until each has been able to pray privately about it. Here they see, in a practical way, reliance on the Lord's leading. You can demonstrate clearly how you all seek His will and follow it. What a valuable lesson for each child to learn. Think of how it will serve him in all his future major decisions.

SATISFYING DIFFERENT NEEDS

When any child becomes a member of a single-parent family, his needs may shift dramatically, even become acute. Some children are more private and need more independence. Others are more dependent and need more cuddling. Some differ in the amount of affection they show and seem to need. Others differ in their abilities to motivate themselves. Each child is different and wants a relationship with you that is styled after his individual needs. You respect and love each one alike, but you do not relate to them all in the same way if their inner needs are to be met.

Understanding your children will help ensure that one child's needs do not dominate so that another's cannot be met adequately. Because the independent child seems to need less attention, it is easy to miss his need when a more dependent child is squeezing him out. The independent child needs attention also.

SHARING RESPONSIBILITIES

When you start the positive work of strengthening your family, a good place to begin is with shared responsibilities. A child can learn responsibility as soon as he is capable of the smallest tasks. When family life involves shared work, each person feels a viable part of the whole. This gives meaning to his place within the family. He is needed, capable and worthwhile. He counts. He is a contributing member, and the family is what it is because of his contribution.

Feeling a real part of the family does not just happen—you

create it in him through having him share the responsibilities. How well he can do the task, though, is not important. This will improve through practice. What is important is that he feels capable. Imagine what happens within the child who is told over and over again, "You can't do that. You never do anything right. No, that's not the way to do it; do it this way. Won't you ever learn?" This child grows up feeling he is a failure before he starts any task, no matter how capable he may truly be.

Needless to say, little hands need little tasks and the freedom to do those tasks at the levels of their abilities. This calls for discernment, for each child is different and functions at different levels. Acquiring the feeling "I am a capable human being" will, in time, release the child's full potential to learn the skills required to perform satisfactorily and successfully. Without that inner feeling he may be hesitant to learn, and he certainly will hesitate to try to do new things. The pain of failure is too great, so how you teach the skill is extremely important. It conveys the feeling to be gleaned from the experience. He needs to hear, "You did a good job. See what you are able to do. That was a hard task and you gave it your best. I want you to feel good about what you did. I am proud of you for the way you did it."

Praise works wonders for a child – for any of us – because the inner child likes to be stroked.[2] The excitement comes in trying new things. It is better sometimes to try something and fail than always to be safe by doing things beneath your ability level. Reaching is risky but trying is also adventurous if the environment is safe for the child. The main lesson to be caught by the child is: To fail at something does not mean you are a failure.

TRUST AND TRUSTWORTHINESS

Family foundations have to include trust – and in good measure. Trust is a gift you share with one another. A growing level of trustworthiness needs to develop in the family and within each individual member. You must be able to depend on one another, not only for basic needs but also for the entire family relationship. The children's certainty you will meet their physical needs is one thing, but being assured you will always love them is another thing altogether.

An early death of a parent or a divorce between parents can lead to a child's basic mistrust of life. Once this is established it takes a lot of effort to reverse it. A major need of your children is to learn basic trust that can help them achieve a good level of trustworthiness. What they sense they can be, they will be able to be.[3]

Truthfulness and personal integrity goes along with trust and trustworthiness. Contrary to popular opinion, truthfulness is not necessarily telling all. It is telling the truth and telling all of it that is necessary for a healthy interpersonal relationship. Personal deception can come through telling an untruth or a half-truth, or by withholding the truth, thus allowing someone to believe something that is not really true. Families have to be based on truth and truth telling. But as Paul said, "[Speak] the truth in a spirit of love" (Ephesians 4:15). You can be so devastatingly frank as to destroy one another; even though what was told was the "truth." Truth telling is both what is told and how it is told.

Jesus was very clear in Matthew 5 that our yes is to mean yes and our no, no. If this is not the case, then what are we to believe? The whole family system tends to collapse. You have to be able to depend on the word of one another.

Children need to learn that lying does not end with simply not telling the truth. What does it do to the level of relating between the persons involved? The betrayal of the relationship has to be seen as part of the consequence.

Young children have a hard time perceiving truth at times, especially when you pressure them for details, chronology and implications. In their panic due to the pressures it is easy for them to resort to falsehood, especially if they sense you are after something about which they are uncertain. The pressure so confuses them it is easy for them to cave in. This is not necessarily a moral weakness on their part. They are in the process of firming up their moral awareness and right now the pressure is too much for them to handle. Help them work it through. Your patience at this point can help them set a life-long pattern of being able to handle pressure and come up with the truth.

WHEN TRUST HAS BEEN BROKEN

Your teen lied to you. Now he wants to simply say, "I'm sorry," and then ask you to restore your trust in him.

It is not your trust that is in question. It is his trustworthiness. He had your trust before; he has it now.

He tries to put the monkey on your back when he says, "You don't trust me. That is why I mess up."

But let the monkey stay where it belongs. Remind your teen that he put it on his own back when he lied to you and proved his untrustworthiness. He can reestablish himself as worthy of your trust only by his actions from now on, but that is up to him. Ask him how he plans to go about doing this. How does he plan to make things right again?

Breaking trust on a repeated basis shows a defect within the person doing the breaking. Let the burden rest there. Do not make excuses for this nor take the responsibility for it. Let the one with the problem wrestle with it while you provide all the encouragement you can. There is always a reason for breaking trust. Outer circumstances only reflect an inner need. Deal with the inner need.

MUTUAL RESPECT

Respect is something each of you has to earn within the family life together. Your children respect you because you demonstrate you are worthy of their respect. The same goes for your respect of them. Because you respect them you do not violate their rights, infringe on their freedoms, or snoop into their secrets. Each person recognizes meaningful boundaries toward each of the others and lives within them. You teach them respect by being respectful.

In years of counseling I have had several occasions where a parent felt justified in violating well-established norms of family life. Through violating certain rights of privacy a parent discovered something that needed to be confronted, but lost a respect level between herself and her child that was extremely difficult to repair. A family needs to be founded on mutual respect, and that has to come first from the parental side. Then you have the right to demand respect from your child, because you have given him yours.

The spiritual values of those within the family are the main source of strength for the family's well-being. They are the core of its emotional health and of its self-image as well as of its self-enablement to be a family. They are the ties that bind the family and really hold it together. Spiritual strength manifests itself in the ways in which each person relates to the others. Each is tethered to the whole with plenty of freedom to develop within his own faith. Each has a private relationship with the Lord at the same time he shares the faith which is common to the family. In this way each member draws great strength from every other member, and this can truly make you a Triple-A Family.

Δ

TAKING ACTION
FAMILY STRENGTHS

1. How do you and your children rate as a Triple-A Family?

2. What strengths are evident in the interpersonal relationships within your family?

3. How much love, affirmation and respect is evident within your family?

4. How is power shared in your family?

5. Do your children get the levels of affection and stroking they seem to need?

6. How do you know your children feel loved, safe, secure and cared about? Please explain.

7. How well does your family nurture/care/affirm itself?

8. In what ways do your spiritual values help strengthen you as a family?

18

ADDING MORE GLUE

In this day and age when families seem to tear apart easily, you need to know yours has enough glue to hold together through thick and thin. That glue has many ingredients but the basic one, the emotional, binds the family together and ties the members to one another. A family is not just for parents or just for children. It is for both. It is "one for all and all for one." You are all in it together.

When you meet each other's needs within the family, loyalties are established, and they stick. Add to these the fun times, the sorrows encountered, and all the other experiences shared, and the glue gets even stronger. You are loyal to others within the family because your lives are so bound together you do not think of yourself apart from what exists among all of you. You are family. You want to be family. You work at being family.

The love shared, gifts given, feelings engendered, and loyalties established are but aspects of a relationship. The relationship itself is the glue holding all together.

A man I know spent several years in a prison camp in the USSR as a political prisoner. During his ordeal he found two sources of strength that saw him through unbearable conditions. The first was his faith. The second was his memories of family. These were like an oasis in a bitter struggle to remain sane as well as alive.[1]

No matter how outside conditions are, we are sustained from within. This is why you want to create for each of your children a memory bank that is rich in the glue of loyal bonding, rich enough to endure forever. (See Luke 2:19.)

WHEN DISTURBING PATTERNS EMERGE

Sometimes in your day-to-day living it may appear that the glue is losing its power. For example, maybe things seemed to be going real well, with only minor ups and downs. You settled in and felt good about what was happening. Then you became aware of little changes, then bigger ones. By now the picture has changed completely. Worse yet, you are not sure why or what is really happening underneath. You sense a need for help. You are running out of things to try.

There will always be change, ebb and flow. Nothing really remains the same in family life as persons change and grow. Many changes will go unnoticed because while the children are changing you are also. But the changes you will notice are those that cause one person to get out of step with the rest. Those changes bring about disturbing patterns that you want to watch out for. They demand action.

Peer pressure may be one source. Problems with one's identity may be another. A tug toward the Ex may be another. Earlier repressed feelings may be still another. The child may not really know what is happening or why he is changing. With an older child it could be drugs. Your wisdom and insight will be needed to uncover the roots. Even if you are not sure what to do at the moment, let everyone know you care, you plan to act, and it is going to be confronted. Don't ignore it; it may not go away. Get the help that is needed and resolve it — for everyone's sake.

AVOIDING NEGATIVISM

Another thing that can dilute the glue is a negative atmosphere. Young children believe everything a significant other in their lives tells them. If you see life as negative, they will too. They trust you. Being an adult you ought to know. This is how they reason. And being an adult you *ought* to know.

They don't need negativism in the home. There is enough of it outside.

Having come through the death of your mate, or a difficult divorce (is there any other kind?), having a bundle of struggles to face, with more bills than income, more work than energy, and more trials than faith, it is easy to become negative. But the children need honesty from you, a compassionate understanding of the real nature of life, positive and negative, and they need to know about God's abilities to keep His own. Faith cannot express itself as negativism and still be faith. Deal with your negatives and bitterness so you can lead your children to see what life in Him really is. They will see it through your eyes until they are able to form their own perceptions. Get them pointed in the right direction.

THE PLACE OF DISCIPLINE

Everything that happens within the family, positive and negative, must be seen in the light of its meaning to the whole. That includes matters of discipline and/or punishment. The purpose of discipline is to assure family harmony, unity and safety. A lack of discipline results in a personal life that is out of control and a family life characterized by confusion, frustration and family chaos.

Goals

Paul Tournier entitled one of his books, *The Whole Person in a Broken World.*[2] This points out the goal of discipline: to assist a person to discover real, authentic, safe and sane forms of relating and living within a world that is broken and at times insane. It is to learn how to order one's inner world so as to live productively, meaningfully and creatively in the outer world of relationships. With this as your goal in disciplining, you now know what skills you need to assure it for yourself and for your children.

Younger children need discipline in order to learn self-discipline. This is how maturity comes. Self-discipline gives a person a sense of unity and direction. A well-ordered family comes from well-ordered personal lives of its members. This begins with you and works down to the youngest. You are modeling your self-discipline that they can imitate and make their own.

If the children have reached adolescence and you are having serious discipline problems, it could be because of your own lack of self-discipline. If you still have to *make* them do something for their own well-being, the lessons they need have not been caught along the way. Discipline teaches self-discipline, which eventually comes from within and is motivated by a sense of well-being.

By moving into good levels of self-discipline, self-control and self-constraint, a person can acquire a master of self that will ensure his living with meaning and purpose. It is not by accident that a part of the fruit of the Spirit is self-control. Paul amplifies this in 2 Timothy 1:7 when he lists it as a spiritual gift. The child part of us is known for its lack of control, thus the need to be controlled. The adult side of us emerges when we learn self-control.

The goal of punishment is to teach the consequences of and personal responsibility for one's actions, but it is also for the establishing and maintaining of family harmony and well-being. Not to punish may mean to allow one family member to infringe on the space and rights of another. On the other hand, to punish is to establish the rights of each as well as responsibility for each. Society exists on the basis of responsibility. So does the family. Take time to jot down your concept of discipline and punishment in relating to your children. Are your views realistic, meaningful and needed? How will these meet your children's real needs? What will result if you continue on the basis of your present concepts?

Consistency

Without sound and consistent discipline, the family would be like a jellyfish—without backbone or direction. It would just float on the whim of the strongest, most aggressive members.

A typical scenario within a troubled family might go like this: Father was perceived as being too strict, so Mother compensated by being a little more permissive. Father reacted to her permissiveness by becoming more strict. She, in turn, reacted to his increased strictness by becoming more permissive.

Now they have divorced, and they continue the same pattern. She feels the children need things a little easier since they have suffered from their father's strictness and from the trauma of the divorce. He assumes that he needs to continue his discipline when they are with him in order to compensate for what they are still receiving from her. This leaves the children confused. They love both parents but resent the differences and the pressures.

The parents are unable to talk with each other and work out what is best for the children, so the overcompensating continues and maybe even intensifies—and the children lose.

Children need consistency, so discipline must be a joint effort, with each parent supporting the other. This is the only way children learn systematically and meaningfully to discipline themselves. If your Ex will not cooperate, and the styles of discipline differ, sit down and explain to your children in nonjudgmental terms what the differences are and why you discipline as you do. It helps them handle the confusion when they understand your reasoning.

Avoiding Extremes

Not only will your children know when you are being extreme in your discipline, but they also will resent and resist it. Your being overly coercive robs your child of personal initiative. He won't know how to act without being yelled at. Some soft-spoken employer will fire him for not getting his work done—he was waiting for the employer to shout because that's what you used to do.

Your child needs punishment for offenses needing correction, but never your punitiveness. There is nothing a child might do that warrants your abusing him. This is not punishment—it is revenge, usually for having been beaten as a child yourself. It is taking out on your child what was done to you by another person, someone you feared.

On the other hand, your being overpermissive fails to help your child put the brakes on himself. He will feel out of control. Sure, he'll enjoy it when it suits him, but he won't appreciate it later in life when he makes demands of an employer and the employer shows him the door instead of giving in as you always did. When you are overpermissive, the child is robbed of any real sense of self-discipline.

The key to discipline is to use enough to accomplish the goal of teaching self-discipline, but never to exert more pressure than is needed. The inner child is resistant to force of any kind, and when what we use has been excessive or inappropriate, the result is an equal amount of resistance which produces a stand-off. The temptation at that point is to exert more pressure, causing more resistance. A lessening of outside pressure and a calling forth of inner pressure can bring about the desired results and avoid additional resistance within the child.

NORMAL PROBLEMS IN DISCIPLINE

The first rule of thumb in disciplining is to understand the needs of the child and discipline toward that end. You can discern them better if you consider these five areas:

1. What are the *needs of the child* that should be addressed in the disciplining process? He needs you to help him live life safely, at the highest level, and in need-satisfying ways. For example, a small child's desire to climb stairs presents a danger as well as a challenge. The challenge is okay; the danger is not. So discipline must be done in a way that preserves the adventure but removes or minimizes the danger.

2. What are *your needs* in the disciplining process? One is to get across the lessons that can lead to self-discipline so you will not have to repeat them the rest of your life.

Another is to teach a child to do for himself what you will not always be there to do for him. Also, you want to raise a child who will be able to care for himself when the time comes.

3. What is the *reason for the power struggle* between you? You say no but the child goes ahead anyway. Is he testing the limits, resenting the limits, or simply ignoring the limits? All of these are normal reactions, and each needs to be addressed for what it is. To confuse them is to miss the point and to react inappropriately.

4. Is the problem a case of *natural stress points?* Your son is now a teen, moving more and more into independence. He strives for increased freedom and you strive for less control. He may try to take more than you are ready to give, or he may not be willing to take all you want him to. These give-and-take natural stress points need to be understood by both.

5. Are you experiencing a *clash of wills?* Dobson writes of the strong-willed child. You'll find few that are not, and some more so than others. I remember having a tug of war with my ten-year-old and feeling like I was losing. I had to remind myself I was the parent and he was the child. We were out of control. Yet not we; it was me. I was trying to control him, not myself. The only one I can control is myself and I was failing to do that. I was getting down to his level and being another ten-year-old. If you find yourself in a clash of wills, it's better to give it up and just take control of you. Then you can help your child with his need.

What is the answer to all this hassle? It is to make reasoning a way of life. That's exactly how God deals with you, so you can deal with your children the same way (Isaiah 1:18). Start reasoning with them as soon as they get beyond the cooing stage.

Children have great gifts. Look how smart they are. They chose you as their parent, didn't they? Plug into their hidden genius and start the wheels turning as early as possible. Share the reasoning aspect of why and wherefore. The time you invest now will pay rich dividends when they reach their teen years. (Of course, when you start reasoning with them, you'd better have good reasons for all you do and say.)

WHAT YOUR FAMILY IS FOR

Early on I shared a definition of love: It is a need-satisfying, dependable relationship. This is what God designed the family to be. It is where each learns how to give love and receive the love of another. It is also where each learns what is meant by "dependable." You are to love and be loved 24 hours a day, 7 days a week, 365 days a year, forever. Here each is provided with the relationships he needs for full and maturing growth.

The emphasis is on being *and* doing. The major emphasis is on being, which then gives rise to the doing. "Doing love" is what family life is all about.

As your children learn to "do love," and as they progress toward maturity, they will go through a great deal of changing, and your parenting skills will need to grow to stay ahead. The only thing constant about a family is change and you need to be prepared. Every Christian ought to be open to change—nothing remains the same except the Lord Himself. He does not change. He is the turning point around which all change happens and makes sense.

The ways in which you and your children can be ready for change and growth include the following:

1. *Learning how to lean.* You lean first on the Lord, then on yourself, then on each other. Leaning is misused only when we lean at a time we shouldn't, but we must remember that even self-sufficient persons have to lean sometimes.

2. *Learning how to stand.* "Standing on your own two feet" is more than an expression. It is a necessity. In the safety of the family, each member learns how to stand, when to stand, and how to be a source of strength to others in their attempts to stand.

3. *Learning how to kneel.* The two knees God gave you can be bent in submission and surrender, and in recognition of your true need. You stand tallest when you kneel.

4. *Learning how to dance.* You can celebrate His presence within you, and in your family, in recognition that all He gives are "good and perfect gifts." The dance of the thankful heart is the most joyous of all.

5. *Learning how to bend.* Get beyond your rigid expectations of perfection, and understand that children are not adults. It's all right to be a child when you are a child. A

day does not have to be perfect to be wonderful, nor does a person have to be perfect to be beautiful. Rigidity is great in a statue but not in a personality. Be flexible!

6. *Learning how to be firm.* Sometimes firmness is called for and bending would be a tragedy. Being firm is not being rigid. Firmness means your gentleness is genuine. Like the old Saturday Evening Post cartoon: "Tough, but oh, so gentle."

7. *Learning how to confront.* Children need to find in you a good mirror in which to firm up their true identity. They need you to let them know when they are wrong as well as when they are right. They need to know when they are being self-destructive or hurting others. They need to know how to discipline themselves and make good choices. They need to know what it means to control themselves.[3]

8. *Learning how to roll with the punches.* Understand that what may seem like the end, the bottom, the limit, the ultimate, the worst, is not always so. Each stage of development has its struggles, and you have far more "copability" than you think. Punches will come, but rolling with them softens the blows.

9. *Learning how to begin again no matter what.* This is the full meaning of God's grace. There are times in family life when you are knocked flat on your face, but you do not have to lie there. You claim His grace, get up, dust yourself off, and begin again. Jesus did this with the cross until He got it up the hill. The good news of the gospel is that there is nothing from which you cannot recover if you are willing to claim His grace. (This is a good time to rehearse all His promises to you as a single parent.)

As a parent you are aware of all that needs to be taught, but don't lose sight of all you can learn, too. Learning comes first. Your children probably will teach you far more than you think you ever taught them. Part of a family's glue is the ability to teach one another and learn from one another.

BECOMING THE BEST YOU

The family is a training ground for lots of things, but at the top of the list is becoming the best you that you can be. The purpose of family life is to assist each member to do just that. Too many families do just the opposite. They tend to bring out the worst in a person. They take a little innocent child and turn him inward on himself, loading him down with all sorts of rejection and self-hate. This can destroy his spirit and discourage him about life.

God's design and purpose for the family, though, is to help bring each member to his best. This does not mean expecting your children to excel where you never did. It means to help them discover their own full potential and be able to motivate themselves toward realizing that fulfillment. As you learn to be the best parent you can be, each child is in the process of learning how to be the best child he can be. As you sharpen your skills, he will sharpen his.

BEING A PARENTAL MODEL

One way that process works is through you as the parental role model. Your children will mimic you — in more ways than you wish. But why not? You are special to them. They want to grow up and become what you are. Of course, they need good modeling from you so they will be on the right track. If you are mature, they will have a head start on becoming mature. If you are open and honest, they will start in that direction, also. Help them choose what is good, truthful, best, beautiful, lasting, and above all, Christian. If you become what you want them to be, they can follow your example freely. This stuff about "Do as I say, not as I do" doesn't work with children. They learn by mimicking what they see.

By following the Lord day by day you have nothing to fear. He will lead you into becoming all you need to be. As they follow you, they will be following Him. The transition from you to Him will be natural when the time comes. Remember how quickly John's disciples transferred their allegiance from him to Jesus when Jesus first appeared? It was because John had prepared them for that shift and when Jesus came on the scene, the shift was natural. They left their work immediately and followed Him (Matthew 4:18-22).

Your following the Lord prepares your children for a natural transition in faith to making Him their true model. The ultimate joy of Christian parenting is leading your children to Christ. (Again, see "Would You Like to Know God Personally" at the back of this book.)

SINGLE-PARENT FAMILY MYTHS

You probably were dealing with these even before the divorce became final. If you lost your mate in death, these myths probably started coming your way soon after the funeral. But for your children they may be yet to come. Their playmates at school and elsewhere will see to it that they do come, and painfully so. Other children who do not understand can be so cruel toward those whose situation they see as different. Those being taunted usually do not fully understand their own situations so they suffer the full impact of these labels.

Myths are usually promoted by those who want to avoid dealing with reality. You must deal with reality, though, and you must help your children deal with it. The best defense in an offense. Preparing your children ahead of time will get them ready to deal with the garbage when they hear it. Rehearse these concepts with them so they can give a good reply for what is happening.

Myth #1: You are a "broken" family.

What is meant by "broken"? What others may indicate is that you are no longer a "whole family," whatever that means. But what lies beneath this is an untruth: It is saying that because the parents have divorced you cannot be whole, as a family or otherwise. The family is "broken"; you are "broken." This is a myth.

Family wholeness does not depend on the number of parents in the home nor does it depend on the marital status of the leaders. Whatever your family is, it is whole, entire, complete.

Myth #2: You cannot be a whole family.

This goes along with #1. Those sharing this myth often speak out of their own insecurities and unwillingness to deal with single-parent families. The church is not immune from this. I know very few "whole" families that are whole, wholeness relating to the emotional health of the home and all those within it. This is why we have so many divorces. Family wholeness has to do with the quality of relationships among those who are in it, not the constellation.

Myth #3: Your children are disadvantaged.

Children from a single-parent family may or may not be disadvantaged, and the divorce, or the death of the other parent, may or may not be a part of it. The myth is that *just because* of these events your children are automatically disadvantaged.

I have seen single-parent families in which the children have virtually blossomed after the divorce when they were not able to before due to negative family life. On the other hand, many have suffered because the divorce or death of a parent left the survivors so emotionally crippled they were unable to cope.

If your children do end up disadvantaged, it will not be simply because of any such event. It goes much deeper than that. The latest statistics indicate single-parent families are producing some excellent achievers, and this may be due to the quality of the relationship between parent and child resulting from their new focus on one another out of the new need.

Myth #4: Your children won't be normal.

I certainly hope not! If normal means average, then you owe yours a whole lot more than that. By "normal," people mean that since the children do not have a full-time mother and father, they cannot be normal. This goes along with #2 and #3, and it comes from the same basic misunderstanding of what constitutes wholeness and normalcy. True, your children have obstacles to overcome, but these can be makers instead of breakers. What matters is what you do with them rather than what you allow them to do to you.

Myth #5: As a divorced person you are a "loser."

Talk about sticking the knife in and twisting it! In a way this is what underlies many of the other myths. Because your marriage broke up, you must be a "loser." If you weren't, why would it have broken up? Now, let's suppose the worst part of this is true and your marriage did break up because you saw yourself as a "loser." As a result things fell apart.

All right, but that was the past. What about the present? You are not seeing yourself as a loser just because your marriage broke up. It started long before that, and in part, helped you choose as you did, do what you did and possibly fail as you did. But now you don't need to see yourself as a loser anymore. You have discovered the truth of who you really are, and that truth has set you free from that perception. The myth says, "Once a loser always a loser." This is not true of you. God's grace has set you free.

Myth #6: Your family doesn't fit in anymore.

Let's face it; there may be a lot of truth to this. Your family does not fit in some places anymore, but that is not because it is now a single-parent family. It's because many churches do not allow single-parent families to fit in. In some quarters you are like an ethnic family walking into a totally segregated congregation. They do not fit in because the congregation will not allow it. God's grace is available to the church, but it is not always appropriated.

Myths die hard. They also have a kernel of truth to them — but only a kernel. They are to be challenged by full truth and reality. To give in to them is to forsake truth and the spirit of the truth. The real truth is: You need not be classified a "broken" family; your family can be whole. Your children need not be disadvantaged; they can be normal or better. You need not be a loser; and your family can fit into any situation where there is health, wholeness, understanding and grace.

Being a whole, cohesive family in this day and age is no small accomplishment. Who knows that better than you? Your struggle is not easy, and it involves many issues. But resolving them brings the kinds of results you are praying and working for. That is the good news.

Δ

TAKING ACTION: FAMILY COHESIVENESS

1. What kinds of loyalties do you see building among family members?
2. Do you consider yourself a positive or negative person? Why?
3. How have you handled defiance among your children?
4. What concerns you most about your style of discipline?
5. What seems to work best in your style of discipline?
6. What are your goals in disciplining?
7. Do you consider most of your discipline problems to benormal or are they due to your being a single parent?
8. What help do you need to enhance your discipline skills?
9. Of the six myths mentioned in the chapter, what ones have you encountered and how have you dealt with them?

19

COMPLETING THE JOURNEY

You are being told from many sources the family is in trouble today. This may be true, but at the present time you have a great opportunity for wholeness because of information now available and because of new discoveries in family theory. It is a time for renewed hope, especially for Christian families.

Single-parent families fit into the picture as well, even with their special needs. I believe they can be whole, and I hope you do, too.

LOVE IS ALL IT NEEDS TO BE

Throughout this book a heavy emphasis has been on assessing the real needs of yourself and your children. Love's desire is to meet those needs for wholeness. That is why this study is so important. Love does not deal hit or miss. It seeks to be very pointed. It seeks to go right to the heart of the matter and work there. The thrust of love is to be need-satisfying in dependable ways.

Love seeks to act consistently. This is a part of its role in dependency. Children need consistency to be assured of dependability. Any lack of dependability leaves them confused, frustrated and frightened. They will not know what to count on or when.

Love cares enough to confront the child when he is wrong and to discipline for adequate correction. It is not so fearful of its own need that it cannot act on the need of the other. Little change will be made unless the problem is confronted.

Love reinforces positive behavior. Paul says, "It rejoices in the truth." So much of parenting can degenerate into correcting negative behavior while little or nothing is said about positive behavior.

The positive needs reinforcing. How does a child know his behavior is acceptable unless it is reinforced? Without making any moral connections like, "You are a good boy [or girl]," the attention needs to be on the behavior: "You did a good job"; or, "What a good thing to do." Doing good things does not make a person good. It is the person you already love doing a good, positive thing.

Love puts the needs of others ahead of its own, but this does not mean its needs are unimportant or to be negated. Love chooses out of its concern for the children and for others. In time the children will learn the loving thing to do because it will have been modeled for them.

Love knows how to act appropriately. It is kind when kindness is called for, forgiving when that is the need, firm when limits are called for, soft and gentle when hurts are being cared for. Love has a built-in antenna called discernment. It picks up signals to which it is programmed to respond. When the message has been received, love springs into appropriate action.

Love also has a special gift for the one loving. It has a built-in ability to assure him not only of the value of the gift, but also that God is in it and that makes it sufficient. Out of His all-sufficiency He allows your gifts to be enough to meet the needs of your children. In this partnership you need not fear failing.[1]

A MEANS TO AN END

What you need to keep in mind throughout the entire parenting process is that your family is never to be an end to itself: It is a means to an end. For you it is preparing your children for life and for their families. For them it will be the preparing for *their* children, their lives, and their families. The purpose of family is linear — it stretches down the corridors of time to all of us who will be taken up into His Forever Family. The ultimate family relationship is enhanced by what we do here in its formation. You are a partner in that final result, a partner with the Spirit of God.

DEVISING GOALS FOR EACH CHILD

When the family foundation is adequate, it becomes obvious to all within it that the preparations will extend well beyond the family itself. You will instill in each a confidence for being able to handle life. By the time of his emancipation from the family each one will be ready for the transition. You will have prepared him.

You will have given him what you yourself may not have had when that day came for you.

Let me list the goals I believe will assist your children in this preparation toward full maturity. What the children accomplish in each of these areas is their choice — providing the teaching and opportunity is your responsibility.

1. A good level of being able to *accept reality* without obvious distortion. When a child breaks the toy he is playing with, he needs to be able to accept the fact that he caused this to happen. It is not someone else's fault.

2. A good level of *harmony*. He needs the ability to get along with others, even when they differ with him. He will understand sibling rivalry for what it is and that will help keep it at a minimum.

3. A growing level of *adaptability*. The older a child becomes, the more he needs to be able to adapt to circumstances without increasing his own personal trauma.

4. An appropriate sense of *independence*. He must understand when it is okay to be dependent, and learn the art of interdependence. Moving into independence, he will do for himself the things he needs to be doing; interdependence comes as he recognizes when he must look to others for help.

5. *Acceptance of his sexuality* and gender. It is okay to be what he is and to perceive himself as a sexual person. It is okay to be his gender. He is worth loving as he is.

6. *Tolerance* for all kinds of differences. This begins in the home, as does prejudice and hatred. These are learned responses. The tolerant child's playmates come in all sizes, shapes and colors, and he loves them all for just being themselves.

7. A sense of *responsibility*. Learning this begins when he is taught to be responsible for himself and then to extend this toward others.

8. *Self-expression*. Each person must have the ability to know what is inside himself. He must be able to share it in meaningful ways so that others may know who he is, how he thinks, and what makes him unique. It is the ability to communicate the self to another for mutual understanding.

9. *Creativity*. Rediscovering this ability, finding the full potential of his God-given creative abilities and talents, is

a part of the maturing process.

10. *Insight*. Self-awareness, or knowing how he is put together and how he ticks, is another term for this, and it leads to understanding others.

11. *Minimum level of floating anxiety*. Anxiety is a part of life, especially in today's world, but reducing it is part of maturing. Being anxious over the unknown is kept at a minimum in the person whose faith continues to move into deeper levels of trust and assurance.

12. A growing *ability to manage aggression*. Anger is also a part of life, but knowing how to deal with one's anger is a sign of maturing, and is needful for every person. Many Christians never really learn how to manage it biblically.

13. Being at *peace* with himself. This is an inner calm that only the mature can know. "It Is Well With My Soul" is the theme hymn of this person.

14. *Consistency of personality*. This is more than "what you see is what you get." What one person sees in him is what all others will see as well, for that is how he is.

15. *Satisfaction* with life, rather than always wishing to change life before he can be content. Change comes because of an inner satisfaction, not just to become satisfied.

16. *Congruence*. What appears on the outside is what is on the inside. What he is experiencing is genuine; it is not a game.

17. *Ability to keep regressions temporary*. Whether dealing with trauma or pleasure, the inner child, who sometimes rises up, is not allowed to remain in control. The situation will be back where it needs to be after some time has been spent in dealing with it.

18. *Capacity for being alone* without being lonely. Children's fears force them to cling. They feel safe only when clinging. Mature adults do not experience these anxieties.

19. *Ability to love and be loved*. This is the ultimate sign of maturing, and forms the basis for all other levels. The others grow through and out of this.

20. *Adequate philosophy of life,* a theology that gives meaning and purpose. It is to understand the calling of God to discipleship, service and ministry and to be His partner for life. It is to be fully human and fully alive within the grandeur of the grace of God shared with him in the person of Christ.[2]

BUILDING AN ABILITY TO LET GO

As you work on these goals for your children, it will pay great dividends to do an occasional expectations check on yourself and them. Most problems arise when your expectations are unrealistic. There are two dangers: expecting too little, and expecting too much. Know the child's abilities and expect him to live up to them. In some areas these will be exceeded; in others it will take more time and practice to reach the norm. But love is patient.

If you find it difficult to let go of some of your expectations, you will have an even harder time letting go of the children when the time comes. Letting go is a gradual process that begins at birth, and it really is a matter of how well you love yourself. A lack of self-love creates a need within you to hold on to your children long after they need to be set free. The ability to let go comes from within you, and is your gift to your children as well as to yourself.

With the loss of a mate, it is easy to form a dependency on your children that makes letting go next to impossible. Letting go becomes easier, though, as you accept the fact that God only loans them to you. Like you, they belong to Him, and in Him you can always belong to one another—not as parent and child, but as friends.

Shifting from parent to friend may soon add a delightful new dimension—becoming a grandparent. The main difficulty at that stage is in trying to figure out how you could have done such a great job parenting, yet your grandchildren have such confused parents! Isn't it a good thing you will still be around to straighten things out?

As children reach adulthood and move out into the world on their own, their needs change, but not the loving ties. The family is where one returns from time to time without any real need to stay. The place to stay is within the new family that is growing up around the maturing person, no longer a child in your home. This is when you start reaping the harvest of joys you have been sowing all along. These are the years you all have worked and prayed for. These are the bonus years of family life.

COMING FULL CIRCLE

In the first chapter of this book I shared with you a deep conviction that the book would be life-changing for you. It has been for me, which is why I wanted to share it with you. *He* wants to change us. That is why He gave us His Spirit to live in us. If you have done what each chapter has called for, you have changed. Neither you nor I can expose ourselves to His truth and not be changed. Keep on changing. Let this be your beginning. You will never get too old to change.

A SPECIAL THANK YOU

Your children may still be very young and thus unaware of what is happening for you. They may sense some change intuitively but not understand what or why. Let me thank you on their behalf until they are old enough to do it personally:

"Thank you for being the parent you are and for the one you are yet becoming. Thank you for meeting my needs and helping me become the person I need to be. Thank you most of all for modeling a faithfulness to Him that allows me to know Him personally. And thank you for being you—my parent. I'm glad God gave me you!"

Δ

TAKING ACTION: RESHAPING YOUR FAMILY

1. On the basis of the definitions in the chapter, use the chart below and on the next page as a guide to assessing your family's health, strength and maturity. On a percentile of 0 to 100, marking with a different letter for each (an *x,* an *o,* etc.), rate your children.

   Ask yourself: Where is each child now in his growth process? How can I assist him best?

   In a few months, come back and do a reassessment, and note the changes. Keep doing this as a check on their progress. When your children are mature enough to benefit from it, share it with them. Use it to affirm them.

   Use the following designations in rating your children:

   25 = below age level, showing need
   50 = at age level, doing well
   75 = ahead of age level, doing great

1. Distorted Perceptions			Acceptance of Reality	
0	25	50	75	100
2. Hostility				Harmony
0	25	50	75	100

3. Rigidity				Adaptability
0	25	50	75	100

4. Pronounced Dependency				Independence
0	25	50	75	100

5. Sexual Confusion				Sexual Acceptance
0	25	50	75	100

6. Intolerance, Prejudice				Tolerance
0	25	50	75	100

7. Irresponsibility				Responsibility
0	25	50	75	100

8. Lack of Self-expression				Self expression
0	25	50	75	100

9. Lack of Creativity				Creativity
0	25	50	75	100

10. Confusion				Insight
0	25	50	75	100

11. Overly Anxious				Minimum of Floating Anxiety
0	25	50	75	100

12. Aggressive				Management of Aggression
0	25	50	75	100

13. In Conflict				Peace With Oneself
0	25	50	75	100

14. Inconsistency of Personality				Consistence of Personality
0	25	50	75	100

15. Dissatisfaction With Life				Satisfaction With Life
0	25	50	75	100

16. Incongruence				Congruence
0	25	50	75	100

17. Inability to Bounce Back				Temporary Regressions
0	25	50	75	100

18. Lonely				Capacity to Be Alone
0	25	50	75	100

19. Indifference				Ability to Love/Be Loved
0	25	50	75	100

20. Inadequate Philosophy of Life				Adequate, Unifying Philosophy
0	25	50	75	100

2. To be most effective in helping your children meet their goals, you should assess your own strength in these areas and determine where you need to take action.

   Use these in rating yourself:
   25 = very immature
   50 = showing a good level of maturity
   75 = very mature
   85-100 = exceptionally mature[3]

   Also ask yourself: What do I see emerging as a pattern in our family? How mature are we as a family?

3. Sit down and write yourself a letter. This letter is to be to you on how you think your child might be on his (or her) eighteenth birthday. This is the letter you want to receive from that child on that special day. Thank you for all you have been, done and shared. It is your child's message to you, looking back over eighteen years of life. See those years through his eyes, not your own. Let the child you have raised reflect back to you his own perception of those years you had together.

   Once you have written your letter, let it be your goal for the years that yet lie ahead. What you have written can be realized. This is what faith is: writing the letter before these years are a reality. This is what grace is: making things happen just as faith has written them.

   On your child's eighteenth birthday, show him the letter—and listen to the reply:

   **"Great! That's exactly what I want to say.
   And . . . thanks!"**

An Open Letter to All Professional Church Leaders

Dear Colleague in Ministry:

Greetings to you in the name of the One who came preaching, teaching and healing.

There is a special segment of people in your congregation who need Jesus' full ministry in their lives. These are the singles, particularly the single parents among your members. I point this group out because they need your sympathetic help and compassionate care.

Being a single parent in our culture is no small task. To be able to fulfill their role as Christian parents effectively, they require your help, support and encouragement.

One way your church can show this is by providing selected reading resources through your library for these single parents' study and help. Most of these people are on limited budgets and your making this material available would be of great encouragement to them.

Another way your church can show concern is through a single-parent support group. A group like this can run itself if you will assist in getting it organized and going. Assigning a staff person the responsibility of liaison between the group and the church is the best procedure because it would show the church's commitment to this ministry.

Still another way to help is to seek ways of integrating single-parent families into the full life of the church. They feel different enough already, so don't add to that feeling. Help to dispel it.

In the case of the death of a spouse bringing about a single parent family, a grief-support group could be a real ministry. With divorce, a divorce-recovery group can be the way to go. Sit down with those involved and explore their needs, and then respond to what you hear.

Single-parent families do have specialized needs, but at the same time they can become whole just as any other family can. Being a church that takes its ministry to families — all families — seriously means more than just providing worship and fellowship experiences. These singles silently cry for support groups, information-sharing times, workshops and ongoing programs designed to meet their real needs. When these things are provided, your church indeed becomes a family church.

The need of your singles and single parents for specialized ministry was yesterday. Today is already late for many of them. Further delays will serve only to deepen their pain. Many have no one to turn to but their church. Be there for them. Act on their behalf. Minister to them and to their little ones. Do it "as unto Him."

This book, *Parenting Solo,* may be used as a study guide for a class or a small group. Why not begin there? It can be set up in just a week or two. Start the group, and they will do the recruiting themselves.

Let me know what happens with your singles and how lives are being changed. Let me rejoice with you. There is no greater thrill than in being involved in His work!

Joy and peace,

Emil

Reference Notes

Chapter 3

1. You may not have thought much about Jesus' parental model as you see Him parenting the Twelve, the little children, and others. He is acting out the Father's essence. Note all the parenting qualities to be found in Jesus and His ministry.

Chapter 6

1. John Powell, *Why Am I Afraid to Tell You Who I Am?* (Allen, TX: Argus Publications, 1967).

Chapter 8

1. Richard J. Foster, *Money, Sex and Power* (New York: Harper & Row, 1980). Note his section on sexual matters.

Chapter 9

1. Divorce is not a sin. God does not give permission to sin. Divorce is a symptom of the breakdown in a primary relationship and each person involved may have sinned against the other. Hardness of heart may be the sin leading to divorce as found in Matthew 19:8. A self-destructive form of relating in a marriage is also a sin.

Chapter 10

1. Adultery is an act, not a state of being. You commit adultery; you do not live in adultery. Once a marriage is contracted it is a valid relationship in God's eyes and in society's.

Chapter 11

1. Dorothy Briggs, *Your Child's Self-Esteem: The Key to His Life* (Garden City, NY: Doubleday, 1967).

2. Sexual identity for a male child is gleaned through interaction with his mother: "It's okay with Mom that I am a boy." With a girl, "permission" is gleaned from relating to her father. When the parent is deceased or absent, a substitute is needed.

Chapter 12

1. Dolores Curran, *Traits of a Healthy Family* (Minneapolis: Winton Press, 1983).

2. The author has a separate chapter on each of the fifteen traits. This is a work of major importance.

Chapter 17

1. The term, "warm fuzzies," is an expression from transactional analysis meaning "good, warm feelings." Claude Stiener is one source.

2. A favorite transactional analysis term for sharing a feeling with another person, either a positive stroke or a negative one.

3. Eric Erikson has a full treatment of basic trust versus mistrust in *Childhood and Society* (New York: Norton, 1963).

Chapter 18

1. Natan Scharansky describes his experience in his book, *Fear No Evil* (New York: Random House, 1988).

2. Paul Tournier, *The Whole Person in a Broken World* (New York: Harper and Row, 1964).

3 See for reference David Augsberger's *Caring Enough to Confront* (Ventura, CA: Regal Books, 1981).

Chapter 19

1. This section is selected from 1 Corinthians 13 and the key aspects of parental love.

2. These items are a result of my doctoral project and are gleaned from many sources.

3. Emil J. Authelet, Jr., *The Maturity Inventory* (Berkeley, CA: American Baptist Seminary of the West, 1985).

Resources
for Further Information

1. Self-Discovery Needs

Briggs, Dorothy. *Celebrate Your Self: Enhancing Your Own Self-Esteem.* Garden City, NY: Doubleday, 1977. This book does for adults what her earlier one does for children.

Dobson, James. *Emotions: Can You Trust Them?* Ventura, CA: Regal Books, 1980. He explores in depth the emotions and their reliability in self-understanding and fulfillment.

Harris, Thomas A. *I'm OK — You're OK: A Practical Guide to Transactional Analysis.* New York: Harper & Row, 1967. This popular work is an excellent introduction to understanding your ego states, especially the inner child of the past. It will give you an in-depth look at transactional analysis terms and their meanings.

Powell, John. *Fully Human, Fully Alive: A New Life Through a New Vision.* Allen, TX: Argus Communications, 1976. This was his first major work and is a must for working on your self-understanding. I have shared many copies and recommend it highly.

——————. *The Christian Vision: The Truth That Sets Us Free.* Allen, TX: Argus Communications, 1984. This takes up where *Fully Human, Fully Alive* leaves off. A little more detailed, it deals more in depth with self-awareness.

——————. *Why Am I Afraid to Tell You Who I Am?* Allen, TX: Argus Communications, 1969. One of Powell's earliest works and still worth reading and studying. Good insights.

Schmidt, Jerry A. *Do You Hear What You're Thinking?* Wheaton, IL: Victor Books, 1983. It covers "the art of talking to yourself."

2. Personal Growth and Maturing

Harris, A. B. and T. A. *Staying OK.* New York: Harper & Row, 1985. It contains much of what they have taught over the years in workshops relating to *I'm OK — You're OK* by Thomas Harris, his first book on transactional analysis.

Jones, G., and Phillips-Jones, L. *Men Have Feelings Too!* Wheaton, IL: Victor Books, 1988. Most men have a difficult time coming to grips with feelings. These authors share some good insights.

Murphree, Jon T. *When God Says You're OK: A Christian Approach to Transactional Analysis.* Downers Grove, IL: InterVarsity Press, 1976. He deals with major theological themes for understanding.

Narramore, Bruce. *You're Someone Special.* Grand Rapids: Zondervan Publishing House, 1978. He helps you construct a biblical self-perception.

Osborne, Cecil G. *You're in Charge.* Waco, TX: Word Books, 1973. Very helpful as are his other works.

Peck, M. Scott. *The Road Less Traveled: A New Psychology of Love, Traditional Values and Spiritual Growth.* New York: Simon & Schuster, 1978. This work requires a lot of reflection but is well worth the journey.

3. Dealing With the Past

Missildine, W. Hugh. *Your Inner Child of the Past.* New York: Simon & Schuster, 1968. This is an important work and is a classic in its field. Make its reading a *must* for you and your children.

Narramore, B., and Counts, B. *Freedom From Guilt.* Eugene, OR: Harvest House, 1974. This appeared originally as *Guilt and Freedom.*

Seamands, David A. *Healing for Damaged Emotions.* Wheaton, IL: Victor Books, 1981. This has a study guide and can be used by a small group wanting to find healing and new directions.

———. *Healing of Memories.* Wheaton, IL: Victor Books, 1985. This book is also out on audio tapes. I recommend it highly.

Walters, Richard P. *Forgive and Be Free: Healing the Wounds of the Past and Present.* Grand Rapids: Pyranee Books, 1983.

Wright, H. Norman. *Making Peace With Your Past.* Old Tappan, NJ: Fleming H. Revell, 1985. I recommend all his books.

4. Dealing With Special Problems

Dobson, James. *Hide and Seek.* Old Tappan, NJ: Fleming H. Revell, 1974.

———. *Love Must Be Tough: New Hope for Families in Crisis.* Waco, TX: Word Books, 1983. All of Dobson's books are worth reading and having in your church's library.

Hart, Archibald D. *Children of Divorce.* Waco, TX: Word Books, 1982. Read this one for new insights into what your children may be experiencing.

Gullo, S., and Church, C. *Loveshock: How to Recover From a Broken Heart and Love Again.* New York: Simon & Schuster, 1981.

Kubler-Ross, Elisabeth. *On Death and Dying.* New York: Macmillan Publishing, 1969.

———. *Living With Death and Dying.* New York: Macmillan Publishing, 1981.

Forward, S., and Buck, C. *Betrayal of Innocence: Incest and Its Devastation.* New York: Penguin Books, 1988.

Vaughan, Diane. *Uncoupling: How Relationships Come Apart.* Nashville: Vintage Books, 1987.

Many good works are available in dealing with incest, abuse, rejection and abandonment. Refer to your local Child Protective Agency for materials and references. The Government Printing Office in Washington, D. C., also has documents available on these topics.

5. Divorce Recovery

Colgrove, Bloomfield and McWilliams. *How to Survive the Loss of a Love.* New York: Leo Press, 1976.

Fisher, Bruce. *Rebuilding When Your Relationship Ends.* San Luis Obispo: Impact Publishers, 1981. This can be used individually or as a guide for a divorce-recovery group. I know of several churches where it is being used.

Gardner, Richard A. *Boys & Girls Book About Divorce.* New York: Science House, 1970.

Hosier, Helen K. *The Other Side of Divorce.* New York: Hawthorn Books, 1975. The cover states it is "A Christian look at the forces at work in divorce and a plea for understanding and compassion."

Lovett, C. S. *The Compassionate Side of Divorce.* Baldwin Park, CA: Personal Christianity, 1975.

Salk, Lee. *What Every Child Would Like Parents to Know About Divorce.* New York: Harper & Row, 1978.

Smoke, Jim. *Growing Through Divorce.* Irvine, CA: Harvest House, 1976. It includes a tape for individual and group use.

Woodson, Les. *Divorce and the Gospel of Grace.* Waco, TX: Word Books, 1979.

6. Remarriage

Brown, B. W. *Getting Married Again.* Waco, TX: Word Books, 1979.

Clinebell, H. J. and C. H. *The Intimate Marriage.* New York: Harper & Row, 1970. Every couple should include this book in their premarital reading. It is also a workbook.

Galloway, Dale. *Dream a New Dream.* Wheaton, IL: Tyndale House Publishers, 1975. It is his personal journey through divorce and remarriage.

Hosier, Helen K. *To Love Again: Remarriage for the Christian.* Nashville: Abingdon Press, 1985.

Muriel, James. *Marriage Is for Loving.* Reading, MA: Addison-Wesley, 1979. This is a workbook and is based on transactional analysis.

McRoberts, Darlene. *Second Marriage.* Minneapolis: Augsburg, 1978.

Powell, John. *The Secret of Staying in Love.* Allen, TX: Argus Communications, 1974.

————. *Why Am I Afraid to Love?* Allen, TX: Argus Communications, 1967.

Purnell, Dick. *Building a Relationship That Lasts.* San Bernardino, CA: Here's Life Publishers, 1988.

Richards, Larry. *Remarriage: A Healing Gift From God.* Waco, TX: Word Books, 1981.

Small, Dwight H. *The Right to Remarry.* Old Tappan, NJ: Fleming H. Revell, 1981.

Wangerin, Walter, Jr. *As for Me and My House: Creating Your Marriage to Last.* Nashville: Thomas Nelson Publishers, 1987.

7. Family Development

Anderson, R. S., and Guernsey, D. B. *On Being Family: A Social Theology of the Family.* Grand Rapids: Wm. B. Eerdmans Publishing, 1985. A good introduction to family systems theory.

Blitchington, Evelyn. *The Family Devotions Idea Book.* Minneapolis: Bethany House, 1982.

Clarke, J. I. *Self-Esteem: A Family Affair.* Minneapolis: Winton Press, 1982.

Curran, Dolores. *Traits of a Healthy Family.* Minneapolis: Winton Press, 1983. The subtitle is "Fifteen Traits Commonly Found in Healthy Families by Those Who Work With Them." This is a work to be studied for a long time to come.

————. *Stress and the Healthy Family.* San Francisco: Harper & Row, 1985.

Hunt, G., and Wakefield, N. *Finding Your Family's Potential.* Omaha, NE: Family Concerns, 1976.

Rhodes, S., and Wilson, J. *Surviving Family Life: The Seven Cries of Living Together.* New York: Putnam's Sons, 1981.

Strommen, M. P. and A. I. *Five Cries of Parents: New Help for Families on the Issues That Trouble Them Most.* San Francisco: Harper & Row, 1985.

8. Single Parenting

Gladen, K., and Gray, J. *Human Uniqueness: A Christian Education Course for Children on Self-Esteem.* Waco, TX: Word Books, 1980. Ask your church to offer this for parents and all children. I give it an excellent rating.

Highlander, Don H. *Positive Parenting: How to Love, Motivate, and Discipline Your Child to Grow Up Happy and Responsible.* Waco, TX: Word Books, 1980.

Juroe, D. J. and B. B. *Successful Stepparenting.* Old Tappan, NJ: Fleming H. Revell, 1983.

Roosevelt, R., and Lofas, J. *Living in Step.* New York: McGraw-Hill, 1976.

Smith, Harold I. *One-Parent Families.* Kansas City, MO: Beacon Hill Press, 1980.

9. Child Development

Briggs, Dorothy. *Your Child's Self-Esteem: The Key to His Life.* Garden City, NY: Doubleday, 1967. This is a major work and should be a *must* for every parent, single or otherwise. Note especially pages 309 and following for a summary and extra resources.

Gesell, Ilg and Ames. *The Child From Five to Ten.* New York: Harper & Row, 1977.

Hancock, M. *People in Process.* Old Tappan, NJ: Fleming H. Revell, 1978.

Krumboltz, J. and H. *Changing Children's Behavior.* Englewood Cliffs, NJ: Prentice-Hall, 1972.

Lanshy, Vicki. *Practical Parenting Tips for the School-Age Years.* New York: Bantam Books, 1985.

10. Specialized Needs

Augsburger, David. *Caring Enough to Confront.* Ventura, CA: Regal Books, 1981. Love learns how to speak the truth in ways that bring healing and new life.

——————. *When Caring Is Not Enough.* Ventura, CA: Regal Books, 1983. Conflict is normal in any relationship. How you deal with it is most important.

Branden, Nathaniel. *If You Could Hear What I Cannot Say.* New York: Bantam Books, 1983. A good workbook for improving communication skills.

Craig, Sidney D. *Raising Your Child, Not by Force but by Love.* Philadelphia: Westminster Press, 1973.

Dobson, James. *The Strong-Willed Child: Birth Through Adolescence.* Wheaton, IL: Tyndale House Publishers, 1981.

Dodson, Fitzhugh. *How to Discipline—With Love: From Crib to College.* New York: Rawson, 1977.

McDowell, J., and Day, D. *Why Wait? What You Need to Know About the Teen Sexuality Crisis.* San Bernardino, CA: Here's Life Publishers, 1987.

11. Family Ministry

Friedman, Edwin H. *Generation to Generation: Family Process in Church and Synagogue.* New York: Guilford Press, 1985. An introduction to family systems and their implications for ministry.

Guernsey, Dennis B. *A New Design for Family Ministry.* Elgin, IL: David C. Cook, 1983.

Otto, Herbert A., editor. *Marriage and Family Enrichment: New Perspectives and Programs.* Nashville: Abingdon, 1976.

Satir, Virginia. *Conjoint Family Therapy.* Palo Alto, CA: Science and Behavior, 1964.

Stewart, Charles. *The Minister as Family Counselor.* Nashville: Abingdon, 1979.

Winn, J. C. *Family Therapy in Pastoral Ministry.* San Francisco: Harper & Row, 1982.

For additional works consult your denominational publishing house for titles and resources for building family ministry in your church.

Would You Like to Know God Personally?

This is an adaptation of the popular Campus Crusade for Christ evangelistic booklet of the same title. You may obtain copies of the booklet at Christian bookstores or directly from the publisher.

The following four principles will help you discover how to know God personally and experience the abundant life He promised.

1 GOD **LOVES** YOU AND CREATED YOU TO KNOW HIM PERSONALLY.

(References contained in these pages should be read in context from the Bible whenever possible.)

God's Love

"For God so loved the world, that He gave His only begotten Son, that whoever believes in Him should not perish, but have eternal life" (John 3:16).

God's Plan

"Now this is eternal life: that they may know you, the only true God, and Jesus Christ, whom you have sent" (John 17:3, NIV).

What prevents us from knowing God personally?

2 MAN IS **SINFUL** AND **SEPARATED** FROM GOD, SO WE CANNOT KNOW HIM PERSONALLY OR EXPERIENCE HIS LOVE.

Man Is Sinful

"For all have sinned and fall short of the glory of God" (Romans 3:23).

Man was created to have fellowship with God; but, because of his stubborn self-will, he chose to go his own independent way, and fellowship with God was broken. This self-will, characterized by an attitude of active rebellion or passive indifference, is evidence of what the Bible calls sin.

Man Is Separated

"For the wages of sin is death" (spiritual separation from God) (Romans 6:23).

This diagram illustrates that God is holy and man is sinful. A great gulf separates the two. The arrows illustrate that man is continually trying to reach God and establish a personal relationship with Him through his own efforts, such as a good life, philosophy or religion.

The third principle explains the only way to bridge this gulf . . .

(A version of the Four Spiritual Laws, written by Bill Bright. Copyright 1965, 1988, Campus Crusade for Christ, Inc. All rights reserved.)

3 JESUS CHRIST IS GOD'S **ONLY** PROVISION FOR MAN'S SIN. THROUGH HIM ALONE WE CAN KNOW GOD PERSONALLY AND EXPERIENCE HIS LOVE.

He Died in Our Place

"But God demonstrates His own love toward us, in that while we were yet sinners, Christ died for us" (Romans 5:8).

He Rose From the Dead

"Christ died for our sins . . . He was buried . . . He was raised on the third day, according to the Scriptures . . . He appeared to Peter, then to the twelve. After that He appeared to more than five hundred" (1 Corinthians 15:3-6).

He Is the Only Way to God

"Jesus said to him, 'I am the way, and the truth, and the life; no one comes to the Father, but through Me' " (John 14:6).

This diagram illustrates that God has bridged the gulf which separates us from Him by sending His Son, Jesus Christ, to die on the cross in our place to pay the penalty for our sins.

It is not enough just to know these truths . . .

4 WE MUST INDIVIDUALLY **RECEIVE** JESUS CHRIST AS SAVIOR AND LORD; THEN WE CAN KNOW GOD PERSONALLY AND EXPERIENCE HIS LOVE.

We Must Receive Christ

"But as many as received Him, to them He gave the right to become children of God, even to those who believe in His name" (John 1:12).

We Receive Christ Through Faith

"For by grace you have been saved through faith; and that not of yourselves, it is the gift of God; not as a result of works, that no one should boast" (Ephesians 2:8,9).

When We Receive Christ, We Experience a New Birth. (Read John 3:1-8.)

We Receive Christ by Personal Invitation

(Christ is speaking): "Behold, I stand at the door and knock; if anyone hears My voice and opens the door, I will come in to him" (Revelation 3:20).

Receiving Christ involves turning to God from self (repentance) and trusting Christ to come into our lives to forgive our sins and to make us the kind of people He wants us to be. Just to agree intellectually that Jesus Christ is the Son of God and that He died on the cross for our sins is not enough. Nor is it enough to have an emotional experience. We receive Jesus Christ by faith, as an act of the will.

These two circles represent two kinds of lives:

SELF-DIRECTED LIFE
S—Self is on the throne
†—Christ is outside the life
●—Interests are directed by self, often resulting in discord and frustration

CHRIST-DIRECTED LIFE
†—Christ is in the life and on the throne
S—Self is yielding to Christ
●—Interests are directed by Christ, resulting in harmony with God's plan

Which circle best represents your life? Which circle would you like to have represent your life?

The following explains how you can invite Jesus Christ into your life:

YOU CAN RECEIVE CHRIST RIGHT NOW BY FAITH THROUGH PRAYER

(Prayer is talking with God)

God knows your heart and is not so concerned with your words as He is with the attitude of your heart. The following is a suggested prayer:

> "Lord Jesus, I want to know You personally. Thank You for dying on the cross for my sins. I open the door of my life and receive You as my Savior and Lord. Thank You for forgiving my sins and giving me eternal life. Take control of the throne of my life. Make me the kind of person You want me to be."

Does this prayer express the desire of your heart?

If it does, pray this prayer right now, and Christ will come into your life, as He promised.

How to Know That Christ Is in Your Life

Did you receive Christ into your life? According to His promise in Revelation 3:20, where is Christ right now in relation to you? Christ said that He would come into your life and be your friend so you can know Him personally. Would He mislead you? On what authority do you know that God has answered your prayer? (The trustworthiness of God Himself and His Word.)

The Bible Promises Eternal Life to All Who Receive Christ

"And the witness is this, that God has given us eternal life, and this life is in His Son. He who has the Son has the life; he who does not have the Son of God does not have the life. These things I have written to you who believe in the name of the Son of God, in order that you may know that you have eternal life" (1 John 5:11-13).

Thank God often that Christ is in your life and that He will never leave you (Hebrews 13:5). You can know on the basis of His promise that Christ lives in you and that you have eternal life, from the very moment you invite Him in. He will not deceive you.

An important reminder . . .

DO NOT DEPEND ON FEELINGS

The promise of God's Word, the Bible—not our feelings—is our authority. The Christian lives by faith (trust) in the trustworthiness of God Himself and His Word. This train diagram illustrates the relationship between fact (God and His Word), faith (our trust in God and His Word), and feeling (the result of our faith and obedience) (John 14:21).

The train will run with or without the caboose. However, it would be useless to attempt to pull the train by the caboose. In the same way, we, as Christians, do not depend on feelings or emotions, but we place our faith (trust) in the trustworthiness of God and the promises of His Word.

Fellowship in a Good Church

God's Word admonishes us not to forsake "the assembling of ourselves together" (Hebrews 10:25). Several logs burn brightly together, but put one aside on the cold hearth and the fire goes out. So it is with your relationship with other Christians. If you do not belong to a church, do not wait to be invited. Take the initiative; call the pastor of a nearby church where Christ is honored and His Word is preached. Start this week, and make plans to attend regularly.

Suggestions for Christian Growth

Spiritual growth results from trusting Jesus Christ. "The righteous man shall live by faith" (Galatians 3:11). A life of faith will enable you to trust God increasingly with every detail of your life.

Steven L. Pogue has written an excellent book designed to help you make the most of your new life in Christ. The title is THE FIRST YEAR OF YOUR CHRISTIAN LIFE, and it is available in Christian bookstores everywhere, or you can call 1-800-854-5659 (714/886-7981 in California) to order from the publisher.

Have You Made the Wonderful Discovery of the Spirit-Filled Life?

This is an adaptation of the popular Campus Crusade for Christ booklet designed to help Christians share with other believers the joy of Spirit-controlled living. You may obtain copies of this booklet at Christian bookstores or directly from the publisher.

EVERY DAY CAN BE AN EXCITING ADVENTURE FOR THE CHRISTIAN who knows the reality of being filled with the Holy Spirit and who lives constantly, moment by moment, under His gracious direction.

The Bible tells us that there are three kinds of people:

1. NATURAL MAN

(One who has not received Christ)

"But a natural man does not accept the things of the Spirit of God; for they are foolishness to him, and he cannot understand them, because they are spiritually appraised" (1 Corinthians 2:14).

SELF-DIRECTED LIFE

S - Ego or finite self is on the throne
† - Christ is outside the life
● - Interests are directed by self, often resulting in discord and frustration

2. SPIRITUAL MAN

(One who is directed and empowered by the Holy Spirit)

"But he who is spiritual appraises all things . . ." (1 Corinthians 2:15).

CHRIST-DIRECTED LIFE

† - Christ is in the life and on the throne
S - Self is yielding to Christ
● - Interests are directed by Christ, resulting in harmony with God's plan

3. CARNAL MAN

(One who has received Christ, but who lives in defeat because he trusts in his own efforts to live the Christian life)

"And I, brethren, could not speak to you as to spiritual men, but as to carnal men, as to babes in Christ. I gave you milk to drink, not solid food; for you were not yet able to receive it. Indeed, even now you are not yet able, for you are still carnal. For since there is jealousy and strife among you, are you not fleshly, and are you not walking like mere men?" (1 Corinthians 3:1-3)

SELF-DIRECTED LIFE

S - Self is on the throne
† - Christ dethroned and not allowed to direct the life
● - Interests are directed by self, often resulting in discord and frustration

1 GOD HAS PROVIDED FOR US AN ABUNDANT AND FRUITFUL CHRISTIAN LIFE.

Jesus said, "I came that they might have life, and might have it abundantly" (John 10:10).

"I am the vine, you are the branches; he who abides in Me, and I in him, he bears much fruit; for apart from Me you can do nothing" (John 15:5).

"But the fruit of the Spirit is love, joy, peace, patience, kindness, goodness, faithfulness, gentleness, self-control; against such things there is no law" (Galatians 5:22,23).

"But you shall receive power when the Holy Spirit has come upon you; and you shall be My witnesses both in Jerusalem, and in all Judea and Samaria, and even to the remotest part of the earth" (Acts 1:8).

THE SPIRITUAL MAN—Some personal traits which result from trusting God:

Christ-centered
Empowered by the Holy Spirit
Introduces others to Christ
Effective prayer life
Understands God's Word
Trusts God
Obeys God
Love
Joy
Peace
Patience
Kindness
Faithfulness
Goodness

The degree to which these traits are manifested in the life depends upon the extent to which the Christian trusts the Lord with every detail of his life, and upon his maturity in Christ. One who is only beginning to understand the ministry of the Holy Spirit should not be discouraged if he is not as fruitful as more mature Christians who have known and experienced this truth for a longer period.

Why is it that most Christians are not experiencing the abundant life?

2 CARNAL CHRISTIANS CANNOT EXPERIENCE THE ABUNDANT AND FRUITFUL CHRISTIAN LIFE.

The carnal man trusts in his own efforts to live the Christian life:

A. He is either uninformed about, or has forgotten, God's love, forgiveness and power (Romans 5:8-10; Hebrews 10:1-25; 1 John 1; 2:1-3; 2 Peter 1:9; Acts 1:8).

B. He has an up-and-down spiritual experience.

C. He cannot understand himself—he wants to do what is right, but cannot.

D. He fails to draw upon the power of the Holy Spirit to live the Christian life (1 Corinthians 3:1-3; Romans 7:15-24; 8:7; Galatians 5:16-18).

THE CARNAL MAN—Some or all of the following traits may characterize the Christian who does not fully trust God:

Ignorance of his spiritual heritage
Unbelief
Disobedience
Loss of love for God and for others
Poor prayer life
No desire for Bible study
Legalistic attitude
Impure thoughts
Jealousy
Guilt
Worry
Discouragement
Critical spirit
Frustration
Aimlessness

(The individual who professes to be a Christian but who continues to practice sin should realize that he may not be a Christian at all, according to 1 John 2:3; 3:6,9; Ephesians 5:5.)

The third truth gives us the only solution to this problem . . .

3 JESUS PROMISED THE ABUNDANT AND FRUITFUL LIFE AS THE RESULT OF BEING FILLED (DIRECTED AND EMPOWERED) BY THE HOLY SPIRIT.

The Spirit-filled life is the Christ-directed life by which Christ lives His life in and through us in the power of the Holy Spirit (John 15).

A. One becomes a Christian through the ministry of the Holy Spirit, according to John 3:1-8. From the moment of spiritual birth, the Christian is indwelt by the Holy Spirit at all times (John 1:12; Colossians 2:9,10; John 14:16,17).

Though all Christians are indwelt by the Holy Spirit, not all Christians are filled (directed and empowered) by the Holy Spirit on an ongoing basis.

B. The Holy Spirit is the source of the overflowing life (John 7:37-39).

C. The Holy Spirit came to glorify Christ (John 16:1-15). When one is filled with the Holy Spirit, he is a true disciple of Christ.

D. In His last command before His ascension, Christ promised the power of the Holy Spirit to enable us to be witnesses for Him (Acts 1:1-9).

How, then, can one be filled with the Holy Spirit?

4 WE ARE FILLED (DIRECTED AND EMPOWERED) BY THE HOLY SPIRIT BY FAITH; THEN WE CAN EXPERIENCE THE ABUNDANT AND FRUITFUL LIFE WHICH CHRIST PROMISED TO EACH CHRISTIAN.

You can appropriate the filling of the Holy Spirit **right now** if you:

A. Sincerely desire to be directed and empowered by the Holy Spirit (Matthew 5:6; John 7:37-39).

B. Confess your sins. By **faith** thank God that He **has** forgiven all of your sins—past, present and future—because Christ died for you (Colossians 2:13-15; 1 John 1; 2:1-3; Hebrews 10:1-17).

C. Present every area of your life to God (Romans 12:1,2).

D. By **faith** claim the fullness of the Holy Spirit, according to:

1. HIS COMMAND—Be filled with the Spirit. "And do not get drunk with wine, for that is dissipation, but be filled with the Spirit" (Ephesians 5:18).

2. HIS PROMISE—He will always answer when we pray according to His will. "And this is the confidence which we have before Him, that, if we ask anything according to His will, He hears us. And if we know that He hears us in whatever we ask, we know that we have the requests which we have asked from Him" (1 John 5:14,15).

Faith can be expressed through prayer...

How to Pray in Faith to be Filled With the Holy Spirit

We are filled with the Holy Spirit by **faith** alone. However, true prayer is one way of expressing your faith. The following is a suggested prayer:

"Dear Father, I need You. I acknowledge that I have been directing my own life and that, as a result, I have sinned against You. I thank You that You have forgiven my sins through Christ's death on the cross for me. I now invite Christ to again take His place on the throne of my life. Fill me with the Holy Spirit as You **commanded** me to be filled, and as You **promised** in Your Word that You would do if I asked in faith. I pray this in the name of Jesus. As an expression of my faith, I now thank You for directing my life and for filling me with the Holy Spirit."

Does this prayer express the desire of your heart? If so, bow in prayer and trust God to fill you with the Holy Spirit **right now.**

How to Know That You Are Filled (Directed and Empowered) by the Holy Spirit

Did you ask God to fill you with the Holy Spirit? Do you know that you are now filled with the Holy Spirit? On what authority? (On the trustworthiness of God Himself and His Word: Hebrews 11:6; Romans 14:22,23.)

Do not depend upon feelings. The promise of God's Word, not our feelings, is our authority. The Christian lives by faith (trust) in the trustworthiness of God Himself and His Word.

This train diagram illustrates the relationship between **fact** (God and His Word), **faith** (our trust in God and His Word), and **feeling** (the result of our faith and obedience) (John 14:21).

The train will run with or without the caboose. However, it would be futile to attempt to pull the train by the caboose. In the same way, we, as Christians, do not depend upon feelings or emotions, but we place our faith (trust) in the trustworthiness of God and the promises of His Word.

How to Walk in the Spirit

Faith (trust in God and in His promises) is the only means by which a Christian can live the Spirit-directed life. As you continue to trust Christ moment by moment:

A. Your life will demonstrate more and more of the fruit of the Spirit (Galatians 5:22,23) and will be more and more conformed to the image of Christ (Romans 12:2; 2 Corinthians 3:18).

B. Your prayer life and study of God's Word will become more meaningful.

C. You will experience His power in witnessing (Acts 1:8).

D. You will be prepared for spiritual conflict against the world (1 John 2:15-17); against the flesh (Galatians 5:16,17); and against Satan (1 Peter 5:7-9; Ephesians 6:10-13).

E. You will experience His power to resist temptation and sin (1 Corinthians 10:13; Philippians 4:13; Ephesians 1:19-23; 6:10; 2 Timothy 1:7; Romans 6:1-16).

Spiritual Breathing

By faith you can continue to experience God's love and forgiveness.

If you become aware of an area of your life (an attitude or an action) that is displeasing to the Lord, even though you are walking with Him and sincerely desiring to serve Him, simply thank God that He has forgiven your sins— past, present and future—on the basis of Christ's death on the cross. Claim His love and forgiveness by faith and continue to have fellowship with Him.

If you retake the throne of your life through sin—a definite act of disobedience—breathe spiritually.

Spiritual Breathing (exhaling the impure and inhaling the pure) is an exercise in faith and enables you to continue to experience God's love and forgiveness.

1. **Exhale**—confess your sin—agree with God concerning your sin and thank Him for His forgiveness of it, according to 1 John 1:9 and Hebrews 10:1-25. Confession involves repentance—a change in attitude and action.

2. **Inhale**—surrender the control of your life to Christ, and appropriate (receive) the fullness of the Holy Spirit by faith. Trust that He now directs and empowers you, according to the **command** of Ephesians 5:18 and the **promise** of 1 John 5:14,15.

* * * * *

To help you make the most of your relationship with God, you may wish to obtain THE SECRET: HOW TO LIVE WITH PURPOSE AND POWER by Bill Bright. This book is available in Christian bookstores everywhere, or you can call 1-800-854-5459 (714/l886-7981 in California) to order from the publisher.

(© Campus Crusade for Christ, Inc. 1966. All rights reserved.)

It's a tough time for the kids, too.

Mom & Dad Don't Live Together Anymore

Help and Encouragement for You and Your Parents

Let authors Gary and Angela Hunt help your child handle the painful situations that are coming his way. In their more than twelve years of working with children and adolescents, Gary and Angela have heard the stories, dried a lot of tears, and counseled many who needed special help. Each chapter openly and honestly addresses a specific need of your child and contains a section especially written for you, the parent.

Mom & Dad Don't Live Together Anymore is about real kids and for real kids—and their single or remarried parent.

Available at your local Christian bookstore.

Or call
Here's Life Publishers
1-800-854-5659
In California call (714) 886-7981

New! From Bestselling Author
Bill Bright

THE
SECRET
How to Live With
Purpose and Power

The inspiring new book that will help you discover a **new dimension** of happiness and joy in your Christian life! **THE SECRET** will show you:

- How to unlock the door to a consistent life of purpose—and power!
- Who the Holy Spirit is—and what He wants to do for you
- How to win the daily spiritual battles you face
- What to do when you fail
- What it really means to be "filled with the Holy Spirit"

Bill Bright, president and founder of Campus Crusade for Christ International, is the author of the Gold Medallion Award-winning **WITNESSING WITHOUT FEAR.** Join him today on a journey that will change your life!

At Christian bookstores everywhere.

Or call

Here's Life Publishers

1-800-854-5659

In California call (714) 886-7981

WARNING: THIS BOOK MAY CHANGE YOUR LIFE!

The word *warning* usually carries with it a negative connotation but not in this case.

I want to share with you what has been burning inside me ever since I began working with singles.

If your pain differs from what I experienced, it is only in degree, intensity or longevity. All single parents face the same fears, the same confusion and regrets. We all feel a little odd, living in a world tailored to dual-parent families.

Every time anyone refers to your family as "broken" you feel a stab in the heart.

You see couples walking along hand in hand and remember when you were like them. You see parents walking along, each holding one hand of a child between them and remember when that was you.

I have been a single parent. I know firsthand the journey from "Marriagetown" to "Pitsville."

I sincerely believe the concepts in this book can change your life, as they have mine.

PARENTING

Solo

DR. EMIL AUTHELET

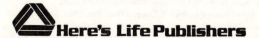

Here's Life Publishers

First printing, April 1989

Published by
HERE'S LIFE PUBLISHERS, INC.
P. O. Box 1576
San Bernardino, CA 92402

© 1989, Emil J. Authelet, Jr.
All rights reserved
Printed in the United States of America

Library of Congress Cataloging-in-Publication Data
Authelet, Emil J.
   Parenting solo : How to enjoy life and raise good kids / Emil J. Authelet.
     p.   cm.
   ISBN 0-89840-197-6 (pbk.)
   1. Single parents.   2. Parenting.   3. Parenting—Religious aspects—
Christianity.   I. Title.
HQ759.915.A95   1988   88-30055
306.8'56—dc 19   CIP

Unless otherwise indicated, Scripture quotations in this book are from the *Good News Bible,* the Bible in Today's English Version, © American Bible Society 1966, 1971, 1976. (Other versions used: KJV, King James Version; NASB, New American Standard Bible.)

For More Information, Write:
L.I.F.E.—P.O. Box A399, Sydney South 2000, Australia
Campus Crusade for Christ of Canada—Box 300, Vancouver, B.C., V6C 2X3, Canada
Campus Crusade for Christ—Pearl Assurance House, 4 Temple Row, Birmingham, B2 5HG, England
Lay Institute for Evangelism—P.O. Box 8786, Auckland 3, New Zealand
Campus Crusade for Christ—P.O. Box 240, Colombo Court Post Office, Singapore 9117
Great Commission Movement of Nigeria—P.O. Box 500, Jos, Plateau State Nigeria, West Africa
Campus Crusade for Christ International—Arrowhead Springs, San Bernardino, CA 92414, U.S.A.

Δ

This book is affectionately dedicated

to Donna, my friend and partner in life and ministry;
to Vicki, John and his wife Colleen,
Jeff and Karen, our children;
to single parents I have known and worked with;
and to the One who loves us all.

Philippians 3:10

Contents

Δ

Acknowledgments

Δ

Much has been gleaned

through my associations with peers such as Ken and Marilyn
Harrower, Jone Bolton, Norm Wakefield and Steven Evanson;

through family and single family conferences
in which I have participated
at Mt. Hermon, Mission Springs, Hartland, Westminster Woods
and Redwood Alliance;

through numerous church family retreats
and many workshops and seminars on family life.

Δ

Special authors have been

John Powell, Dorothy Briggs, Dolores Curran, Hugh Missildine,
Cecil Osborne, David Seamands, David Augsberger
and many others.

Δ

I also wish to thank Here's Life Publishers and its staff

through Dan Benson and Leslie Stobbe
for their confidence and invaluable help.

Δ

I especially wish to acknowledge

the editorial assistance of Jean Bryant
and
the thorough and diligent work of my wife
for her reading of the manuscript many times over
and for her gentle criticism and help
while seeking to maintain a loving relationship with a husband
who has a frail ego.

Δ

All of these have contributed more than help.
They each have given of themselves.

Part I

CONVERSATIONS WITH A SINGLE PARENT

An in-depth look at the person you are
and how this affects your parenting skills

THE SINGLE-PARENT JOURNEY, WITH MEANING

WARNING: THIS BOOK MAY CHANGE YOUR LIFE!

I want you to know this right from the start.

The word *warning* usually carries with it a negative connotation but not in this case. I sincerely believe this book can be life-changing for you in many positive ways. I'm glad you're reading it because what I want to share with you has been burning inside me ever since I began working with singles. It makes me want to put my arms around every single parent I meet and whisper God's word of encouragement. Single parenting can be a lonely journey but I want more than that for you. Let me put an arm around you and tell you what helped change me and my life.

LET'S GO FOR A WALK

I know the pain you may be experiencing. It can be deep and intense, and the confusion can seem overwhelming. We will talk about many aspects of your struggle, but right now I want to invite you to take a walk with me so we can get better acquainted.

My favorite place to walk winds along a trail through some giant redwoods, mountain oak, laurel and madrone trees. I like it because it's quiet. It's secluded, and it's relaxing. The trees are some of God's most magnificent handiwork. Their size makes me feel so small and my problems even smaller. The fern and vines and flowers edge the lush carpets of each meadow. Fallen trees, rooted two thousand years ago, make my beginning seem so new. The birds sing when I don't feel like singing, and they remind me of God's promise of a new song. We can get acquainted here, you and I, as we walk together in the midst of God's grandeur and power.

If your pain differs from what I experienced, it is only in degree, intensity or longevity. All single parents face the same fears, the same confusion and regrets. We all feel a little odd, living in a world tailored to dual-parent families. Every time anyone refers to your family as "broken" you feel a stab in the heart. You see couples walking along hand in hand and remember when you were like them. You see parents walking along, each holding one hand of a child between them and remember when that was you. I have been a single parent. I know firsthand the journey from "Marriagetown" to "Pitsville."

What I want to share will not only enhance your parenting skills and help you become a more adequate single parent but it also can change the way you see and understand your past, freeing you of its crippling tyranny. It can change your present fears of failure and inadequacy, and the feeling of not being worth loving. It can change your future by helping you find ways to meet your needs, and your dreams can become more than fantasies. It can bring total changes and you will realize more and more what Jesus promised you through His gift of "abundant life." If I had known years ago what I have since discovered, my life would have been so different. Let me share my discoveries with you so you can make the necessary changes *now*!

ABOUT THE JOURNEY

We'll travel at a pace that is comfortable for you. We can stop and cry together whenever you feel the need; we can rejoice at some points and celebrate at others; and we can share our doubts as we go. The Lord will accompany us each step of the way, and our constant prayer will be for Him to do the leading and the pace-setting. I've taken this journey with hundreds of single parents and each goes at a different pace. I need to tell you also that some have turned back because changes do not come easily. When it gets really tough, stop and take a deep breath, look up through the trees to God's blue sky of promise, and heave a sigh of prayerful trust. Then, by God's grace, we will move on.

We will divide our journey into two segments, coming full circle as we complete it. In the first part we will talk about *you* and who you are. You need to see the *person* the single parent is before you examine the single parenting process. I'm sure you are flooded with questions about how to accomplish your super task of single parenting. Little Johnny and Susie need all they can receive from you right now, and you are rightly concerned about meeting their needs. This may tempt you to skip to the second segment and leave the first for later, but I've been along this path before, many times, and I'm asking you to trust me when I say you need to talk first about *you*.

Let me illustrate this by reminding you of something you may have experienced in the past. You are seated in a jet, waiting for takeoff. The steward is going through the routine you've heard so often. All of a sudden, you *hear* it—for the first time: "In case of a sudden loss of cabin pressure, an oxygen mask will automatically drop from the compartment immediately above your head . . . anyone traveling with a small child, first fit your own mask in place before attending to your child."

Your parenting instincts cry out, "My *child* first, *then* me!" But if you were to lose consciousness, who would care for your child? Put your mask on first, and then you'll be able to put the children's masks on, however many you have. This is what I'm talking about. Look at the person first, then at the process.

YOUR CHILDREN'S REACTIONS

You are the only person you have to offer to your children. It is out of who you are as a person that you parent them. They will react more to what they perceive is happening with you than to what actually may be happening with them. You are their lifeline; they are dependent on you. Take the time to adjust your own mask; breathe in the clear oxygen of God's truth about you. Then you will be ready—and more able—to help your children with their needs.

THE PERSON YOU ARE

Most everyone I know sees me differently from the way I see

myself. They all claim to know me, but if you listen to each one's description, you will hear variations of some sort in every one. What makes it even more confusing is that none of them agree with my description of myself.

How do you see yourself? Why do you see yourself that way? What if you do not see yourself as you really are? It's possible you know, to live with yourself for thirty years and still not know who you are. In 2 Corinthians 13:5 Paul wrote about finding or examining our true inner selves. Well, if you're not who you think you are, who are you?

Part of the journey I want you to make with me is discovering your *true* self. I didn't really find my true self in any depth until I was well into my thirties, yet by then I had married, selected a profession, brought a son into the world, and developed a dream for my life. This may be true of you also. Or perhaps you are now being forced by a divorce or the death of your mate to begin that in-depth self-examination. Let's walk it together.

How will you know when you have found that true self? What will you be? How will you know you've made the real discovery? Will you like that "me" you find? And who have you been walking around in if it isn't you?

These are all good questions, and we will find the answers to every one. Let me give you a clue as to where we will go if we don't get detoured. When you discover the real you, you will first experience a deep, inner sense of God's peace in being you. No more of those lousy feelings about yourself. It will be okay to be you. Next, you will realize a love for that beautiful person in your mirror that will make you reach out, put your arms around that you and say, "I'm glad I'm me!" Then a surge of hope will stir in you, bubbling up from deep within until it engulfs your whole being, the hope of becoming the person you know God wants you to be, the person you want your children to have as their parent.

A QUESTION

You've been preparing for this journey and I haven't even asked you this question yet. *How are things going for you?* Let me guess.

Physically, you're exhausted. Between working, maintaining a home, caring for the kids, hassling over visitation rights and child support, dealing with the Ex's family, and not sleeping well, you